MONT BLANC

by Claire Eliane Engel

KNIGHTS OF MALTA

THEY CAME TO THE HILLS

A HISTORY OF MOUNTAINEERING IN THE ALPS

translations into English

POMPADOUR by Jacques Levron

PARIS IN COLOUR by Marcel Brion

ROYAL CHATEAUX AND PARKS OF THE ILE DE FRANCE
by Jacques Levron

THE MASSACRE OF ST BARTHOLOMEW by Henri Noguères

MONT BLANC

An Anthology
Compiled by
Claire Eliane Engel

ILLUSTRATED

RAND McNALLY & COMPANY
CHICAGO · NEW YORK · SAN FRANCISCO

Rand McNally and Company edition published in the
United States and possessions in 1965

Library of Congress Catalog Card Number: 65-15356

English Edition © George Allen and Unwin Ltd 1965

*This anthology was originally published in France
under the title MONT BLANC
© Editions d'Art et d'Histoire, Paris, 1965*

PRINTED IN GREAT BRITAIN

CONTENTS

ILLUSTRATIONS

INTRODUCTION

For rather less than three centuries travellers have been observing mountains and describing them. From a historical point of view, this is all rather recent, for we have to discard a few old stories that are of no significance in respect of mountain lore: for instance, Noah landing on Mount Ararat, or the unfortunate Baron Dompjulien de la Villa de Beaupré's attempt on Mont Aiguille in 1492 at the behest of Charles VIII. (No one knew what the King said when he heard of the successful ascent!)

Today, however, increasing numbers of people are attracted to mountains for a variety of very personal reasons, and there is no easy phrase or obvious explanation for this strange passion for activity, hunger, thirst, cold, danger and lack of sleep. Possibly it has its origin in the deliberate search for an ordeal.

Mountaineering was conceived, rather diffidently, at the end of the eighteenth century, and was born in the middle of the Victorian era, an age intent upon comfort, stability, conformity; it was thus an answer to the ageless quest for what restless minds seek constantly: the unknown, the unexpected and the dangerous. The first mountaineers were mostly scholars who had left their libraries or laboratories to probe the mystery of the lonely hills. Officially, they were doing scientific research, and they carried scientific instruments to places where they could not go unaccompanied. Yet it is obvious that de Saussure, who was certainly very fond of his barometers, was fonder still of Mont Blanc, though he was disappointed on reaching its summit. As early as 1861, Leslie Stephen quarrelled with one of his Alpine Club colleagues, John Tyndall, because he flatly refused to pretend he loved mountains merely for scientific reasons.

From that time on the matter was settled, and it was permissible to like mountains merely because 'they were there'.

Their main attraction, in many cases, was the lure of danger. Both World Wars have underlined this feature of the human mind, since two lost generations accepted despair and consequently ignored all ordinary caution. An avalanche, or a bullet, or the unredeemed tedium of years in prison? The avalanche was cleaner and quicker. There were climbs done for sheer love of danger, as for instance the unforgettable struggles of German parties on the north faces of the Grandes Jorasses and the Eiger shortly before the Second World War. Those suicidal climbs have been repeated along several new routes and, as usual, they have lost some of their terror. To recapture it, they have been repeated in winter at a temperature of about −30°C. As the years pass, one grows accustomed to a certain kind of danger. Is the mountain really tamed? No one knows. Anything may happen on a mountain, even when it has been climbed several thousand times, as Mont Blanc and the Matterhorn have been. Man becomes used to danger, but you never know if a mountain becomes used to man.

One may also detect a certain ascetic longing, more or less conscious, a will to master one's body, to test one's strength and submit it to the power of the mind. That is what optimists who do not climb call the 'moralizing effect' of mountaineering. The only moral element which can be found on a mountain is the mountaineer's, and mountaineering quarrels are among the fiercest. When François Mauriac wrote in his foreword to Jacques Boell's *High Heaven*: 'Above a certain height it is impossible to nourish evil thoughts; there are some thoughts which cannot flourish except in the lowlands,' he obviously did not know what he was writing about. Eighteenth century optimists had already sung that song and had been given the lie by history. Man is man at any altitude.

Yet, big climbs require a cool head, tireless application, a strong team spirit – however small the team is – and a perfect mastery of one's nerve: and that means much.

As for mystical contemplation, it is never consciously indulged in, at least not when actually climbing. Yet attempts at probing the problems of the world can be detected even in the works of some agnostic writers of the nineteenth century: having refused any religious revelation, they looked for an alternative in a cosmic understanding of the universe, and actually found it.

Mountains impart one certainty: aesthetic pleasure. High altitude landscapes are beautiful and little known. They can hardly be revealed to the uninitiated: painting always failed and photography is hardly more successful. Such landscapes are made of contrasts and contradictions. You expect to find clashing colours and shapes and actually find just the reverse. Colours are a delightful blending of delicate tinges such as lavender blue, pale pink, mauve, beige, and silver grey, melting away in a sun-vibrating distance. Stark precipices are touched up with exquisite shades. Sunset and moonshine bathe the landscape in fairy-like splendour. Under the worst possible conditions, storms compel admiration, even at times when ice-axes hiss and gibber with static. You expect to find a rough, uncouth world of clashing shapes, and you discover a manifold, refined architecture which conjures up an impression of triumphant poise. Mountains are an organized, almost intellectual world. Their powerful and architectural harmony is made of strict lines and surfaces, or pure and rigid reliefs. The human mind has tried to grasp this perfect synthesis, not easy to explain, and a line by Baudelaire accounts for its strange fascination:

> 'Je suis belle, ô mortels, comme un rêve de pierre. . . .'
> (I am fair, o Mortals, as a dream cast in stone. . . .)

14

Introduction

In the history of mountaineering, Mont Blanc always played a leading part, on account of its central, striking position. It is seen from afar, and it looms up on the horizon of a big city, Geneva. Actually, centuries elapsed before men were conscious of its presence, and it was named for the first time in 1742 by Pierre Martel.

One must resolutely ignore a letter by St Francis de Sales, dated 1606, in which the mountain bears its present name, though it is reprinted from time to time. For it is one of the numerous forged letters, penned by a Genevese cheese merchant, which found their way into the saint's *Complete Works*.

Yet, if Mont Blanc was not yet named, it was part of the horizon and many visitors, who were not particularly attracted by the beauties of nature, still alluded to 'hoary mountains' or 'frightful hills' looming in the distance. So did Théodore Beza in his translation of Psalm LXI; also Marc Lescarbot and Bishop Gilbert Burnet. In 1673 Henry Justel wrote to the Royal Society to tell its members that a wandering Capuchin monk had discovered, in the vicinity of Geneva, 'a mountain of ice and crystal'. By that time, René la Pays had already been to Chamonix and had written about the valley in a way which was thought ridiculous at a time when the Baroque style had few admirers; it is a provincial baroque, yet very charming nevertheless.

Maps were inaccurate and were not improved for many years. Yet, this dream-like horizon gradually became intriguing and visitors began to speculate about it. William Windham, who was studying French in Geneva, took seven friends with him and sallied forth. One of them was a professional explorer, Richard Pococke. The party wanted to discover what lay at the foot of those surprising hills and, as Windham intended to join the army, he organized his expedition in a military manner. He was right to do so, since the Geneva border was far from peaceful. He wrote a limpid, humorous account of his journey. The next year, a few young Genevese, led by Pierre Martel, an optician, followed the same route at a time when things were even less quiet. Martel also wrote an excellent account and made history, since one of his sentences runs thus: 'The two other points are the Mont Mallet Aiguille . . . and Mont Blanc, which is reported to be the highest of the Glacières and possibly of the Alps.' Mont Blanc had been born.

For the next twenty years visitors were not very numerous. In 1745 a twenty-five-year-old Knight of Malta, Michel Sagramoso, climbed up to the Jardin de Talèfre, probably with crystal hunters: a most enterprising feat, quite in keeping with Sagramoso's general attitude to life, for his was a daring, non-conformist mind. In 1760 Horace-Benedict de Saussure came to Chamonix for the first time and that was the turning-point of his career. A great gentleman and a great scholar, he became for the next forty years the life and soul of alpine research. The eighteenth century was attracted by scientific valour: de Saussure was one of the most daring and most conscientious scholars. In his innumerable notes on Mont Blanc and its range, and the four big volumes of his *Journeys among the*

15

Alps, can be found some of the finest descriptions ever written of those areas.

Little by little people began to wonder if Mont Blanc could be ascended. At first the answer was no. But Marc-Théodore Bourrit, a vain and venomous man who yet was passionately fond of a mountain he never succeeded in describing well, in spite of countless attempts in a great many books, said its ascent was possible. His enthusiasm eventually converted de Saussure. The first ascent was made in 1786 by the young Chamonix doctor, Michel-Gabriel Paccard, with a guide – or rather a porter – Jacques Balmat. Paccard was totally indifferent to publicity and he climbed Mont Blanc out of scientific interest and for sheer love of the mountain. He had been studying it for several years, as he sometimes acted as a sort of amateur guide. He had climbed fairly high with Thomas Blaikie and had been William Beckford's guide. Bourrit was enraged at having been forestalled on the summit (which he was never to reach), and began a violent and rather nauseating argument about the ascent. This was the first big mountain quarrel and by no means the last. In 1787 de Saussure reached the summit in his turn and the mountain was publicized all over the world. A modern equivalent would have been the ascent of Everest by the Duc de Broglie.

From then on, Mont Blanc was revealed to the world. No one ever seemed to know whether the mountain was in Switzerland or in Savoy, but visitors flocked to Chamonix during the summer months, though very few of them cared to repeat de Saussure's feat. The valley of Chamonix became one of the sights to be seen. De Saussure took Sir William Hamilton up to Montenvers; another year, when coming down after a long day in the mountains, he found the young Chevalier Francois de Pange having a bath in his own room. Both men started laughing, the younger one apologized, dried himself and retired to another room to dress. Joseph Michaud, who was to write a learned history of the Crusades, attempted to ascend Mont Blanc and went as far as the Grand Mulets. All through the Romantic period, the greatest writers visited Chamonix.

By now Mont Blanc had become more than a well-known part of a landscape. De Saussure, who was a very conscientious scholar, always refused to indulge in philosophical musing about it, but some of his pages are among the finest meditations ever written about a natural object the secret of which he was attempting to reveal. The mountain was still waiting for its poet, who eventually came on July 23, 1816: Percy Bysshe Shelley, who very quickly, it seems, scribbled *Mont Blanc*, by far the finest poem ever inscribed to the great mountain. His complex, intensely living lines throb first with terror and then with overwhelming joy. Romantic poetry did not stay at that level and Mont Blanc did not inspire many good poems. Some of the worst were written by Victor Hugo. The last years of the romantic era failed to produce any striking interpretation of the mountain and its mystery.

This was to come from completely different quarters: mountaineering was to endow it with the strength and the colour it lacked. The poetry of mountains was to be sought off the beaten tracks, and the first mountaineers – Englishmen, most of them – were going to create the imagery, the interpretation, the notions through which mountains finally entered literature. With widely different styles, J. D. Forbes, John Tyndall, Leslie Stephen, A. W. Moore and Edward Whymper were to understand and make understood the aspects of a still unknown earthly kingdom – a kingdom which was reserved for those worthy of it, through the ordeal of long climbs which were still part exploration. Some of them longed for a scientific revelation. Others were intent only on finding physical pleasure and the fulfilment of a personal longing. The wide, keen sympathy felt by Théophile Gautier was of the same kind, so also was Ruskin's passion for the 'cathedral of the earth', despite his hatred for mountaineers and mountaineering.

They were not particularly worried by Ruskin's rebukes and the romance of mountaineering continued. C. T. Dent and Mummery tackled the 'gaunt bare slabs', and as years elapsed men ceased looking for the easiest route to the summit, concentrating on all the routes, preferably the most difficult and the most direct. The fantastic architecture of the Chamonix Aiguilles provided climbers with a great variety of spectacular pitches. Soon came 'the last alpine problem' – there was always another! – the north face of the Grandes Jorasses, and the various pillars on the south face of Mont Blanc. Frantic years elapsed, during which climbs were carried out with grim determination and a furious will to win in spite of everything. There were suicidal teams who went all out for death or glory. From Courmayeur or Chamonix ropes went up, facing the big mountain as if engaged in war. With Cassin, Esposito, Bonatti, Gaston Rebuffat, Lionel Terray, Guido Magnone, Ledoux, Pierre Mazeaud and others mountaineering technique came closer and closer to perfection. Many died in the contest: Louis Lachenal, Livacic and others. The dividing line between the professional and the amateur became less and less clear. Gaston Rebuffat was elected to the Alpine Club.

Summer mountains, winter mountains. Early in the century Chamonix saw its first skiers – very tame ones. Then, many years later, it became obvious that something had to be done to organize skiing in a beautiful but not very propitious valley. Telepheriques were strung over steep slopes, reaching the Flégère, the foot of the Index, the Aiguille du Midi, the Brévent, finally to the Col du Géant. It was almost too great a success. Ruskin, who said (one does not know why) that 'the true beauty of the Alps lies only where all can see it, the child, the cripple and the old man', would be aghast today.

Now the problem of winter mountaineering is solved. Most of the big summits have been ascended in winter. One of the latest and most striking achievements was Walter Bonatti's winter ascent of the Grandes Jorasses with amazing courage and skill.

Several mountain anthologies have already been published. As mine is concentrated on one group of mountains, I had to select a special way of dealing with it. A merely chronological order would have been monotonous. Travellers who came to Chamonix around 1780 said much the same thing in much the same way as those who came around 1840. So did the first climbers of Mont Blanc. I decided it would be better to group quotations under various headings, concentrating on themes which have always attracted attention. It enables the reader to compare various renderings. It is meaningless to speak of progress, even in mountaineering. We can only grasp an evolution and a succession of themes. Nowadays, no one would dare to describe the Mer de Glace or even the Col du Géant, which are reached by train or telepherique; it is very likely that a number of tourists see in those radiant places merely a railway station. At the Col du Géant a gendarme asks for passports, which may be necessary, but rather out of place and slightly exasperating at that altitude. Too great an intimacy has destroyed part of the respect to which mountains are entitled.

I never intended to quote everybody in my anthology. First of all, one never can find everything, and it is not to be hoped for. It is impossible by rigid rules to select texts likely to please any reader. Any choice can be argued and faulted. I have merely tried to gather together contrasting impressions on a fairly well-defined subject, so that one can achieve a synthesis of the reactions of travellers who, for about 300 years, have come to Chamonix and its valley.

A few texts are unpublished and many are little-known. I have not aimed to provide nothing but new extracts – which was impossible – but I have provided some completely new documents and others which throw new light on older texts.

I have avoided reviving the endless argument concerning the first ascent of Mont Blanc. After D. W. Freshfield, C. E. Matthews, Dr Dubi, H. F. Montagnier, E. H. Stevens, Graham Brown, Sir Gavin de Beer and my own books, the subject is finished. Yet I am publishing one new document about that first ascent.

In order to avoid long biographical notices in each chapter, I have contrived a biographical and bibliographical index: it has its good and bad aspects. I hope it may be useful. In compiling my book, I have been constantly helped by M. E. Roux-Devillas, who suggested several new extracts. Mm. Jacques Boell, Gaston Rebuffat, Edouard Wyss-Dunant and the curators of the Geneva Library, Mm. Borgeaud, Georges Sonnier and Gaston Rebuffat gave me unpublished material. Mr. Boyd Alexander allowed me to use an extract from Beckford's diary which he had just published. I want also to mention Wilfrid Noyce, with whom I discussed the outlines of this book a few months before he left for the Pamirs, where he was killed.

ACKNOWLEDGEMENTS

For permission to use extracts from copyright material thanks are due to the following:

Faber and Faber Ltd., for the poem *St Gervais* by Michael Roberts; A. & C. Black Ltd., for 'The Sentinelle Rouge' from *Climbs and Ski Runs* by F. S. Smythe; Methuen & Co. Ltd., for 'Bivouac' from *First on the Rope* by R. Frison-Roche, and for the poem *A Rock called Le Père Eternel* by G. Winthrop Young; Hodder and Stoughton Ltd., for 'A Storm on the Aiguille Noire' from *Nanga Parbat Pilgrimage* by Hermann Buhl; J. M. Dent & Sons Ltd., for 'The Huts' from *Ten Great Mountains* by R. L. G. Irving and 'The North Face of the Dru' from *Starlight and Storm* by Gaston Rebuffat; Trinity College, Oxford, and Hodder and Stoughton Ltd., for 'The Brenva Route' from A. E. W. Mason's *Running Water*; the *Alpine Journal* for 'The Mont Maudit Route' by George Leigh-Mallory; Rupert Hart-Davis for two passages from *On the Heights* by Walter Bonatti, and one from *Gervasutti's Climbs*; the Museum Press for 'The West Face of the Dru' from Guido Magnone's *The West Face*; Victor Gollancz Ltd., for 'Twentieth Century Guides' from *Conquistadors of the Useless* by Lionel Terray; William Heinemann Ltd., for 'An Accident on the Verte' from *The Gods Are Angry* by Wilfrid Noyce; Georges Sonnier and Albin Michel for passages from their two books *Terre du ciel* and *Où règne la lumière*, and some unpublished material; Max Adelbert and Durel for a passage from their *Le royaume des hautes terres*; Armand Charlet for an extract from his *Ma vocation alpine*; Pierre Dalloz and Hartmann for the passages entitled 'Early Morning' and 'Zenith'; Edouard Frendo for 'The Central Spur of the Grandes Jorasses'; General Jacques Faure for unpublished material; Jacques Boell and Arthaud for 'The Highest Battle in the World'; Bernard Pierre for 'The Dièdre of the Sorrows'; and *Les Alpes* for Dr Wyss-Dunant's contribution.

Except where otherwise stated, the translations are my own, with the assistance of Malcolm Barnes.

The sources of the illustrations are as follows. Photographs were in the main provided by the photographers named in the list on pages 11 and 12. Otherwise 1, British Museum; 2, 7, 21, 28, 29, 30, 39 Bibl. Pub. et Universitaire, Geneva; 3, 4, 26, 41, 42, Geneva Museum; 9 and 10, the collection of the late Sir John Herschel; 11, 12, 23, my own collection; 13, 48, 59, the collection of M. F. Roux-Devillas; 15, Saussure's *Journeys through the Alps*; 24, Gaston Rebuffat; 36, 37, 38, the Alpine Club collection, London; 47, the collection of M. R. Jourdan; 49, the National Portrait Gallery, London. My thanks are due to all concerned for their co-operation.

C.E.E.

1

MONT BLANC FROM AFAR

GLACIERS

Behind us a long range of inaccessible rocks separated the esplanade where we stood from that part of the Alps named the *Glacières*, because huge ice summits, which are constantly increasing in height, have covered them since the beginning of the world. Those mountains are so high that, half an hour after the sun has set, their summits are still shot by its rays, the scarlet tinging the white domes to a beautiful colour which can be seen from afar off.[1]

La Nouvelle Héloise

MONT BLANC SEEN FROM THE DOLE

The magnificent panorama descried from the summit of the Dôle covers the whole range of the Alps. Over one hundred leagues of it can be seen, stretching from Dauphiny to the St Gothard. In the middle of the range rises Mont Blanc; its snowy summits are higher than all the rest, and even when seen from twenty-three leagues away they strike one with awe because of their very great height. The curve of the earth and the effect of perspective unite to lessen the height of more distant mountains and they really do get smaller to right and left of Mont Blanc as their distance from the monarch increases. To enjoy this view to the full, you should see it as I was lucky enough to do one day when thick cloud shrouded the lake, the hills along its margin and even the lower mountains. Only the summit of the Dôle and the High Alps raised their heads above this mighty veil; a bright sun was shining above the cloud, and the Alps, lit both by rays of

[1] J. J. Rousseau never went to Chamonix. In 1753, he heard of the valley through Jean-André and Guillaume-Antoine Deluc, the two naturalists who were devoted to the mountains and had visited the whole neighbourhood.

23

the sun and the light reflected from the cloud, were seen in their greatest splendour a huge distance away. Yet there was something terrible and strange in that very situation; I felt as if I were alone on a rock in the middle of a stormy sea, very far from a continent edged by a long ridge of inaccessible cliffs. Little by little the cloud sailed up, first folding me into its gloom and then, when it soared above my head, it suddenly unveiled to me a beautiful view over the lake and its smiling shores.

BENJAMIN DISRAELI, LORD BEACONSFIELD

SUNSET

. . . Nor is there indeed in Nature a sight more lovely than to watch, at decline of the day, the last embrace of the sun lingering on the rosy glacier of the White Mountain. Soon, too soon, the great luminary dies; the warm peaks subside into purple and then die into a ghostly white; but soon, ah!, not too soon, the moon springs up from behind a mountain, flings over the lake a stream of light and the sharp glaciers glitter like silver.

. . . The effect of sunrise is perhaps still more lovely. The high peaks are those which the sun loves most. One by one, the mountains, according to their elevation, steal into darkness and the rosy tint is often suffused over the peaks and glaciers of Mont Blanc while the whole world below is enveloped in the darkest twilight.

Contarini Fleming

JULIUS KUGY

MONT BLANC SEEN FROM COURMAYEUR

So it came about that in August 1887 I travelled up the Aosta valley. . . . From Aosta I saw Mont Emilius and the Grand Combin. Soon the north ridge of the Grivola came in sight; wrought in pure ice, and rising like the glistening edge of a whetted scythe to the slender summit, it put all else into the shade. Monks from the Great St Bernard were travelling in our diligence, their clever dark eyes, set

1 - *Vues de Savoie.*

1 - *Views of Savoy.*

2 - *Vue du fameux Mont Blanc dans le Haut Faucigny.*

2 - *The view of the celebrated Mont Blanc in the Haut-Faucigny.*

3 - *Le Mont Blanc.*

3 - *Mont Blanc.*

4 - *Le Mont Blanc vu de Sallanches.*   4 - *Mont Blanc seen from Sallanches.*

5 - *Le Glacier des Bossons.*   5 - *The Glacier des Bossons.*

in weather-beaten faces, regarding all nature in joy and gratitude. At one point about half-way up, where the beautiful valley of the Dora Baltea makes its great bend, there was a sudden stir among the company. Something had arisen before us, and it filled the background of the valley. It was neither cloud, nor rock, nor ice. It was all these in one. A fabulous structure of cloud, rock, ice, and snow, a picture great beyond the richest fantasy, a cathedral borne on giant granite columns, an altar lit by the glory of heaven, a dome standing brilliant in the firmament. 'Ah! *le Mont Blanc!*' cried one of the monks. It was a cry from the inmost heart, with a ring of ecstasy. He bent forward with arms upraised and a light in his eyes, as in prayer, to greet the vision from another world. All of us had risen. And in solemn tones, as if to proclaim honour and praise to the highest, his voice trembling with inward emotion, the eldest among them turned to us all: '*Oui, c'est le Mont Blanc, Messieurs, le Mont Blanc dans toute sa majesté!*' There was no one of us but would have bowed himself in reverence.

Alpine Pilgrimage, translated by R. L. G. Irving

2
THE APPROACH

I. THOSE WHO LIKE MOUNTAINS

RENÉ LE PAYS

CHAMONIX SEEN BY A BAROQUE WRITER

From Chamonix in Faucigny; May 16, 1669

I confess, Madam, I did not do what I promised to do, though I had a great many opportunities. From the depths of my despair when I left you I had sworn to throw myself down the nearest precipice. Yet for a fortnight now I have been up and down the most dangerous mountains in Savoy; I rode along the edge of a great many precipices and I have not hurled myself down them so far. I might tell you that I have been so busy that I forgot, but I must not deceive you. The delight of seeing your portrait in that terrible country always held me back when I was about to fulfil my promise. But I cannot bring myself to die in a place where I can see your pleasant semblance to my heart's desire.

It would certainly give you much trouble to guess the portrait of which I speak; you would go first to your jewel box, to see whether I stole the miniature you so often denied me. Yet, note that I did not derive this pleasure from the painting: Nature herself is the artist. In a word, Madam, I see here five mountains which are your living image.

Do not laugh! These pictures are a better likeness of you than the Judith and the Pallas in your cabinet. Five mountains of pure ice from head to feet, ice which can be termed perennial. According to local tradition, it is well-known that it has been frozen since the beginning of the world. Neither the heat of some five or six thousand summers nor the waters of the Flood could melt it, except for a few spots where one now finds crystals and gems. Yet in truth it is dangerous to go and look for them. Misers or inquisitive people have often been overwhelmed in summer under the havoc worked by crashing snow. I have been shown the remains of some of them who have died, encased in ice, and their relatives, to comfort themselves, say that they could not have been given a more gorgeous or resplendent tomb than the one Nature devised for them. By the way, Madam,

29

nothing can be more beautiful than those mountains when they are struck by the sun; the various faces which Nature gave them reflect the light of that magnificent orb in so many ways that it seems there are millions of suns of various colours.

Is it possible to find a more life-like portrait of you? This perpetual ice, those jewels which may be found in you were one bold enough to melt the ice, the dire peril such a hero would have to face, and finally the sun which lies in your eyes – are they not so many perfect likenesses to those icy mountains which I can henceforth regard as your very finished portrait? Five times Nature made for you what an illustrious scholar made for Alexander but once. You are painted here over five mountains, and this is a much greater glory for you than if Apolles or Praxiteles should return to life to etch your features on copper or carve them in marble.

Finally, Madam, those portraits are such perfect images of you that, to revenge myself for your cruelty in so often refusing to give me your miniature, I have a good mind to hang one of those mountains round my neck as a medal or, if I fail, to hang myself on the mountain, so as to die affixed to your portrait. Yet, if I must die of cold, better to face the ice of your heart than that of the mountains. Thus, Madam, I am resolved to get out as quickly as possible from this terrible country and repair to you, to die at your feet. There I mean to keep my promise; besides, you would not be quite satisfied with my death, were your cruel eyes unable to gloat upon it.

Amours et amourettes[1]

WILLIAM WINDHAM

ACCOUNT OF A JOURNEY TO THE GLACIERS OF SAVOY IN THE YEAR 1741

Dear Sir,

The story of our trip to the Glaciers of Savoy, which you wanted me to write for you, will be very straightforward. I will not try to embellish it with brilliant descriptions, though the beauty of the views and of the situations we saw in those little-frequented places deserve to be described by one able to unite a poetic imagination with a taste for painting.

---

[1] The five mountains of ice are the five big glaciers which came down almost to the valley floor and were increasing in the middle of the seventeenth century. See below, the note relating to Bishop d'Arenthon d'Alex.

I will limit myself to a faithful account of our journey. I am going to tell you very simply the observations we made and add a few suggestions which may be useful to those who in the future may feel the same curiosity as ourselves, and enjoy an opportunity to make more accurate comments. It is a very great pity that such a striking natural curiosity is so little known, and though Scheuchtzer, in his *Iter Alpinum*[1], describes the Swiss Glaciers, I feel there is a great difference between them and those of Savoy.

I had wanted to make the trip for a long time, but I always had to postpone it, because it was difficult to find companions. Luckily, in June 1741, an Englishman named Pococke arrived in Geneva : he had travelled all over Egypt and the East. I told him of what tempted my curiosity and, as he did not mind a difficult journey, he showed a great desire to make it, and so we planned our party. When other friends saw that we had made up our minds, they came with us.

As we were told everywhere that we would find nothing we needed in that country, we took pack horses with us, loaded with all sorts of food supplies and a tent which proved most useful, though the bad impression we had been given of the neighbourhood proved to be rather exaggerated.

I had provided myself with several scientific instruments for measuring heights and making observations, in the hope that Mr Williamson, Lord Haddington's tutor and a clever mathematician would come with us; but his dread of fatigue made him abandon the trip, so I left the instruments at home, as there was no other person in our group able to make the observations.

We left Geneva on June 18, 1741, a group of eight masters and five servants, all well provided with weapons; we were followed by pack horses, and that made us look quite like a little caravan.

On that day we got no further than Bonneville, within four leagues of Geneva, according to the way they reckon in that country; yet we took six hours to cover the distance. The place is situated at the foot of the Môle mountain, and on the bank of the Arve, surrounded by high mountains, covered with forests and fine meadows, in very pleasant surroundings. There is a rather fine stone bridge, but a flood had demolished part of it. We found an inn which proved fairly tolerable but for the beds.

The next day – June 19th – we left very early and crossed the Arve. We rode between the Arve and the mountains, which provided us with pleasantly diversi-fied and lovely landscapes. One reckons two leagues from Bonneville to Cluse but we took three hours and a half to cover them. Cluse lies at the bottom of a moun-tain gorge, and the ranges unite there, leaving just a narrow bed for the Arve which for a league is strangled between high mountains.

Before coming to Cluse there is a sort of hermitage on a rock on the right, and we climbed up there to look at the view, which is delightful; then we crossed the

[1] *Ouresiphoïtes, Itinera per Helvetiae alpinas regiones*, 1708. Scheuchtzer was a Swiss scholar and a Fellow of the Royal Society.

Arve over a stone bridge. We rode for an hour and a half along a narrow path between the Arve and prodigiously high rocks, which seemed to be cleft to allow the river to flow through. Apart from the beauty of the prospect, we were much amused by the number of echoes and the way they answered the cracks of our whips or the pistol-shots we fired while we rode. On either side we saw beautiful waterfalls that fell from the top of the rocks into the Arve. One of them is more beautiful than all the rest: it is called the Nant d'Arpenaz; it is a big torrent which hurls itself from the top of a very high precipice. All my companions agreed that it was higher than the Salève; for myself, I was not sure. The Terni waterfall[1] does not fall anything like so far, though, when we saw the former, there was not such a wide sheet of water as in Terni. The local peasants swore that at certain seasons there was a much greater volume of water.

After a three hours' ride from Cluse we reached Pont-St-Martin, opposite Sallanches on the other side of the Arve. We did not enter it, but camped in a fine meadow near the bridge to rest. Unknown to us Pococke had brought with him an Arab dress[2] which he put on while we were busy preparing dinner. At first we did not recognize him, but as soon as we discovered who he was, we immediately set a sentry at the tent's door and we behaved towards him with the greatest show of respect. Such an extraordinary scene was quickly noticed and rumoured in Sallanches, and within moments the whole town came out to look at us, and their various surmises amused us very much. Yet, as several ladies of quality had come to see us, we admitted the joke and departed in haste.

After a four hours' ride over bad paths, and having to ford very bad torrents, we came to a little village named Servoz. Our horses suffered much because there were no stables and they were tied out all night; moreover, they had no fodder but freshly mown grass. For ourselves we had brought everything we needed; we were therefore all right and we slept very well on straw in a barn.

We were on our way at daybreak and, after having crossed the Arve again over a very bad wooden bridge, and climbed up and down a very steep mountain[3] where we had plenty of trouble dragging our horses, which constantly cast their shoes and barely escaped toppling into the Arve at the foot of the rocks, we reached a fairly pleasant valley where we crossed the Arve a fourth time by a stone bridge, where we got our first view of the glaciers. We rode on to Chamonix, a village on the Arve in a valley where there is a priory of the canons of Sallanches. We camped there and, while refreshments were prepared, we questioned the peasants about the glaciers. They first showed us the tips of them that came down into the valley and could be seen from the village; they looked like white rocks, or huge icicles, formed by water dropping from the mountains. This

---

[1] Near Spoleto. Windham had been travelling in Italy.

[2] In Constantinople he had been painted in that costume by Liotard. The portrait is in the Geneva Museum.

[3] Les Montées.

did not satisfy our curiosity, and we thought we had come too far to stop at that.

We then asked the peasants several questions, to know whether, by ascending the mountain, we could see more. They said yes, but most of them made it sound very difficult and exhausting. They said that no one went there but crystal hunters and those who sought ibexes and chamois, and that all the visitors who had come to Chamonix had been satisfied with what we had already seen. A nice old man, the prior of the place, who was most polite to us, strongly advised us not to go higher. There were others who suggested that it would all be very easy, but we noticed that after having agreed between themselves to act as our guides, they expected we would soon get tired, when they would get their money without much trouble. Yet our curiosity got the better of us and, relying on our strength and courage, we decided to undertake the ascent of the mountain. We hired several peasants, some to act as guides, and some to carry our wine and food. They were so sure that we would not reach the top that they took candles, flint and steel to make fire in case we were exhausted and had to spend the night on the mountain.

To prevent the most agile of the party from exhausting the rest by hurrying, we ruled that no one might pass those in front, and that the one in the lead should walk slowly and regularly, that whoever felt tired or breathless might call a halt, and finally that, on finding a spring, we should drink wine mixed with water and fill our bottles for the next stage. The regulations were so useful that, had we not made them, the peasants would probably have been right in their surmises.

We started at twelve noon on June 22nd, and we crossed the Arve over a wooden bridge. Most maps[1] put the glaciers on the same bank as Chamonix, but they are wrong. We soon reached the foot of the mountain and began ascending a very steep path through a wood of fir trees and larches. We often stopped for a short rest, to recover our breath, but that did not prevent us from ascending fairly quickly. After crossing the forest, we reached a sort of meadow scattered with big rocks which had fallen from the mountain. The slope was so steep that we had to use holds and iron-shod sticks to secure a footing. Our path crossed the slope and we had to pass several places where avalanches had fallen and had caused terrible havoc. It was a shambles of uprooted trees and big rocks resting apparently on nothing at all. When we trod on them everything toppled down. We could look straight down to the bottom of the slope, and its steepness, together with the height we had reached, made a frightful sight, which well might have caused giddiness. At last, after a very hard climb of four and a half hours, we came to the summit of the mountain, from which we enjoyed a view of the most extraordinary scenery.

We were on top of a mountain which, as far as we could make out, was at least twice the height of the Salève. From there we had a perfect view over the glaciers.

---

[1] There were at least three of them, and all were bad.

I confess I feel very awkward because I do not know how to give you an idea of the view, and not knowing, among all I have seen, anything bearing the faintest resemblance to it. The description by travellers of the Greenland Seas seems to come nearest. You must picture for yourself a lake churned up by a violent wind and suddenly caught by the frost; yet I do not know whether it would really resemble what we saw.

The glaciers are three big valleys forming a Y, the tail of which falls towards the Val d'Aosta, and the two branches towards the Valley of Chamonix. The place we had reached was between the two branches, whence we clearly saw the valley which formed one of those branches.

Unluckily, I had forgotten my compass and I could not get my bearings, but I think the glacier runs more or less north-south. Those valleys, though situated at the top of a very high mountain, are surrounded by other mountains, higher still, the bare, steep rocks of which rise to immense heights, looking more or less like a Gothic building[1], and infinitely higher than the summit on which we stood. Nothing grows there, snow lies throughout the year, and our guides told us that neither chamois nor birds reach those summits.

During the month of August crystal hunters go to the foot of the rocks and tap with their pick-axes. If they hear a hollow sound they work hard and break the rock open; they find caves full of crystal. We wished we could have gone, but the season was too early and the snow had not yet melted.

We observed the valley as far as the eye could see. The height of the surrounding rocks prevented us from reckoning how wide it was, but I think it might be something like three-quarters of a league. We did not stop at that. We had about 400 steps to climb down to reach the bottom. It was extremely steep, over hard earth covered with pebbles and small stones which gave us no foothold, so that we came down, half falling, half sliding on our hands and feet. We stepped on to the ice – it was not difficult. The ice was quite rough. We found a huge number of cracks; we could step over some of them, others were several feet wide. They were so deep that we could not even see the bottom. Crystal hunters are sometimes lost there; after a time their bodies are recovered, well preserved in the ice. Our guides all swore to us that the cracks constantly change and that the ice has some motion. While ascending we heard rumblings like thunder and our guides told us it was caused by new cracks opening, though none did so while we were on the ice. I cannot decide whether it was that or avalanches or falling rocks that made the sound. Yet, travellers have remarked that in Greenland the ice cracks, making a noise like thunder, so that our guides might well be right. As inhabitants of uncultured countries are always very superstitious, they told us very ridiculous tales of wizards, and such things who hold their sabbath on the glacier

---

[1] Windham is much in advance of his time. The Gothic Revival started only in 1760.

and dance to the tune of instruments; we would have been greatly surprised if there had not been such legends there.[1]

Ibexes, in troops of fifteen or sixteen, often run about the glaciers. We saw none: there were a few chamois and we shot at them, but we were too far away to have any luck.

Water kept dripping from the glacier, and our guides told us it was most wholesome; they said it could be drunk continually without any ill effect, even when feeling very hot.

The sun shone with great strength, and the glare from the ice and the surrounding rocks was such that there was plenty of water in holes in the ice, but it always freezes at night.

Our guides swore to us that in their fathers' time the glaciers were much smaller and that there was even a way across the valleys leading to the Val d'Aosta, which could be reached within six hours, but the glacier had increased very much, the way was now choked and the ice was yearly getting thicker and broader.

At the side of the glacier we found blocks of ice which we first mistook for rocks; they were as big as houses and were separated from the glacier. I cannot understand how that had come there.

After having been for about half an hour on the ice and having formally drunk the health of Admiral Vernon[2] and the triumph of the British armies, we very laboriously climbed back to the summit we had come down from, the earth slipping from under our feet at each step. From there, after a short rest, we started our descent and reached Chamonix at nightfall, surprising local people and our guides very much; they confessed to us they had been sure we would fail in our attempt.

Our curiosity being perfectly satisfied, we left Chamonix the next day and, having slept at Sallanches, reached Bonneville on the 23rd. The place was so near the Môle that we had a fancy to ascend it, so we left Bonneville at daybreak the next day to do so.

We thought that after the glaciers any mountain would be easy for us; yet it took us five long hours to reach the summit of the Môle; the slope was extremely steep, though after the first two-thirds of the way a fine grassland is reached which stretches to the summit, which is perfectly spear-pointed, the mountain being a sort of sugarloaf, very steep on the side facing away from Geneva. From the top one has a very charming view, on one side over the Lake of Geneva and the surrounding regions, on the other over steep mountains which provide a most picturesque prospect. After a rest, we descended the mountain and went to Annecy to spend the night, and the next day returned to Geneva. Those who will make the journey in future should not leave before mid-August; they would

[1] Those legends are known all over the Alps, in Zermatt, Saas Fee, Kandersteg, etc.
[2] He had captured Porto-Bello on November 6, 1739.

find far less snow on the mountains and might visit the crystal mines and shoot ibexes. They would also find harvested oats and their horses would not have so rough a time. Though we met nothing dangerous, yet I would advise them to carry weapons; it is a simple precaution and it may be useful sometimes; one is never the worse for it. Barometers, to ascertain the height of the mountains, might be useful, if there are mathematicians in the party, and also a portable telescope. A tent is not required, except if one intends to look at everything in the greatest detail and to make observations. In that case, it might be erected on the mountain named Montenvers, if one must spend the night, for it is not very cold up there; it might be possible then to see whether the ice cracks change each day, as we had been told. One might also observe the glacier and make many curious records. A person who could draw would have much to do, either on the way or on the spot. Finally, clever people could do many things we did not do. The only credit we claim is that of opening the way to inquisitive travellers.

Cooked and salted meat should be carried, also bread and wine, for nothing of the kind can be found in most places or very little of it, which is bad. We bought live cattle which we had slaughtered and cooked on the spot. One must be provided with halters to secure the horses, horseshoes for each hoof and all that is required to shoe them, as they constantly lose their shoes, and one must constantly watch one's companions' horses, to see whether they cast a shoe.

With such precautions any journey is pleasant and easy, even in the wildest country, and one is able to examine anything strange they may display.[1]

Translated from the French original. *Mercure Suisse*, 1742

ALEXANDRE DE LA ROCHEFOUCAULD D'ENVILLE

GIANTS AND DRAGONS

It was much worse than fighting against giants, winged dragons, sheep or windmills; he had to walk through a dreadful country, on paths full of stones that were falling from the mountains, ford torrents, stand up to the voracious insects which swarm in Savoy inns: his courage made him victorious over all these trials. . . .

The glacier looked like a narrow sea which, when churned by a violent wind, was suddenly frozen. On one side it goes down to the vale of Chamonix over a very steep slope; and on the other it unites with another glacier which comes down between Mont Blanc and the Aiguille du Midi. Those two glaciers together

---

[1] The last paragraphs may well have been written by Pococke, who was used to really wild countries.

form a huge ice valley which, according to what the peasant told us, runs parallel to the valley of Chamonix. We could not see this, because we would have had to ascend mountains which were beyond the skill of anybody but Savoyards. According to what they told us, this big valley is as smooth as a mirror, some five leagues long and almost one broad, without a crack, but others say that there are big cracks which divide it into roughly square compartments.[1]

Published in *La Montagne*, 1893

MARC THÉODORE BOURRIT

MONT BLANC SEEN FROM THE ALLEE BLANCHE

As I had strayed from the path I was to follow to enter the Allée Blanche, this shepherd set me right. In front of me was a great curtain in the form of a steep mountain; from its summit I was to discover a view of the High Alps.

I can never explain the emotion I felt when I descried Mont Blanc and the mountains which lie on the same plane. It was the opening of a new world, like nothing I had ever seen. Just imagine this great alpine dome, supported by magnificent rocks, with two superb pyramids in front, the tallest in nature, surrounded by inaccessible glaciers over which the sun's rays were directed. So, I exclaimed, this is the threatening mountain which has survived the centuries and defies the glaring sun, the storms and the power of the elements!

Is there any transparence, any gleam, any whiteness which can be compared to such ice? What a magnificent dècor those surrounding mountains afford! How many majestic shapes! What a variety of colours and material! The first pyramid was of pinkish porphyry, the other was of granite. Nearer the giants stood hills of granite studded with shining crystals; further on were other ice mountains and hoary summits, the perpendicular layers of which were intermingled with waterfalls, glaciers and snow slopes. They seemed to kneel to Mont Blanc in homage. Above them all was the most superb sky, and to it they all seemed to be sailing, seeking to share its permanent purity. What wonderful majesty there was in all that landscape! What power could tear such tremendous masses from the earth and hurl them 2,000 *toises* upward? How long have they been there? Were they formed at the beginning of the world? . . . One cannot meditate over those immense objects or contemplate those huge products of nature without awe or respect. But I leave more experienced observers to solve their great problems.

Itineraire de Genève, des Glacières de Chamonix

[1] The young Duke left Geneva for Chamonix on July 30, 1762, together with Jean Jalabert, J. L. Claparède and J. L. Pictet.

Mont Blanc

HORACE-BÉNÉDICT DE SAUSSURE

VIEW FROM THE BUET

Those immense and ageless rocks, blackened by the water which drips from their flanks, striped with shining ice and snow, when seen on a fine day, through the transparent atmosphere of those high hills, afford the most magnificent prospect one can imagine. Certainly, the view from the summit of Mount Etna[1] is broader and more pleasant, but that over the range of the Alps which one descries from the top of the Buet is probably more astonishing: it stirs up a deeper emotion in the soul and gives a philosopher more to ponder upon. If one does not limit one-self to gazing at the snow and ice and contemplating the reassuring prospect of the eternity of the streams to which they give birth, if one ponders upon the formation of mountains, their age, their succession, the forces which piled so many stones so high above the rest of the world's surface; if one probes into the origin of those elements, the revolutions they went through and those which are still ahead of them. What an abyss of thought! Those, and those only, who have enjoyed such meditations on the tops of the high Alps know how deeper, wider and more illuminating they are than when one is pent up between the four walls of a study.

Voyages dans les Alpes

ANDRE CHENIER

ELEGY

There are times when a poor wretch may manage to smile through his tears and find some pleasure in his grief. . . . So does Savoy hide, among her hills, which are winter's permanent home, the flowers of spring together with the riches of summer. The traveller who has reached the barren summits wonders. Beside the rocks which have been piled up by countless centuries, shine the hard, sharp waves of frozen sea. On that glittering path he can scarcely stop himself from slipping with his iron-shod stick. He hears the rumbling voice of the abyss. All around him spreads a jagged mass of summits, either bare or densely covered with snow, the sons of huge Mont Blanc, which sits over their heads, as high above them as they themselves are above the abyss. But he soon climbs down to the valley at their feet; under his eyes are spread soft, delightful vales, meadows and

[1] De Saussure had ascended Mount Etna in 1772.

38

pastures, the fresh children of the dew, Trient, Cluses, Magland, a cluster of moist havens and green hillocks, above wayward brooks overgrown with lofty larches, those old inhabitants of the hills.[1]

Elégie VII

WILLIAM BECKFORD

REGION OF ICE AND CRYSTAL[2]

I am just returned from the region of ice and crystal, from the source of the Arveyron and the silent retired valleys at the base of Mont Blanc. The image of my dearest William pursued me even into these days of solitude. I passed three evenings in a thick forest of larch whose intermingled branches are fringed with heavy moss, totally abandoned to my reveries. Would to God I might converse with you once more upon the subject dearest to my heart. . . . Where shall I now wander like a melancholy ghost too full of the remembrance of the world it has left to taste the pleasures of that into which it is entering.

Letters

THE ARVEYRON[3]

We leaped several rapid branches of the torrent, and, advancing between high masses of crystalline ice, saw the enchanted grotto of the Arveyron before us. It had not been open, according to the account of our guides, more than ten days and was widening every hour. Large glittering drops were trickling from the azure vault, and every now and then a fragment detached itself, fell with the sound of thunder into the torrent. We were too much absorbed in contemplating the celestial blue of the arch to notice for some time the rapid increase of the waters round us; but at length, half stunned with their roar, we made a precipitate retreat.

England's Wealthiest Son, William Beckford (Boyd Alexander)

[1] André Chénier and the two brothers de Trudaine were on their way from Geneva to the Rhone Valley, over the Col de la Forclaz 1784.
[2] Letter to Mrs Peter Beckford, Geneva, July 28, 1783. The 'William' referred to was William Courtenay.
[3] Beckford's *Diary*, 1783. One of his guides in Chamonix was Dr Paccard.

39

Mont Blanc

MARIA JOSEPHA HOLROYD

(LADY STANLEY)

MONTENVERS AND TETE NOIRE

August 1791. The road from Sallanches to Chamonix is beautiful; many torrents
to pass, some so rapid that we were carried over them and the char-à-bancs were
held up by six or seven people. The 'Torrent Noir' is very terrific. For Lady
Webster's amusement there came a thunderstorm, attended with violent rain;
which last was the most inconvenient part of the story, as the only covering to
the char-à-bancs is an awning of sail-cloth, which is soon penetrated by the rain.
At Servoz we stopped to see a bas-relief of Mont Blanc which was very well
executed, and the worst part of the storm was while we were there, but it continued raining all the evening. . . . We arrived at Chamonix at half-past nine,
wet through. A dram of brandy was administered to us, and we none of us found
any bad effects from our adventures.

Thursday, we went to the Glacier des Bois, and the Source of the Arveyron.
Rode upon mules. Friday, after many different opinions and resolutions on the
subject, Mama, Lady W. and Louise[1] agreed to let us go to the top of Montanvers
without them, as everybody said the fatigue was very great. Sir John Macpherson
and Mr Hawkins, the son of an Irish Bishop, are at Chamonix, and went with
us. They are very pleasant, lively men, and made the expedition much pleasanter.
We were four hours ascending the mountain, through woods of fir trees, with
frequent views through the trees of the beautiful valley and the mountains on
the opposite side. Most of the way was so steep we were obliged to walk. From
the top of the Montanvers we went upon the Glacier des Bois, from its size called
the Mer de Glace.

It is a beautiful scene, such as no description can give an idea of. The glacier
takes a fine turn amongst the mountains, and has exactly the appearance of a
very rough sea. We carried a cold dinner and champagne with us and drank the
Prince of Wales's health in Blair's cabin, built by an Englishman of that name.
The descent was very steep and rendered worse by heavy showers of rain which
made it very slippery. We did not go back the same way, as we wished to see the
Source of the Arveyron again, which bursts out of a beautiful cave of blue ice at
the foot of the Mer de Glace. We arrived at the inn at six o'clock like drowned
rats, with some reason to be fatigued, as we had walked the whole time, an hour
and a half excepted, when we rode upon mules.

Saturday morning it was agreed that Sir George and Lady Webster and Mama
and Mr Pelham should return by Geneva, and that we should pursue our journey

---

[1] Her younger sister. Maria Josepha is writing to her aunt Serena.

40

6 - *Le Pont St-Martin.*

6 - *The Bridge at St Martin.*

7 - *Vue du Couvercle.*

7 - *The Couvercle.*

8 - *View from the Col des Montets (The Aiguille Verte)*.

8 - *Vue du Col des Montets (L'Aiguille Verte)*.

N° 334

9 - Le Couvercle.

9 - The Couvercle.

J.Herschel del. Cam. Luc. Aug 17. 1821   The "Couvercle" a granite block above the Jardin. Mont Blanc

10 - Le Dru.

10 - The Dru.

over the Col de Balme, attended by Sir J. Macpherson, Mr Hawkins and Levadé[1] The whole day's journey having to be performed on mule or on foot, the married ladies thought it would be too much fatigue for them. This and the next day I enjoyed the scenes and myself thoroughly; the country was beautiful beyond all expression; everybody was in good humour, and we knew from one five minutes to another what we meant to do – a state of happiness we had not arrived at since Lausanne.

We left Chamonix at half past six, and from that time to half past six at night were either walking or riding à la Française, upon mules, up and down almost perpendicular mountains, with the most delightful view all round us.

Letters of Lady Stanley of Alderley (née M. J. Holroyd)

JACQUES DELILLE

MONT BLANC

Hail to thee, pompous Jura and dreadful Montenvers! Huge heaps of snow and ice, and shapeless pillars of the temple of frost! You blinding prisms, whose blue faces challenge the sun, reflects its colour and throw purple and golden gleams over their shining mass. Winter, from his throne of ice, gloats at the sight of the day star embellishing his palace and attending his court. Among those huge phenomena, those moving scenes and awful sights, imagination never allows thought to languish or eyes to rest.

Yet, woe to overbold men who venture among those deserted horrors, if with a prudent noise of their fire tubes they probe those wintry snows. Sometimes, a minute cause has terrible consequences. Often, a bird resting on those hills loosens a particle of snow. This tiny weight is forcibly increased with more tiny snow flakes. Snow gathers round them. Its mass increases constantly; air vibrates, and all at once, in a tremendous fall, the frightful weight of accumulated winters topples from rock to rock, and its huge collapse makes distant abysses tremble; villages are crushed, forests are torn away; one looks in vain for vanished cities and by the distant blast of collapsing Alps travellers are overwhelmed before they are touched.

L'Homme des champs (third canto)

[1] Gibbon's librarian in Lausanne.

Mont Blanc

MONTENVERS

. . . The following day was fixed for this excursion. La Luc and his party arose at an early hour and, having taken a slight breakfast, they set out towards the glacier of Montanvers, which lay at a few leagues' distance.

It is unnecessary to describe the high enthusiasm of Adeline, the more complacent pleasure of La Luc and the transports of Clara, as the scenes of this romantic country shifted to their eyes. Now, frowning in dark and gloomy grandeur, it exhibited only tremendous rocks and cataracts rolling from the heights into some deep and narrow valley, along which their united waters roared and foamed, and burst away to regions inaccessible to mortal foot; and now the scene arose less fiercely wild. 'The pomp of groves and garniture of fields' were intermingled with the ruder features of nature, and while the snow rose on the summit of the mountain, the vine blushed at its foot.

Engaged in interesting conversation and by the admiration which the country excited, they travelled on till noon, where they looked round for a pleasant spot where they might rest and take refreshment. At some little distance, they perceived the ruins of a fabric which had once been a castle: it stood nearly on a point of rock that overhung a deep valley, and its broken turrets, rising from among the woods that embosomed it, heightened the picturesque beauty of the object. . . .[1]

They seated themselves on the grass under the shade of some high trees, near the ruins. An opening in the woods afforded the view of the distant Alps – the deep silence of solitude reigned. For a time they were lost in meditation.

. . . 'The stillness and total seclusion of this scene,' said Adeline, 'these stupendous mountains, the gloomy grandeur of this wood, together with that monument of faded glory on which the hand of time is so emphatically impressed, diffuse a sacred enthusiasm over the mind and evoke sensations truly sublime.'

When they arose to depart, 'I am unwilling,' said Clara, 'to quit this charming spot. How delightful would it be to pass one's life beneath these shades, with the friends who are dear to one!' La Luc smiled at the romantic simplicity of the idea.

They now mounted their horses, and soon after arrived at the foot of Montanvers. The emotions of Adeline as she contemplated in various point of view the astonishing objects around her, surpassed all expression; and the feelings of the whole party were too strong to admit conversation. The profound stillness which reigned in these regions of solitude inspired awe and heightened the sublimity of the scenery to an exquisite degree.

[1] Mrs Radcliffe may have remembered a description of the Castle of St Michel, near Servoz.

42

'It seems,' said Adeline, 'as if we were walking over the ruins of the world,
and were the only persons who had survived the wreck.[1] I can scarcely persuade
myself that we are not left alone on the globe.'

'The view of these objects,' said La Luc, 'lifts the soul to the great Author, and
we contemplate with a feeling almost too vast for humanity, the sublimity of His
nature in the grandeur of His works.' La Luc raised his eyes, filled with tears, to
heaven and was for some moments lost in silent adoration.

They quitted these scenes with extreme reluctance; but the hour of the day
and the appearance of the clouds, which seemed gathering for a storm, made them
hasten their departure. Adeline almost wished to have witnessed the tremendous
effect of a thunderstorm in these regions.

The Romance of the Forest

P. B. SHELLEY

THE VALE OF CHAMOUNI

July 22, 1816. . . . Our route still lay through the valley, or rather, as it had
now become, the vast ravine, which is at once the couch and the creation of the
terrible Arve. We ascended, winding between mountains whose immensity
staggers the imagination. We crossed the path of a torrent which three days
since had descended from the thawing snow and torn the road away.[2] We dined
at Servoz. . . .

. . . From there three leagues remain to Chamouni. Mont Blanc was before
us – the Alps with their innumerable glaciers on high all around, closing in the
complicated windings of the single vale – forests inexpressibly beautiful, but
majestic in their beauty – intermingled beech and pine, and oak, overshadowed
our road, or receded whilst lawns of such verdure as I have never seen before
occupied these openings and gradually became darker in their recesses. Mont
Blanc was before us, but it was covered with cloud; its base, furrowed with
dreadful gaps, was seen above. Pinnacles of snow intolerably bright, part of the
chain connected with Mont Blanc, shone through the clouds at intervals on high.
I never knew – I never imagined what mountains were before. The immensity of
those aerial summits excited, when they suddenly burst upon the sight, a senti-
ment of ecstatic wonder, not unallied to madness. And remember this was all one

[1] This sentence is practically translated from de Saussure's description of the view from Les
Rognes. See below p. 65.
[2] The summer of 1816 had been abnormally wet.

scene, it all pressed home to our regard and our imagination. . . . We were travelling along the valley, when suddenly we heard a sound as the burst of smothered thunder rolling above; yet there was something earthly in the sound, that told us it could not be the thunder. Our guide hastily pointed out to us a part of the mountain opposite from whence the sound came. It was an avalanche. We saw the smoke of its path among the rocks, and continued to hear at intervals the bursting of its fall. It fell on the bed of a torrent which it displaced, and presently we saw its tawn-coloured waters also spread themselves over the ravine, which was their couch. We arrived at Chamouni at six o'clock.

We did not, as we intended, visit the Glacier des Bossons today although it descends within a few minutes' walk of the road, wishing to survey it at least when unfatigued. We saw this glacier which comes close to the fertile plain as we passed; its surface was broken into a thousand unaccountable figures: conical and pyramidical crystallizations, more than fifty feet in height, rise from its surface, and precipices of ice, of dazzling splendour, overhang the woods and meadows of the vale. The glacier winds upwards from the valley, until it joins the masses of frost from which it was produced above, winding through its own ravine like a bright belt flung over the black region of pines. There is more in all these scenes than mere magnitude of proportion; there is a majesty of outline; there is an awful grace in the very colours which invest these wonderful shapes – a charm which is peculiar to them, quite distinct even from the reality of the unutterable greatness.

July 24. Yesterday morning we went to the source of the Arveyron. It is about a league from the village; the river rolls forth impetuously from an arch of ice and spreads itself in many streams over a vast space of the valley, ravaged and laid bare by its inundations. The glacier by which its waters are nourished, overhangs this cavern and the plain, and the forests of pine which surround it, with terrible precipices of solid ice. On the other side rises the immense glacier of the Mont-envers, fifty miles in extent, occupying a chasm among mountains of inconceivable height and of forms so pointed and abrupt that they seem to pierce the sky. From this glacier we saw, as we sat on a rock close to one of the streams of the Arveyron, masses of ice detach themselves from on high and rush with a loud dull noise into the vale. The violence of their fall turned them into powder, which flowed over the rocks in imitation of waterfalls, whose ravines they usurped and filled.

In the evening I went with Ducré, my guide,[1] the only tolerable person I have seen in this country, to visit the Glacier des Bossons. . . . The verge of a glacier, like that of Bossons, presents the most vivid image of desolation that it is possible to conceive. No one dares to approach it; for the enormous pinnacles of ice which perpetually fall are perpetually reproduced. The pines of the forest, which bound

---

[1] Ducray, very likely.

it at one extremity, are overthrown and shattered to a wide extent at its base. There is something inexpressibly dreadful in the aspect of the few branchless trunks which, nearest to the ice rifts, still stand in the uprooted soil. The meadows perish, overwhelmed with sand and stones. Within this last year, these glaciers have advanced 300 feet into the valley. Saussure, the naturalist, says that they have their periods of increase and decay; the people of the country hold an opinion entirely different; but as I judge, more probable . . . the glaciers must augment and will subsist at least until they have overflowed this vale.[1] . . . Do you, who assert the supremacy of Ahriman, imagine him throned among these desolating snows, among the palaces of death and frost, so sculptured in this their terrible magnificence by the adamantine hand of necessity, and that he casts around him, as the first essay of his final usurpation, avalanches, torrents, rocks and thunders and above all these deadly glaciers, at once the proof and the symbols of his reign – add to this, the degradation of the human species. . . . This is a part of the subject more mournful and less sublime; but such as neither the poet nor the philosopher should distdain to regard. . . .

July 25. We have returned from visiting the glacier on Montenvers or, as it is called, the Sea of Ice, a scene in truth of dizzying wonder. The path that winds to it along the side of a mountain, now clothed with pines, now intersected with snowy hollows, is wide and steep. The cabin of Montenvers is three leagues from Chamouni, half of which distance is performed on mules, not so sure footed, but that on the first day the one which I rode fell in what the guides call a *mauvais pas,* so that I narrowly escaped being precipitated down the mountain. The guide continually held that which Mary rode. . . . We arrived at Montenvers, however, safe.

On all sides precipitous mountains, the abodes of unrelenting frost, surround this vale; their sides are banked up with ice and snow, broken, heaped high, and exhibiting terrific chasms. The summits are sharp and naked pinnacles, whose overhanging steepness will not even permit snow to rest upon them. Lines of dazzling ice occupy here and there their perpendicular rifts, and shine through the driving vapours with inexpressible brilliance; they pierce the clouds like things not belonging to this earth. The vale itself is filled with a mass of undulating ice, and has an ascent sufficiently gradual even to the remotest abysses of these horrible deserts. . . . It exhibits an appearance as if frost had suddenly bound up the waves and whirlpools of a mighty torrent. . . . The waves are elevated about twelve or fifteen feet from the surface of the mass, which is intersected by long gaps of unfathomable depth, the ice of whose sides is more beautifully azure than the sky. In these regions everything changes and is in motion. . . . The echo of rocks, or of the ice and snow which fall from their overhanging precipices, or roll from their aerial summits, scarcely ceases for one moment. One

[1] This is Buffon's theory.

45

would think that Mont Blanc, like the god of the Stoics, was a vast animal, and that the frozen blood for ever circulated through his stony veins.

We dined on the grass in the open air. . . . The air is piercing and clear.

History of a Six Weeks' Tour

MARY SHELLEY

THE ARVEYRON

We had chosen a fair moonlight, but our journey thither had been long, and the crescent sank behind the western heights by the time we had accomplished our purpose. The snowy mountains and blue glaciers shown in their own light the rugged and abrupt ravine, which formed one side of the Montenvers was opposite to us, the glacier on our side; at our feet Arveyron, white and foamy, dashed over the pointed rock that jutted into it, and, with whirring spray and ceaseless roar, disturbed the still night. Yellow lightning played upon the vast dome of Mont Blanc, silent as the snow-clad rock they illuminated; all was bare, wild and sublime, while the singing of the pines in melodious murmuring added a gentle interest to the rough magnificence. Now the rise and fall of icy rocks clove the air; now the thunder of the avalanche burst in our ears.[1]

The Last Man (1826)

JOHN HOBHOUSE, LORD BROUGHTON

BYRON IN CHAMONIX[2]

August 30, 1816. . . . Came down into the valley to the village of Les Houches, where our guide took us up a pine wood to the right of the glacier;[3] rather a painful ascent. We climbed up the side of the ice and came on the plain, where we had to cross some deep and broad crevasses in which we heard the ice spring roaring below. Above us were the snow precipices of the mountain rising into the

---

[1] The plot of the novel is very dramatic, but for Mary the whole landscape was bathed in her remembrance of the days she had spent there in 1816 with Shelley.

[2] The expedition took place between August 29th and September 1, 1816. Byron and Hobhouse were accompanied by Scrope Davies and Polidori, Byron's young Italian doctor.

[3] The Glacier des Bossons.

clouds; below the masses, vertically split, of the glacier itself, stretching down to the cornfields.

Going down the other side of the glacier was not a little perilous, especially to Byron, who slid down an ice-ridge. We left this wonder of the world, descending through another pinewood and returning to our carriage, having crossed the glacier in one hour and a quarter which is a quarter of an hour less than usual.

. . . After dinner we went in char-à-bancs up the valley to the source of the Arveyron . . . and we scrambled up to the stream under its masses, and were warned not to approach the fountain under the ice itself, as the glacier was never tranquil . . . but Scrope Davis picked his way over the torrent to the fountain and we all adventurously followed and put our heads under the overarching ice and saw the rushing fountains below for a moment.

On coming to this spot we saw the very summit of Mont Blanc, *la Bosse du Dromadaire*,[1] a white boss just distinguished from the clouds and stretching upwards beyond the flight of an eagle. I never saw anything that gave me an idea of intense height before.

Recollections of a Long Life

VICTOR HUGO

THE VALLEY OF CHAMONIX

The valley of Chamonix is displayed lengthwise to the traveller who arrives from Sallanches. The three parishes into which it is divided, Les Houches, Chamonix and Argentière, reveal at intervals, along the narrow vale, their shining slate steeples. On the left, above an amphitheatre of gardens, chalets and tilled fields, the Brévent raises its pinewoods and crags almost vertically, while round them the wind winds and unwinds the clouds as if they were threads on a distaff. On the right stands Mont Blanc, the summit of which throws a strong light upon its ridges, that stand out against the dark blue sky above the high glacier of Taconnaz, and the Aiguille du Midi which raises its thousand steeples like a many-headed Hydra. Lower down, at the hem of a huge bluish cloak cast by Mont Blanc across the trees and fields, down to Chamonix, the outlines of the Bossons (*buissons*) Glacier stands out, the magnificent structure of which appears at first as something both impossible and unbelievable. It is unquestionably richer and possibly stranger than that weird Celtic monument at Carnac, the

---

[1] The 'white boss' is the actual summit; the 'Bosses du Dromadaire' are slightly lower, above the Dôme du Goûter.

47

three thousand stones of which, curiously arrayed across the plain, do not form a building. Just imagine huge prisms of white, green, purple or bluish ice, clustered together and assuming the strangest attitudes, some of them leaning, others standing erect, setting their dazzling cones against the dark background of larches. You might think it a city of obelisks, columns and pyramids, a collection of temples and vaults, or a palace that fairies have built for spirits; and I am not surprised to hear that the primitive inhabitants of the country have often thought they have seen supernatural beings fluttering between the glacier steeples when the dawn restores light to the alabaster columns.

Beyond the Bossons Glacier, opposite the Priory of Chamonix, stands the rounded wooded hill of Montenvers; higher on the same plane soar the twin peaks of the Pélerins and the Charmoz, which look like magnificent medieval cathedrals, with towers, turrets, lanterns, needles, steeples, big and small; between them the Glacier des Pélerins spreads its waves, resembling white curls on the hoary brow of the mountains.

The background fits the magnificent picture. The eye cannot tire as it scans the various planes of this vast mountain architecture, finding things to admire everywhere. First, there is a forest of gigantic larches covering the far end of the valley. Above it, the end of the Mer de Glace bends around the Montenvers like an enfolding arm and drops its marble-white blocks, its huge waves, its crystal towers, steel dolmens and diamond hillocks, raises its sheer silver walls and in the middle of the plain opens the dreadful mouth from which the Arveyron pours, to end a mile lower like a torrent.

Behind the Mer de Glace, lording it over all the surrounding mountains, soars the Dru, a granite pyramid of one single block, fifteen *toises* high. The horizon on which one scarcely descries the Col de Balme and the rocks of the Tête Noire is crowned with a lace-work of snow-covered summits, against the whiteness of which stands out this prodigious, solitary, grey obelisk of the Dru. When the sky is clear, its slender shape and dark tinge make it look like the solitary steeple of a ruined church; one might think that the avalanches which from time to time fall from its walls, are so many doves fluttering down to its deserted ledges. When it is vaguely descried through a veil of mist, one takes it for Vergil's Cyclop sitting on the mountains, and the uncertain whiteness of the Mer de Glace are the sheep he counts as they file past his feet.[1]

Victor Hugo, raconté par un témoin de sa vie

---

[1] Victor Hugo and his wife were accompanied by Charles Nodier and his wife, and Baron Taylor. Victor Hugo was twenty-three. 1825.

The Approach

CHARLES DICKENS

THE VALLEY OF CHAMONIX

August 2, 1846

I begin my letter[1] tonight, but only begin, for we returned from Chamonix in time for dinner just now, and are pretty considerably done up. We went by a mountain pass not often crossed by ladies called the Col de Balme, where your imagination may picture Kate and Georgey[2] on mules for *ten hours at a stretch*, riding up and down the most frightful precipices. We returned by the pass of the Tête-Noire which Talfourd knows, and which is of a different character, but astonishingly fine, too. Mont Blanc, and the Valley of Chamonix, and the Mer de Glace and all the wonders of that most wonderful place are above and beyond one's wildest expectations. I cannot imagine anything in nature more stupendous or sublime. If I were to write about it now, I should quite rave – such prodigious impressions are rampant within me. . . . You may suppose that the mule travelling is pretty primitive. Each person takes a carpet bag strapped on the mule behind himself or herself: and that is all the baggage that can be carried. A guide, a thoroughbred mountaineer, walks all the way, leading the lady's mule; I say the Lady par excellence in compliment to Kate; and all the rest struggle on as they please. The caravan stops at a lone hut for an hour and a half, in the middle of the day, and lunches brilliantly of whatever it can get. Going by that Col de Balme pass, you climb up and up and up for five hours and more, and look – from a mere unguarded ledge of path on the side of the precipice – into such awful valleys that at last you are firm in the belief that there can be nothing earthly overhead. Just as you arrive at this conclusion, a different (and, oh Heaven! what a free and wonderful) air comes blowing on your face; you cross a ridge of snow; and, lying before you (wholly unseen till then), towering up into the distant sky, is the vast range of Mont Blanc; with attendant mountains diminished by its majestic side into mere dwarfs tapering up into innumerable rude Gothic pinnacles; deserts of ice and snow; forests of firs on mountain sides, of no account at all in that enormous scene, villages down in the hollow, that you can shut out with a finger, waterfalls, avalanches, pyramids and towers of ice, torrents, bridges; mountain upon mountain until the very sky is blocked away, and you must look up overhead to see it. Good God! what a country Switzerland is,[3] and what a concentration of it is to be beheld from that one spot!

---

[1] To Forster!   [2] Dickens' wife and son.

[3] This is just possible, as Dickens was standing near the hut which is still on Swiss territory, the frontier being a few inches away; but Dickens does not seem to suspect that the valley belonged, not to Switzerland, but to Savoy.

And (think of it in Whitefriars and in Lincoln's Inn!) at noon on the second day from here, the first day being but half a one by the bye, and full of uncommon beauty, you lie down on that ridge and see it all! . . . I think I must go back again (whether you come or not!) and see it again before the bad weather arrives. We have had sunlight, moonlight, a perfectly transparent atmosphere with not a cloud and the grand plateau on the very summit of the Mont Blanc so clear by day and night that it was difficult to believe in intervening chasms and precipices, and almost impossible to resist the idea that one might sally forth and climb up easily. I went into all sorts of places; armed with a great pole with a spike at the end of it, like a leaping pole, and with pointed irons buckled on to my shoes, and am all but knocked up; I was very anxious to make the expedition to what is called 'The Garden': a green spot covered with wild flowers, lying across the Mer de Glace; but I could find no Englishman at the hotel who was similarly disposed, and the Brave *wouldn't* go. No, sir! he gave in point blank (having been horribly blown in a climbing excursion the day before), and couldn't stand it. He is too heavy for such work, unquestionably. In all other aspects I think he has exceeded himself on this journey. . . . He was (next to me) the admiration of Chamonix.

Forster's *Life of Dickens*

MICHAEL ROBERTS

ST GERVAIS

Coming out of the mountains of a summer evening,
travelling alone;
Coming out of the mountains
singing.

Coming among men, and limousines,
and elegant tall women, and hotels,
with private decorative gardens,
Coming among dust,

After the distant cowbells, bringing
memory of mule-tracks, slithering snow,
wild pansies, and the sudden
loose clattering of rock,

The Approach

I remembered Sunday evenings, church bells and cinemas
and clumsy trams
searching interminable streets
for quiet slums, the slums where I,

remembering St Gervais and the gorges, linger, bringing
in the worn shell of air, the pines,
the white-cloud-vision of Mont Blanc, and up
beyond les Contamines, the seven shrines.

Poems

ANONYMOUS

EXORCISING THE MOUNTAINS

The inhabitants of a parish called Chamonix displayed a singular trust in their bishop's blessing. Chamonix is on the Valais frontier, among large mountains laden with ice and snow in summer as well as in winter. They are so high that their summits seem to reach the clouds, and they are as high as the sight can reach. Ice and snow, which always hang from their tops, perpetually threaten the surrounding districts with eradication, and each time the bishop went to those places the inhabitants begged him to exorcise and bless those icy mountains.[1] About five years before his death they sent him a delegation to implore him to visit them once more, fearing that, as he was getting older each day, old age might deprive them of the happiness of seeing him again. With touching devotion they offered to pay all his expenses during his journey, and assured him that since his last visit the glaciers had retreated more than eighty paces. The bishop was delighted with their faith and answered: 'Yes, my good friends. I shall come, even if I have to be carried, to join you in prayer.' He went and was greeted with a delight equal to those good people's faith and trust in him. He did what he had been asked to do. I have an affidavit made under oath by the most eminent people of the place, in which they swear that, after Jean d'Arenthon's blessing, the glaciers have retreated half a quarter of a league from the point they reached before he blessed them, and that they have ceased to cause destruction in the way they used to do.

Anonymous. *La Vie de Messire Jean d'Arenthon d'Alex*

[1] It seems that glaciers increased greatly at the end of the seventeenth century. At the same period, glaciers were also exorcised at Saas Fee.

CHATEAUBRIAND

A JOURNEY TO MONT BLANC[1]

When clouds are driven away by the wind, mountains seem to hide behind that fleeting curtain; they are alternately veiled or unveiled; at times, a cluster of trees suddenly peeps out through a gap in a cloud, like an island suspended in the sky; at other times a rock slowly appears ghostlike, descried little by little through thick mist. A disheartened traveller hears nothing but the wind droning among the pines, torrents crashing into glaciers, the rumble of a falling avalanche, and sometimes the whistle of a frightened marmot that has seen a hawk in the sky.

When the sky is cloudless and the whole circle of mountains visible, there is but one detail worthy of attention: mountain summits standing so high in the air, have a purity of outline, a distinctness in their relief and profile which are lacking at lower altitude. Those gaunt summits, under the transparent canopy of the sky, resemble superb geological specimens, fine coral trees, chains of stalactites preserved in a case of pure crystal. Mountain dwellers try to discover familiar figures among these elegant spires: hence names such as *les Mulets, les Charmoz* or *les Chamois*; other names are borrowed from religion, the *Summit of the Cross,* the *Altar*,[2] the *Glacier des Pélerins*: artless names which are proof that, though men are obsessed by their needs, they still like to have reminders everywhere of what may comfort them.

Mountain landscapes are supposed to be sublime, possibly on account of their size. But what is we can prove that this very real size is unnoticed by the eye?

What nature has built is appraised like any work of art: to enjoy its beauty it must be seen from the right angle; otherwise shapes, colours and proportions vanish. Surrounded by mountains, one is practically within touching distance of the object and the optical field is too narrow; hence dimensions lose their scale. This is so true that one is constantly misled about heights and distances. Ask any traveller: does he think Mont Blanc looked very high from the Valley of Chamonix? Often in the Alps a huge lake looks like a small pond; you think you are within a few steps of the top of a slope and you take three hours reaching it; a whole day is hardly long enough for you to get to the other end of a gorge which you thought you could almost touch with your hand. Consequently, the heights of mountains, so loudly praised, are only perceived through the weariness they make you feel. As for the landscape, it looks no bigger than any other.

Besides, those mountains which lose their apparent size when they are too near are yet so huge that they dwarf all that could embellish them. Thus, by

[1] When Chateaubriand went to Chamonix he was accompanied by his wife, hence his exasperation. 1805.

[2] 'Le Reposoir': one of the summits of the Warens range, above Cluse.

contradiction, everything looks smaller in the Alps, both the whole and the details. Had nature made trees one hundred times bigger on mountains than in the plain, if streams and waterfalls forced out a hundred times more water, such huge forests and torrential waters could create a most majestic effect on those broad ribs of the earth. There is no such effect: the frame of the picture increases beyond range, while rivers, forests, villages and cattle retain their normal size. So there is no longer any proportion between the whole and the detail, the stage and the setting. Mountains, being on a perpendicular plane, become a constantly raised ladder, on which the eye compares tiny objects with a huge background. For instance, the highest pines are hardly perceived on the steep sides of a glen on which they lie like flakes of soot. Across those stark black woods rain water carves small parallel yellow lines; the broadest torrents, the tallest waterfalls, resemble narrow threads of water or a bluish haze.

Those who have seen diamonds, topaz, or emeralds in glaciers are luckier than I was: my imagination failed to discover such treasures. The snow of the lower Glacier des Bois, mixed with granite dust, looked to me like ashes. Several places on the Mer de Glace could be mistaken for chalk or gypsum quarries; only the crevasses display some of the colours of the rainbow, and when ice lies on the rocks it looks like bottle-glass.

Besides, the white veils draped over the Alps are most unpleasant – they make everything near them look black, even the sky, the azure of which looks dirty. Do not believe for one moment that this unpleasant trick is atoned for by the beautiful effect of the sun on the snow. The colours assumed by mountains in the distance are unperceived when you are at their feet. The grandeur of sunset over the summits of the Savoy Alps is only perceived by those who live in Lausanne.[1] As for the traveller in the Valley of Chamonix, he vainly waits for this gorgeous display. What he sees, as from the bottom of a funnel, is a tiny scrap of a hard blue sky, deprived of sunset or sunrise; a sad place into which the sun scarcely peeps at midday, over a barrier of ice.

. . . Only at a single moment do mountain landscapes recover their natural majesty: when the moon shines. The inherent quality of this half-light, deprived of any glimmer and of all colours but one, is to magnify objects by isolating them, and to destroy the gradation of colours which link together the different parts of a picture. Consequently, the firmer and more definite the mountain relief is, the longer its outline, the better this white light brings out the shadow lines. That is the reason why great Roman monuments as well as fountains look so fine when the moon shines on them.

Grandeur, and consequently the kind of sublimity it creates, are unperceived when among mountains. Now let us see whether there is anything eminently graceful there.

---

[1] Mont Blanc cannot be seen from Lausanne.

Usually one gazes in wonder at the Swiss valleys; but let it be noted, they are deemed pleasant only by comparison. Of course, when the eye is weary of wandering over sterile plateaus or crags covered only with some reddish lichen, it falls back with delight upon a little verdure and vegetation. But of what does that verdure consist? A few wretched willows, a few furrows of barley or oats which grow with difficulty and ripen late; a few trees, yielding hard and bitter fruit. If a vine painfully strives to live in a little, south-facing shed, well protected from northern blasts, you are requested to marvel at its extraordinary fecundity. When you ascend the neighbouring rocks, the large outlines of the mountains dwarf the tiny valley. Huts can scarcely be perceived, and small tilled fields look like a clothier's sample card.

Much is made of mountain flowers, violets one can pick on the edge of a glacier, or strawberries which blush in the snow, etc. They are delightful but hardly noticeable, and have no effect whatever: those ornaments are too tiny for such giants.

Finally, I may have been very unlucky, but I never discovered among those celebrated chalets, made illustrious thanks to J. J. Rousseau's imagination, anything but dirty hovels full of cattle dung or the stink of cheese and fermented milk; they are inhabited only by wretched mountaineers who feel themselves exiled and long for the time when they can go down to the valley.

Little dumb birds, hovering from icicle to icicle, a few pairs of choughs or hawks, give scarcely any life to snow or stone wastes where falling rain is almost the one single motion discernible to the eye. What luck when the woodpecker, giving a storm warning, raises its cracked voice in the midst of a cluster of pines! Yet this sad sign of life makes the surrounding atmosphere of death even more oppressive. Chamois, ibexes and white rabbits have been practically destroyed; even marmots are becoming rare, and the little Savoy sheep may lose his treasure. On the summits wild animals have been replaced by herds of cows which long for the plain as much as their herdsmen. Sprawling among the thick grass of the country of Caux they would look equally fine, and they would have the added advantage of reminding you of the descriptions of Greek and Latin poets.

I can only speak of what I feel among mountains. It is, according to me, very unpleasant. I cannot feel happy where I see everywhere weary men and their exhausting labour, which a harsh earth refuses to repay. The mountaineer who feels his trouble is more sincere than the traveller; calls the plain 'the good earth' and does not pretend to believe that the rocks he vainly moistens with his sweat is the better part allotted by Providence. If he loves mountains very much, this is just because of the marvellous connections God created between our sufferings, the thing which causes them and the places where we experience them; it depends on childhood recollections, the first emotions of the heart, the sweetness and even the harshness of our homes. More solitary than other men, more serious as he suffers much, the mountaineer puts more stress than other men on his sentimental life. One must not ascribe to the charm of the place he lives in the great love he feels for his country: it springs from the concentration of his thoughts and his own frugality.

Yet are not mountains the place to dream in? I wonder. I very much wonder whether it is possible to go dreaming when a mere walk is exhausting; when the care with which you must watch your steps completely engrosses your mind; the lover of solitude who would '*bayer aux chimères*'[1] when going up to Montenvers might well fall into some well, like the astrologer who claimed he could read above his head and could not watch his feet. . . .

Finally, if we believe Rousseau[2] and those who repeated his blunders, without inheriting his eloquence, when one reaches a mountain summit one feels a new man. . . . Would to God it were true! How sweet it would be to get rid of one's trouble by climbing a few feet above the level of the plain! Yet the human soul is independent of air and landscape; a heart heavy with pain is equally heavy on a mountain or in the plain. The men of antiquity, who must always be referred to when seeking the truth, did not think like Rousseau about mountains; on the contrary, they thought of them as the abode of pain and suffering. If Julie's lover forgot his sorrows among the rocks of Valais, Eurydice's husband lived with his pain among the mountains of Thrace. In spite of the Genevese philosopher's talent, I doubt if St Preux's voice will last as long as Orpheus' lyre. . . . Finally, another more beautiful and more sacred Antiquity gives us similar instances. The Scriptures, which knew human nature better than pseudo-wise men, always show the great unhappy prophets and Jesus Christ Himself ascending a mountain on a day of sorrow. . . . It was on the Mount of Olives that Jesus Christ drained the cup filled with all the sorrows and tears of men! . . . Well, how could Jean-Jacques himself in good faith believe in this wholesome influence of the high mountains? Did he not linger in pain and passion over the mountains of Switzerland?

Voyage au Mont Blanc

MME VIGÉE-LEBRUN

MOUNTAINS AND PAINTING

After having passed St Martin and Bonneville, we reached Sallanches through a road bordered on the right by large and superb rocks, the rich varied tinges of

---

[1] La Fontaine (Chateaubriand's note) – 'to stand gaping at chimeras'.
[2] Obviously, the whole attack upon mountains is aimed at Rousseau.

11 - *Les Aiguilles vues de Charlanoz.*

11 - *The Aiguilles seen from Charlanoz.*

12 - *Le Mont Blanc vu des Praz.*

12 - *Mont Blanc seen from Les Praz.*

← 13 - *La sortie des Emigrés, par Fioux.*

← 13 - *Emigrants escaping from France.*

14 - « *Divers animaux qui habitent ces montagnes* ».

14 - *Various mountain animals.*

15 - *Le Glacier de la Brenva.*

15 - *The Brenva Glacier.*

16 - *Vue de la Vallée de Chamonix.*

16 - *The Valley of Chamonix.*

which were lit by the sun. We ascended them to the top to enjoy the beautiful view over the dome of Mont Blanc, and the Aiguille du Goûter. The setting sun was casting golden tints upon the higher parts of that huge mass; the lower reaches of the range had the colour of iris and opal, for the only light over that part of the glaciers was the reflection from the sky. Finally, that great mass was obscured from the left by high, pine-clad mountains in complete shadow; so were the plains at their feet, which created a contrast and heightened the effect of Mont Blanc. It was not essential but it served to complete the picture. I attempted to paint that reflection. I seized my crayons, but to no avail; neither colours nor pastels can reproduce those radiant tints. . . .

We went up to Sallanches. After breakfast we left at once for the valley of Chamonix, which resembles nothing of what I had seen before. On either side stand high mountains covered with dark fir-trees. On the right, ascending, those dismal forests are interspersed with huge glaciers. Above them can be seen Mont Blanc, its dome and the Aiguille du Goûter, together with other glaciers. The spring of the Arveyron, dirty-coloured, spurts out from below a huge ice cave; everywhere, this wild place astonishes but does not charm the gaze. After lunch, as the weather was very fine, we arranged to see the Mer de Glace. I must tell you that there were masses of travellers going there at the same time. To avoid the shouting, chattering crowd, I let them go a little ahead. Thus I left alone with my guide, to keep away from the noise and the bustle. We were about to start the ascent towards the Mer de Glace. After about an hour's ride, I came up to a very narrow path above a high precipice, with no barrier of any kind. There I heard M de Brac shouting to me: 'In God's name, Mme Le Brun, don't go any further, please!' I immediately rode down with my guide, and he took me to the Bossons Glacier, the finest in the valley. I was delighted. Those numerous, enormous ice canopies are of a transparent kind when seen at close range. . . . I settled down to paint the glacier, resting my portfolio against my companion's back. I was parched with thirst. My guide had a little bottle of wine. He gave me some, adding a little piece of ice to cool it. Having rested while painting, I went down to the foot of the glaciers. My guide looked for strawberries for me: they were delicious. While walking back, I stopped again to paint a part of those mountains at the foot of which a torrent flows; seeing a splendid cluster of trees in a meadow, I also wanted to draw them at once: I think it is the least wild spot in the valley.

Souvenirs 1807

Mont Blanc

ALEXANDRE DUMAS

THE MER DE GLACE

The Montenvers path is one of the worst I know; especially at the end of the season, when it has been worn out by pedestrians and mules. The narrow parts of the path crumble away, the level surface disappears and leaves a slope instead. It is as if one were walking along a slate roof at a height of some 2,000 feet; a false step, mere lack of concentration, a failing foothold and you topple into the source of the Arveyron, the rumble of which rises from the foot of the precipice. You can hear the stones rushing down, as if to show you the way, that had been merely displaced but have been carried away by their weight alone.

It is up that delightful path that one climbs for about three hours; then one perceives a hut among the trees. This is a halt for the mules. Twenty steps higher a little house stands above the Mer de Glace: this is the travellers' inn. If I were not afraid of being accused of partiality for the human race, I would say that quadrupeds are much better cared for than bipeds, since they find fodder, straw, oats and hay in their stable, the equivalent of a four course meal, while the bipeds in their hotel can only get milk, bread and wine, which is not even the equivalent of a bad lunch.

Besides, one's first wish on reaching the plateau is not to eat, but to embrace in a look the broad prospect which surrounds one. Right and left the Charmoz peak and the Aiguille du Dru soar like mountain lightning conductors; before one is the Mer, an ocean turned to ice in the midst of a raging gale, with waves of a thousand shapes, sixty or eighty feet high, and cracks four or five hundred feet deep. After having looked at the view for a few moments you are in France,[1] even in Europe, no longer; you are in the Arctic Ocean, beyond Greenland or New Zemblia, on a Polar Sea, near Baffin Bay or the Bering Straits.

When Payot[2] thought we had looked at the view from afar long enough, he decided it was time to get us moving; so he started walking towards the Mer de Glace, about sixty feet below, down a path far narrower than the one up to Montenvers; it was in such a state that I wondered whether I should not use my iron-shod stick to balance myself rather than to lean upon. As for Payot, he walked as if he were on a main road and did not bother to look round to see if I were following.

'Look here, my dear fellow,' I shouted after a short time. 'Is there no other path?'

'Oh, so you're going to sit down?' he remarked. 'What do you think you're doing there?'

[1] Of course, the valley was not French at that time; it still belonged to Savoy.
[2] His guide.

'What am I doing? Well, I'm giddy, that's all. D'you think I was born to become a cock on a steeple? You're a bad lot anyway! Come and give me a hand. I'm not going to try to look more clever than I am.'

Payot immediately climbed back to me and held out the tip of his stick. Thanks to his help, I reached a rock safely, some seven feet below, overlooking a sort of fine sand ridge which surrounds the Mer de Glace. When I had reached it, I uttered a deep 'Ah!', which had as much to do with a need to breathe as with the relief of finding myself on the level. Then my pride returned as danger receded, and I tried to show Payot that, if I was a bad climber, I was a better jumper and, in an off-hand way, without saying anything to anybody, just to see how he would react to my nimbleness, I jumped from the rock on to the sand. . . .

With Payot walking in front, and I following him, we walked for about a quarter of a league on that sea, the breadth of which one cannot ascertain when among its waves, the horrible creakings of which seem like mysterious wailings from the middle of the earth. I don't know whether it arises from a nature more excitable or more nervous than that of other men but, when I stand among such mighty upheavals of nature, and though I know there is no real danger, I experience a sort of physical terror, seeing myself so small and lost among things so great. A cold perspiration wets my brow, I grow wan, my voice breaks and, if I could not retreat far from the place which overwhelms me, I would certainly faint. Consequently, I was not frightened, as there was no danger, and yet I could not stay among those crevasses which yawned at my feet or those waves poised above my head. Grasping my guide's arm, I said: 'Let's go!'

Impressions de voyage en Suisse (1832)

JULES MICHELET

'MONT BLANC, THAT GREAT MISER. . . .'

Let us consider the terror which then surrounded it: Chamonix was quite unknown, even in the country to which it belonged. Lower down one did not choose this long and dreary valley to go round the mountains. Passers-by, walking up the corridor of Notre-Dame de la Gorge (a path towards Italy), when they happened to be curious went up the Prarion and took a look at Mont Blanc. But what a terrible sight it was! One is very near it, within a stone's throw. It does not look – as it does from afar – like a huge corpse laid out with its head and its feet resting on other Alps. Seen from near and from below, it stands alone, like a huge white monk swathed in an icy cope and cowl, dead and yet standing.

59

Others[1] see in it a splinter or a piece of that dead star, the pale and sterile moon, a planet of death above our own planet.[2]

Its wide snow cap looks like a cemetery. The monuments are the dark pyramids, contrasting with the snow. Those aged daughters of the fire object to the ice; according to them, this white pall is nothing in comparison with the dark fathomless world below it.

If one goes towards the foot of the mountain through the valley of Chamonix, one steps into a dead end, dark and dismal for eight months out of twelve. Do not judge it by its appearance during the few sunny days, when it is invaded by a noisy crowd. The valley is caught between the Forclaz of the Prarion and the other Forclaz of the Tête Noire. You feel quite shut in. Chateaubriand realized that beneath this gigantic foot one can hardly breathe. How much more comfortable one feels on Mont Cenis or St Gothard! their summits, however stern, are yet the broad paths along which life flows. How many horses, herds and even migrating birds have used them! Mont Blanc leads nowhere: it is a hermit, alone in its solitary dream.

A strange Alpine riddle. While all the Alps speak through innumerable streams, while the St Gothard generously pours its four rivers north, south, east and west, with great parts to play in the world, Mont Blanc, that great miser, scarcely produces two small torrents (which only enlarge lower down by collecting other streams). Are there underground rivers? One can see only that it receives much and gives very little. Can we believe that, discreetly, this silent hoarder seals up the treasure of its hidden life against the future thirst of a drying world?

La Montagne

[1] Possibly Théophile Gautier.
[2] For Michelet high mountains were a realm of death, and it would be madness to trespass upon them.

3
MOUNTAIN LIFE

JAMES D. FORBES

THE OPENING OF A SUMMER CAMPAIGN

Mere change of scene and active exercise produce fatigue at last, unless the mind have some wholesome employment as well as the body; and most of those who have made the trial will probably regard amongst the happiest periods of their lives those in which a favourite study has been pursued in the retirement of mountain scenery. Mornings of active exercise, from sunrise till afternoon, and evenings of quiet thought and speculation, with here and there a day interposed of easy society with intelligent travellers, or employed in reducing and digesting the knowledge previously acquired by observation, give the sense of living twice over. The body and the mind are alike invigorated and refreshed; weariness from fatigue and weariness from inactivity, are forgotten, together with the other evils of our more artificial existence. The student in his closet exhausts his powers by one kind of toil, whilst the fox-hunter and dear-stalker exhaust them by another; both call it pleasure; but the one is all too exclusively speculative, the other too exclusively active. Let speculation and action minister to one another; then, like a well-compacted body, the members act in harmony – the double exercise prevents fatigue. Happy the traveller who, content to leave to others the glory of counting the thousands of leagues of earth and ocean they have left behind them, and established in some mountain shelter with his books, starts on his first day's walk amongst the Alps in the tranquil morning of a long June day, brushing the early dew before him, and, armed with his staff, makes for the hilltop – begirt with ice or rock, as the case may be – whence he sees the field of his summer's campaign spread out before him, its wonders, its beauties, and its difficulties, to be explained, to be admired, and to be overcome.

> *Ignotis errare locis, ignota videre,*
> *Flumina gaudebat; studio minuente laborem*

> *Travels through the Alps*

63

GEORGES SONNIER

DAYBREAK

Jean had been silent for a long time. It was getting colder, a portent of dawn. I was so exhausted that I probably dozed off. When I awoke it was as if I had dreamt all he had told me and the very hours we had lived.

It was daylight. The shadows round us were slowly taking shape, like things emerging from depths of translucent water. For the first time I could see the ledge on which we had spent the night; with its two slabs at right angles completely shutting in the view and all the surrounding emptiness, it was one of the most anonymous places I had ever seen, with its perfectly simple outline, and one of the most elementary. Obviously, there was nothing there to move either mind or heart, and yet I shall never forget it.

A few years before, in Germany, I had seen *Tristan*. The scene of the third act was a sloping floor, the two unequal sides of which met at the back of the stage, the apex of a triangle. There was nothing beyond but a veil of mist, through which came, from time to time, the heart-rending call of the *cor anglais*. I had been greatly moved by the *décor* of Tristan's death, mostly because of its bareness, its abstract and boundless quality. 'An obvious and bare place, resembling a cemetery of dead seasons' (Saint-John Perse, *Exil*). By strange coincidence, our night shelter had been similar.

Far away, the sun, still out of sight, soaring up to us from the other side of the world, was sending long rays of light which permeated the sulphur-coloured dawn clouds. . . . Gates were open to the light. . . . Its level rays, wherever they touched the mountain, conjured up brand new relief and shapes. They revealed and magnified all its secret architecture.

Below us a pattern of seracs and crevasses drew a strange mosaic on the glacier – the unaccountable fragment of a big jigsaw puzzle. A blue crevasse made a hollow look even deeper. Caught by some ascending air current, little clouds were soaring, straight up, shot with colour and light, and then floated half-way up the summits in the quiet air. We were waiting.

Suddenly, through the pervading silence, the deep warbling of springs, which had been silenced at nightfall, became audible again.

The day was breaking. One more day. . . . Luckily, the weather was fine. That was the answer to all our questions; time for joy and action when, in spite of a gnawing pain and crushing weariness, everything becomes suddenly shot with wonderful certainty. Hail to thee, O world of adventure!

As the sun had now reached us, we started climbing down.

Terre du ciel

17 - *Vue de la vallée
du Mont Anvers.*

17 - *The Valley of
the Mont Anvers.*

18 - *L'Allée Blanche.*

18 - *The Allée Blanche.*

HORACE-BENEDICT DE SAUSSURE

SUNSET SEEN FROM LES ROGNES[1]

Behind our hut was a low rock ridge of about forty feet. I selected it to lay out my observatory. . . . The beauty of the evening and the grandeur of the view I enjoyed at sunset made me forget a slight annoyance. The evening haze which, like a thin veil, was softening the glare of the sun and partly hiding the huge expanse at our feet, was casting a beautiful crimson band on the western horizon, while in the east the snow and ice of Mont Blanc, shot with this light, were displaying the grandest and strangest aspect. As the vapour was flowing down and condensing, this zone was becoming narrower and more vivid; finally, it was quite scarlet, while at the same time small clouds, sailing above this line, were shot with such a dazzling light that they shone like stars or fiery meteors. I went back to the same place when night had fallen; by that time, the sky was perfectly pure and cloudless, vapour was nowhere to be seen, but at the bottom of the valleys the stars were shining but not twinkling and they cast over the mountain summits a pale, faint gleam sufficient to bring out masses and distances. The repose and deep silence cast over this huge expanse, and increased by my imagination, inspired me with a sort of terror; I felt as if I were the sole survivor in the universe, the dead body of which I saw lying at my feet. However sad such ideas can be, they are so attractive in a way that it is difficult to resist them. I gazed more often at this dark solitude than at Mont Blanc, the shining and almost phosphorescent snow of which conjured up ideas of motion and life. But the air was so sharp on this isolated ridge that I was soon compelled to go back to the hut.

Voyages dans les Alpes

NIGHT ON THE COL DU GEANT[2]

The sixteenth evening, the last we spent upon the Col du Géant, was supremely beautiful. All the high peaks seemed to have conspired to make us regret parting from them. The cold wind that had made most of our evenings here so comfortless,

[1] September 12, 1785. Saussure was bivouacking on the Rognes, to attempt the ascent of Mont Blanc over the Aiguille du Goûter. He was accompanied by Bourrit and his son; through their slowness and inefficiency the attempt failed the next day.

[2] July 18, 1788. Saussure had spent a fortnight on the Col du Géant to complete observations which he had begun the year before, when ascending Mont Blanc.

refrained from blowing. The crests that towered above us, and the intervening snows, put on the loveliest shades of rose and carmine. Over Italy a broad band of purple extended along the whole horizon, and above the band the full moon rose in queenly majesty, vermilion-tinted. The air around us was as pure and perfectly limpid as Homer imagines that of Olympus to have been, while the valleys, filled with the vapours that had formed there, looked like abodes of the deepest darkness.

But how shall I find words to describe the night that followed on this lovely evening, when the twilight ended and the moon shone in solitary glory, pouring floods of silvery light upon the immense amphitheatre of snow and rock that encircled our humble shelter. These fields of snow and cliffs of ice, too dazzling to be looked at in the day, what a wondrous and enchanting spectacle they present under the soft beams of the torch of night! What a magnificent contrast the dark granite rocks afford, standing out in sharp bold outlines against the gleaming snow! Was ever such a moment given for meditation? What pains and hardships are not repaid in full by moments such as these! The soul of man is lifted up, a wider, nobler horizon is offered to his view; surrounded by such silent majesty he seems to hear the very voice of Nature, and to become the confidant to whom she tells her most secret operations.

Voyages dans les Alpes

SIR LESLIE STEPHEN

SUNSET ON MONT BLANC[1]

Thus distinctly drawn, though upon so minute a scale, every rock and slope preserved its true value, and the impression of stupendous height became almost oppressive as it was forced upon the imagination that a whole world of mountains, each of them a mighty mass in itself, lay couched beneath our feet, reaching across the whole diameter of the vast panorama. And now, whilst occupied in drinking in that strange sensation, and allowing our minds to recover their equilibrium from the first staggering shock of astonishment, began the strange spectacle of which we were the sole witnesses. One long delicate cloud, suspended in mid-air just below the sun, was gradually adorning itself with prismatic colouring. Round the limitless horizon ran a faint fog-bank, unfortunately not quite thick enough to produce that depth of colouring which sometimes makes an Alpine sunset inexpressibly gorgeous.

[1] August 6, 1873. Leslie Stephen and the painter Gabriel Loppé ascended Mont Blanc so as to be on the top in time to watch the sunset.

The weather – it was the only complaint we had to make – erred on the side of fineness. But the colouring was brilliant enough to prevent any thoughts of serious disappointment. The long series of western ranges melted into a uniform hue as the sun declined in their rear. Amidst their folds, the Lake of Geneva became suddenly lighted up in a faint yellow gleam. To the east a blue gauze seemed to cover valley by valley as they sank into night and the intervening ridges rose with increasing distinctness, or rather it seemed that some fluid of exquisite delicacy of colour and substance was flooding all the lower country beneath the great mountains. Peak by peak the high snowfields caught the rosy glow and shone like signal-fires across the dim breadths of delicate twilight. Like Xerxes, we looked over the countless host sinking into rest, but with the rather different reflection, that a hundred years hence they would probably be doing much the same thing, whilst we should long have ceased to take any interest in the performance.

And suddenly began a more startling phenomenon. A vast cone, with its apex pointing away from us, seemed to be suddenly cut out from the world beneath; night was within its borders and the twilight still round; the blue mists were quenched where it fell, and for the instant we could scarcely tell what was the origin of this strange appearance. Some unexpected change seemed to have taken place in the programme; as though a great fold in the curtain had suddenly given way and dropped on to part of the scenery. Of course a moment's reflection explained the meaning of this uncanny intruder; it was the giant shadow of Mont Blanc, testifying to his supremacy over all meaner eminences. It is difficult to say how sharply marked was the outline and how startling was the contrast between this pyramid of darkness and the faintly-lighted spaces beyond its influence; a huge inky blot seemed to have suddenly fallen upon the landscape. As we gazed, we could see it move. It swallowed up ridge by ridge, and its sharp point crept steadily from one landmark to another down the broad Valley of Aosta. We were standing, in fact, on the point of the gnomon of a gigantic sun-dial, the face of which was formed by thousands of square miles of mountain and valley. So clear was the outline that, if figure had been scrawled upon glaciers and ridges, we could have told the time to a second; indeed, we were half-inclined to look for our own shadows at a distance so great that a whole village would be represented by a scarcely distinguishable speck of colouring.

The huge shadow, looking even more strange and magical, struck the distant Becca di Nona, and then climbed into the dark region where the broader shadow of the world was rising into the eastern sky. By some singular effect of perspective, rays of darkness seemed to be converging from above our heads to a point immediately above the apex of the shadowy cone. For a time it seemed that there was a kind of anti-sun in the east, pouring out not light, but deep shadow as it rose. The apex soon reached the horizon, and then to our surprise began climbing the distant sky. Would it never stop, and was Mont Blanc capable of overshadowing not only the earth but the sky? For a minute or two I fancied, in a bewildered way, that this unearthly object would fairly rise from the ground and climb upwards to the zenith. But rapidly the lights were out upon the great army of mountains; the snow all round took the livid hue which immediately succeeds an Alpine sunset, and almost at a blow the shadow of Mont Blanc was swallowed up in the general shade of night.

The display had ceased suddenly at its culminating point and it was highly expedient for the spectators to retire. We had no time to lose if we would get off the summit before the grip of the frost should harden the snows into an ice-crust; and in a minute we were running and sliding towards the familiar Corridor. Yet as we went the sombre magnificence of the scenery seemed for a time to increase. We were between the day and the night. . . . The western heavens were of the most brilliant blue with spaces of transparent green, whilst a few scattered cloudlets glowed as if with internal fire. To the east the night rushed up furiously, and it was difficult to imagine that the dark purple sky was really cloudless and not blackened by the rising of some portentous storm.

The Playground of Europe

II. NIGHT

J. W. VON GOETHE

MOONLIGHT[1]

It grew darker and darker as we approached the valley of Chamonix, and when we entered it we could only perceive its broader outlines. The stars were coming out one after the other; above the summits before us a light was revealing itself, the source of which we could not understand. It was light, but resembling the Milky Way in its lack of distinctness and glow, and it seemed nearer than the Pleiades. We could not take our eyes from it and, as our position changed, we saw it above all the mountains surrounding us, as a pyramid in which a light might have been hidden. It shone through the night like a glow-worm and we realized at last that it was none other than Mont Blanc. It had a strange, supreme beauty; it covered us with light and the stars were massing round it. It had not their twinkling glimmer, but it looked like a vast shining body, belonging to a higher sphere. It was difficult to believe that it had earthly roots.

Reisen

GEORGE SAND

STARS[2]

What I am sure of is that this line of bonfires, set like beacons all along the ravines (to prevent hoar-frost at dead of night, provided me with a beautiful sight. . . . They pierced with red spots and pillars of dark smoke the veil of

---

[1] In the autumn of 1779.
[2] Letter to Charles Didier. George Sand went to Chamonix in August 1836, with Liszt, Marie d'Agoult, Major Pictet and Gustave de Gévaudan. She was bored stiff.

69

silver haze in which the valley was wrapped and hidden. Above fires, smoke and haze the Mont Blanc range revealed one of its highest granite belts, ink-black and snow crowned. That fantastic background to the picture seemed to sail in sheer nothingness. Above a few windswept summits, in a pure cold sky, big stars could be seen. Those mountain peaks, thrusting towards the sky a black, narrow horizon, made the stars look brighter still. The fiery eye of the Bull, the grim Aldebaran soared above a dark needle which looked like the crater of a volcano out of which this hellish spark had just sprung. Further on, Fomalhault, a bluish, pure and melancholy star, was floating down towards a snow-white dome, like a tear of compassion and mercy wept by the sky on the poor valley, but about to be snatched half-way down by a perfidious glacier sprite. Having coined those two metaphors and feeling mightily pleased with myself, I closed my window, but when looking for my bed, the position of which I had lost in the pervading darkness, I acquired a bump on my forehead which I banged on the corner of the wall. So I got sick of metaphors during the days that followed. My friends were kind enough to pretend they missed them very much.

Lettres d'un voyageur

JOHN RUSKIN

MOONRISE

28th June, half-past ten. I never was dazzled by moonlight until now; but as it rose from behind Mont Blanc du Tacul, the full moon almost blinded me : it burst forth into the sky like a vast star. For an hour before, the aiguilles had appeared as dark masses against a sky looking as transparent as clear sea, edged at their summits with fleeces of cloud breaking into glorious spray and foam of white fire. A meteor fell over the Dome as the moon rose; now it is so intensely bright that I cannot see the Mont Blanc underneath; the form is lost in its light.

Praeterita (1844)

Mountain Life

GUIDO REY

A BIVOUAC ON THE DRU[1]

When I had calmed a little and rested, I suddenly heard through the air confused gibbering voices, sailing up from the valleys or down from the summit; they came from very far, drew near, became more powerful and swiftly faded away in the distance.

They sounded like souls sighing, hurrying away through the darkened air. Out of this immense hollow and powerful choir a shriller cry would emerge, a yell of rage or a moan which was soon hushed into silence; then another voice answered. It was the eternal dialogue between the mountains and heaven; yet, on that very evening all the mountain voices, great and small, seemed to fly towards this one tiny human being, standing alone, high up, lost in the lap of the mountain, to tell him a long, wonderful tale as old as the hills.

I trembled strangely with eagerness and fright; the atmosphere of time and place were conjuring up in me a primeval horror, the unconscious heritage of ageless ancestors who had lived without fire or shelter.

In my trembling fibres some part of the soul of some weird quarternary ancestor, who had lived at the terrible time of glaciation, would awake.

Then all became silent; the evening wind had stopped and the last gleam had died; the hills looked dead. Now was gone the sweet light which gives the glaciers a voice; which in its course makes them alter their shapes and colours; which enlivens shadowy hollows and make the summits shine; which softens or hardens the mountain face, underlining its features and touching it up with glee.

At night the powerful limbs of the mountains become motionless, as if stiffened by the eternal cold; the great face hardens into an expression of changeless mystery.

We had to spend a whole night clasped in the arms of the huge corpse; instinctively, I folded mine over my chest, to feel the warmth of my body and protect it against that fierce icy embrace. Just to hear a human voice I started chatting with my companions, but we stopped short: we had nothing to talk about. One of us would move from time to time, to free an arm or a leg which hurt, or to find a more comfortable seat, moving from side to side on the bare slab. When one man moved, he disconcerted all the others, and it took a long time for the group to grow quiet again.

How often had I nestled against friendly limbs which had kept me warm during an ice-cold night of 4,000 metres!

And I began to think of my former companions in adventure, most of them

[1] In 1905, after a perfectly easy climb.

dead; two of them, two faithful guides, were buried not far from us, under the Mont Blanc snow, and I felt as if an endless time had elapsed and I had lived two lives, always walking and sleeping at night on rock slabs under the stars.

A sweet melancholy gripped my heart as I thought of those I had lost on the way, and I felt as if they were coming to me through the silence, along the edge of the ridge, up from the dark bottom of the valleys. I heard the stones they kicked down. They were already quite near. And surprised at seeing me there, they asked in a friendly voice: 'What! Are you here again?' And I wished I could clasp them to my breast, as I had done on days of victory gone by, keeping those friendly souls beside me to chatter about the past all night long; but they moved on and soon disappeared beyond the infinite ridge.

Alpinismo Acrobatico

FRANK SMYTHE

THE SENTINELLE ROUGE[1]

The air was very still. Not a breath of wind whispered around the stern figure of the Sentinel above. It seems absurd to invest a mere rock with the attributions of sympathy and understanding, but all that night a friendly presence encompassed us, watching over the two little things that were men who shivered and kicked on that hitherto untrodden mountainside.

On these occasions amid the sublimity of Nature's inmost sanctuaries, where no human being has stood before, the mind is capable of asserting itself above the discomforts of the body, and the most prosaic of men will find his thoughts wandering in realms of strange fancies. The forces of the World are vast, and sometimes inexorably cruel; they care little for weaklings; but to those who deliberately set themselves to wrest from them their secrets, they are often kind. . . .

One other incident of that eventful night I remember vividly. To induce warmth we brewed several cups of tea, and during one brewing we were startled to hear three long-drawn moans come up from the Brenva Glacier. Each moan was several seconds in duration and seemed expressive of the utmost agony. They were inhuman in tone and yet unlike any mechanical noise or siren that we had ever heard. I can offer no explanation. Glacier ice, under pressure, makes curious noises; it sometimes cracks, grates and booms in the night, but I have never before

[1] August 1927. Frank Smythe and Graham Brown were opening a new route in the face of the Brenva.

heard a noise resembling those three extraordinary moans. The effect was weird in the extreme, and to us it seemed as though the very spirits of the lost and the damned were abroad in the night.

Climbs and Ski Runs

R. FRISON-ROCHE

THE BIVOUAC

Twilight set the West afire with violent, livid streaks, like a display of Northern Lights above the shadowy valleys. They felt like castaways stranded on a polar ice-floe, at the edge of a sea of shadows that was already lapping their snowy reef. Now only a few points held the light; the 4,000-metre summits, five or six glowing centres that kept watch, like so many lighthouses, over the sleep of men below. One after another they went out; and at last there were only two left – Monte Rosa to the east, Mont Blanc to the west. Monte Rosa dimmed its light, then vanished into darkness, and finally the invisible watchman, decreeing it was now time for all to rest, extinguished the last gleams illuminating the dome of Mont Blanc, knowing very well how dangerous sleep would be at such a temperature. So they made themselves very busy; they carefully unlaced their crampons (the straps were beginning to freeze), put their feet in their sacks, muffled their faces in their helmets, all but their eyes, then with nothing left to do, they began to sing. Under the brilliant night sky of the high peaks, they bawled away at the tops of their voices.

Pierre went through his whole repertory: mountain songs, drinking songs, and even an occasional aria from an opera. Georges, who could not sing a note in tune, provided the bass. When they had sung everything they knew, they stopped, quite exhausted, and dozed off for a bit; but not for long, the cold woke them up and the singing began again; it was better than just sitting with chattering teeth.

Nights are short at the end of June, when you are 4,000 metres up. As light slowly filtered back they began to suffer in earnest from the cold. They lit the spirit stove and warmed up a fresh brew. They were still numb from the night's exposure, and prayed for the sun, that would surely not be long now. Mont Blanc was already aglow – and a warm puff reached them, encircled them, and brought them back to life. Snow that had been grey and livid now sparkled from every crystal. They left their fox-hole, took great breaths in the sunlight and slapped each other vigorously on the back, till they were ready to face the descent.

First on the Rope, translated by Janet Adam Smith

73

GASTON REBUFFAT

UNDER THE STARRY CANOPY

Only two centuries ago the slender rock or ice needles, frozen above the living planet, were merely Earth's signals to Heaven. Now they have been tamed and hold a place in our heart. For they are not there merely to be climbed. Climbing for climbing's sake has gone so far that we are in danger of forgetting which summit we are climbing.

Mountains, chiselled by wind, frost and centuries, stand against the blue sky.

They have a shape, a form, and their own elegance. That is the reason why some of them attract us at first sight; they are beautiful and we go to them of our own accord.

With their crown of legend, they have a history, a name and now a life. They are not only pleasant to look at: they actually live.

Just like the huge expanse of space, and more than the rest of the planet, they are drawn into Earth's great revolution around the Sun. What is the use of those empty lands, marked in brown and white on the maps? Nothing grows there, and there is nothing to sell. Those useless spaces, the Earth's waste lands, are gardens for man's delight. Our youth was in need of a revelation, and on the hills, fighting against storm and frost during our first climbs, and face to face with the silence, we felt as if we had been born anew.

This had nothing to do with the idea of 'living dangerously'. We were not in quest of stark adventure and even less of suicide; but like flowers, men need something to fertilize them.

A few years ago, during a winter day that was fine but deadly cold, with a friend I plodded up with great effort – because of the deep snow – towards the Grépon. There are various routes to the summit, but we wanted to reach it, if possible, over the finest of all, the celebrated Knubel crack. In the summer, the 'Knubel' is extremely difficult and seldom ascended; in the winter, under its coat of shining ice-glaze, it had never been attempted. We had studied it. It was one of those difficult cases where feelings have to be discarded and one's strength has to be pitted only against the difficulties. We had decided to make the ascent, since we were sure we could do so safely; but we were also very well aware that we should have to put everything we had into the struggle. There is usually a slight hesitation when tackling a precipice, knowing that one cannot risk a mistake; yet at the same time, one feels an extraordinary surge of life when both body and soul are united in the effort. In spite of overhanging rocks and the ice which makes them feel like glass, one rises slowly, feeling one's perfect poise on this perpendicular, indifferent, yet slightly changed rock.

A few days later we were on the Col du Midi, at the top of the Vallée Blanche.

74

Ascending the Aiguille du Midi from there is child's play: an easy hollow, an almost horizontal ridge, then the summit rocks. In the summer, innumerable parties halt each day at this viewpoint. But it was winter and, within a few feet of the top, the easy snow ridge, which had been hollowed out by the wind, had become a deadly cornice. To move along it was still perfectly easy, like walking along a level road, without any acrobatic effort. But the road was hollow, rotten to the core; it might dissolve into an avalanche. We hesitated, and then gave up. A few days after having successfully carried out an extremely difficult ascent, we did not complete a climb which was becoming dangerous.

The high hills had trained us.

On another March day we were due back at the Col du Midi by midday, which meant that we had to cross the huge ice hollow of the Vallée Blanche, a distance of several kilometres at a height varying between 10,000 and 11,500 feet, a route we had followed any number of times and which is much frequented in summer.

But there was a howling storm that barred all progress, so we were stuck. Then the weather suddenly cleared. The sky had been restored to us, and we could see the mountains. We were full of joy to start again, but half-way up the clouds closed in again and snow began to fall, wiping out the tracks. We felt as if blind, unable to see more than a few feet around us. We decided on a direction, believing we were walking straight ahead, but there were crevasses across the route and we had to walk round them. The Vallée Blanche is criss-crossed with crevasses. One always thinks that one recognizes this protruding piece of ice or that line of séracs, yet everything in the end looks alike.

Nevertheless, some power, not really born out of our recollections, but some instinct rather, took charge; our feet, more than our helpless eyes, lead us on. We realized that we were not mere visitors, but belonged to the glacier, the snow and the clouds. And we arrived on the Col du Midi.

During the summer, a deadly morning dawned, trapping parties who were climbing on the greatest precipices of the Alps. Fine weather, good conditions and encouraging weather forecasts had incited climbers to attempt very difficult routes, which required one or two nights in the open. The weather was perfect when they left. In the evening they would curl up in their sleeping-bag under the stars, but they suddenly forsook them. Like fruit that rots while travelling, the night turned bad, lost its substance, and in the morning the great festival of sunrise was postponed to another day. The sky breathed heavily and spread the avalanches out.

Man must adapt himself: it is his fate, the result of an increasing number of difficulties arising when mountains and bad weather meet, when he feels himself filled with power, poise, and a sense of friendship which are always his, but of which he is just becoming aware. Then he confronts the weather.

I will never forget one still-born dawn, on the day before we had attempted the Eigerwand in radiant weather, but now the Eigerwand was merely a spring-board to nothingness. We were within 300 metres of the top. The precipice was a death-trap, and we knew it. All those who had been caught in storm had attempted to descend and had died: the way out was upwards. Our first movements had nothing of the spontaneity of other days. The animal in us was angry. It was cold, snow drifted up our sleeves and down our necks; our fingers were awkward, our feet became frost-bitten, our wet clothing was already turned into a carapace as stiff as armour. Yet gradually some warmth crept back into us; the same gift which made us retreat from the rotten cornice gave us the answers. Strength flowed through us and had to be properly used against wind, snow and cold. It was not a short-lived excitement, but we were led to realise that wind, snow and cold were not enemies but obstacles. Thanks to this strength we succeeded, with prudence, in a most hazardous attempt. Avalanches roared down, but from time to time, at long intervals, there was a lull and our party slipped between two torrents of snow which could have carried it away like so many twigs. To the now ice-cold rock snow stuck even when it was sheer; yet for no obvious reason we were able to go through, in spite of everything.

When night fell we were very miserable because we had to stop moving: we had to keep awake, tied to pitons. We shared a few sweets, a few pieces of sugar, a little luke-warm water made from melted ice. We were dead-tired but we had to keep awake, just as in our crevasse on Annapurna. The night was endless.

Yet, having refused to sleep or die, we finally emerged on the summit in a silent landscape. A few men were blissfully happy, for throughout the ascent the storm and the snow they had felt deep in their hearts the great fulfilment: a life lived to the full in close touch with the elements.

JOHN TYNDALL

A BLIZZARD ON THE SUMMIT[1]

Climbing zigzag, we soon reached the summit of the Mur, and immediately after-wards found ourselves in the midst of cold drifting clouds, which obscured every-thing. They dissolved for a moment and revealed to us the sunny valley of Chamouni; but they soon swept down again and completely enveloped us. Upon the Calotte, or last slope, I felt no trace of the exhaustion which I had experienced last year, but enjoyed free lungs and a quiet heart. The clouds now whirled wildly round us, and the first snow, which was caught by the wind and spit bitterly against us, cut off all visible communication between us and the lower world. As we approached the summit the air thickened more and more, and the cold resulting from the withdrawal of the sunbeams became intense. We reached the top, however, in good condition, and found the new snow piled up into a sharp *arête*, and the summit of a form quite different from that of the *Dos d'un Ane*, which it had presented the previous year. Leaving Balmat to make a hole for the thermometer, I collected a number of batons, drove them into the snow, and, drawing my plaid round them, formed a kind of extempore tent to shelter my boiling-water apparatus. The covering was tightly held, but the snow was as fine and dry as dust, and penetrated everywhere; my lamp could not be secured from it, and half a box of matches was consumed in the efforts to ignite it. At length it did flare up, and carried on a sputtering combustion. The cold of the snow-filled boiler condensing the vapour from the lamp gradually produced a drop, which, when heavy enough to detach itself from the vessel, fell upon the flame and put it out. It required much patience and the expenditure of many matches to relight it. Meanwhile the absence of muscular action caused the cold to affect our men severely. My beard and whiskers were a mass of clotted ice. The batons were coated with ice, and even the stem of the thermometer, the

[1] September 13, 1858. John Tyndall and Sir Alfred Wills were accompanied by Auguste Balmat and several other guides and porters.

bulb of which was in hot water, was covered by a frozen enamel. The clouds whirled, and the little snow granules hit spitefully against the skin wherever it was exposed. The temperature of the air was 20 Fahr. below the freezing point. I was too intent upon my work to heed the cold much, but I was numbed; one of my fingers had lost sensation and my right heel was in pain; still, I had no thought of forsaking my observation until Mr Wills came up to me and said that we must return speedily, for Balmat's hands were *gelées*. I did not comprehend the full significance of the word; but, looking at the porters, they presented such an aspect of suffering that I feared to detain them longer. They looked like worn old men, their hair and clothing white with snow, and their faces blue, withered and anxious-looking. The hole being ready, I asked Balmat for the magnet to arrange the index of the thermometer: his hands seemed powerless. I struck my tent, deposited the instrument and, as I watched the covering of it up, some of the party, among whom were Mr Wills and Balmat, commenced the descent.

I followed them speedily. Midway down the Calotte I saw Balmat, who was about a hundred yards in advance of me, suddenly pause and thrust his hands into the snow, and commence rubbing them vigorously. The suddenness of the act surprised me, but I had no idea at the time of its real significance: I soon came up to him; he seemed frightened, and continued to beat and rub his hands, plunging them, at quick intervals, into the snow. . . . He at length became exhausted by his own efforts, staggered like a drunken man, and fell upon the snow. Mr Wills and myself took each a hand, and continued the process of beating and rubbing. I feared that we would injure him by our blows, but he continued to exclaim: '*N'ayez pas peur, frappez toujours, frappez fortement!*' We did so, until Mr Wills became exhausted, and a porter had to take his place. Meanwhile Balmat pinched and bit his fingers at intervals, to test their condition; but there was no sensation. He was evidently hopeless himself; and, seeing him thus, produced an effect upon me that I had not experienced since my boyhood – my heart swelled, and I could have wept like a child. The idea that I should be in some measure the cause of his losing his hands was horrible to me. . . . At length returning sensation in one hand announced itself by excruciating pain. '*Je souffre!*' he exclaimed at intervals – words which, from a man of his iron endurance, had a more than ordinary significance. But pain was better than death, and, under the circumstances, a sign of improvement. We resumed our descent, while he continued to rub his hands with snow and brandy, thrusting them at every few paces into the mass through which we marched. At Chamouni he had skilful medical advice, by adhering to which he escaped with the loss of six of his nails – his hands were saved.

Glaciers of the Alps

GEORGES SONNIER

A STORM ON THE REQUIN

When leaving the (Requin) hut at dawn, a warm puff of wind, coming from the glacier, struck us in the face. It was a bad omen. But it was a short climb and we went on. The Glacier d'Envers du Plan was in very bad condition, yet we reached the rock quickly. I have nothing to say about the climb. I was quite staggered, hardly believing what I saw, when I suddenly landed on a narrow slab, after which there was nothing but emptiness all round: it was the summit. Was this all there was? The Requin? Relieved, and even slightly disappointed, I yet relished an unexpectedly easy victory.

In front of us stood the dizzy cluster of the Aiguilles. I extended my hand towards them. . . . What was the matter? I felt an unbearable pricking in my finger tips. They started to hum, and my wet rope-soled shoes also hummed. I looked at my companion, his hair was standing on end, drawn towards the sky. I felt my own hair doing the same. Small bluish flames were hovering round us, springing out of the rocks they caressed.

We knew what it meant: we were in the very centre of a developing storm. In one single leap we left the summit, racing into empty space. Twenty seconds later we reached, seven metres below, the base of the summit block and my companion was about to fix the first double rope in the Fontaine chimney. At that very moment we heard a short and dry explosion. I looked at the guide with a questioning eye. He nodded; we understood each other without a word: the lightning had struck the summit. That was obvious. . . . It had been a matter of twenty seconds, thirty at most, and it would find us there. How little does life hang upon! Relaxed and perfectly unconcerned we smiled, happy to have played that trick on fate. I was surprised at feeling so calm and so completely unmoved. In point of fact, I could not feel how great the danger had been. I just marvelled at our luck.

Où règne la lumière

HERMANN BUHL

A STORM ON THE AIGUILLE NOIRE

I was for pushing on to the summit as quickly as possible and Martin agreed. Soon heavy raindrops, mingled with hailstones, were pattering down, though it didn't last long and the mist presently lifted; but the sky above was blacker and more threatening than ever. It seemed as if the weather was bound to make fools of us, though we still hoped to reach the summit before the thunderstorm broke.

A vain hope for, even before we reached the subsidiary summit, the full force of it was unleashed on us. The sluices of heaven were opened; hail and rain poured down upon us, with snowflakes intermingled. A fierce gale, breathtaking in its ferocity, blew up. We crossed the subsidiary summit, roped down to a saddle, and raced up the ridge towards the summit; by now we were in the middle of a lovely snowstorm. The gale was driving solid walls of snow- and ice-crystals horizontally across the ridge, lashing them into our faces. The organ notes of the storm boomed among the crags, howling around the faces: so thick was the pother that we could hardly see ten yards ahead. Suddenly the profile of a ridge loomed up – the East Ridge. We must have been quite near the summit of the Noire then! The last bit to the top, though, where East and South Ridges meet, shoots up like a tower.

What on earth was happening –? My friend looked at me in astonishment. A high-pitched murmur filled the air, a most uncanny sound – but one I recognized at once. It was a static charge of electricity in the air, presaging the discharge of lightning. Everything around us was in a high state of tension. This was no time for hanging about; it was a signal for us to get off the ridge and down as far as possible in the shortest possible time, renouncing all ideas of our climb.

While we were still deliberating, a bright flash enveloped us and we were struck by a force which almost lifted us off our feet; a hot blast of air flapped at us. There we stood, half-blinded, concussed and deaf from the ensuing thunder-clap. The next followed with hardly an interval, and then another and another; an ear-splitting, all enveloping noise filled the Witches' Cauldron about us. Added to the thunder crashes was the howling of the wind, the lashing of the hail and the water roaring down like a tidal wave. We were caught in the hell of a high thunderstorm; flash upon flash, roar upon roar, as we raced like hunted animals down the upper part of the ridge, seeking at least to escape from the immediate danger zone. The blizzard hurled whole waves of sharp ice-crystals in our faces – which became so painful that we could hardly keep our eyes open. In a trice the rock was covered in a perilous glaze of ice. Steep cliffs kept on forcing us back on to the crest of the ridge from the slight shelter we had found on the South Face. Up there that ghastly murmur was always about us and with us.

The thunder gradually passed over, but the gale did not abate. Whenever the mist lifted we could catch a glimpse of what lay ahead of us. It was an endless way down and Time raced wildly. Dusk began to fall and we found ourselves engaged in a race with Night. Soaked as we were, we couldn't possibly bivouac. Every time we thought we had reached easier ground, the short respite was followed by another steep downward dip; such disappointments are a feature of the Western Alps.

21 - *La Dent du Géant.*

21 - *The Dent du Géant.*

22 - *La Montée de M. de Saussu...*

22 - *M. de Saussure ascending Mont Bla...*

We could hear from the rushing of the waterfall that there was still a steep pitch between us and the ravine at the bottom. We were going separately now, each picking his own line, until gullies down which we could not see brought us to a halt. We certainly couldn't rope down into that kind of unexplored pit – all experience, bitterly won, enforced that lesson. We tried gully after gully for a way out, but in vain. Were we going to have to bivouac after all? The thought chilled us to the very marrow.

We went feeling our way round in the dark. By a miracle I stumbled on an *abseil* sling, a clear pointer to the right way down. We roped down several pitches, most of them turned to waterfalls. Not that we cared; we were soaked through to the skin already. At last we reached the bottom. Just seventeen hours after leaving the Noire Hut, we found blessed shelter under its roof again. We had it all to ourselves; and while the storm raged outside, we were soon in a deep sleep. We had earned it.

Nanga Parbat Pilgrimage, translated by Hugh Merrick

IV. LIGHT AND SHADOW

THÉOPHILE GAUTIER

A PAINTER'S VIEW[1]

When coming out of the valley of Magland we were dazzled with admiration: Mont Blanc unveiled at last, and it was so magnificently splendid, so different from any earthly colour or shape, that we felt as if the gates of a dream world had suddenly been opened wide. It looked as if a huge piece of the moon had fallen from the sky. The gleam of the snow, lit by the sun, would have turned to black all the comparisons in my *Symphonie en blanc majeur*.[2] It was an ideal white, white proper, the white of the light which shot on the Christ of Mount Thabor. Splendid clouds, of the same hue as the snow, which were only discernible through their shadows, sailed up and down the mountain sides like angels on Jacob's ladder, among torrents of light, and, reaching higher than the sublime summit, they extended into the sky, looking as if, with their immense wings, they were about to fly into infinity. At times the veil of clouds tore open, and through the wide gap old Mont Blanc was descried on his balcony as the King of the Alps, bowing to the hills, his subjects. He condescended to show himself for a few minutes, then closed his curtain. This mixture of cloud and snow, this silver chaos, those waves of light breaking into white streaks of lightning, those phosphorescent diamonds, would require words that human language lacks, and which could only be found by the dreamer who wrote the Revelation in the ecstasy of his vision.

. . . One cannot imagine the colour the earth assumes when completely barren, near mountain summits, and just below the eternal snow-line. Those tinges have a delicacy, a transparency, a radiance which would turn into mud the colours of the freshest palette: pearl grey, lilac, smoke, China pink, amethyst, purple, turquoise, like the backgrounds of the Paradise Breughel paints in his

[1] In the summer of 1868, Théophile Gautier and his mistress, Ernesta Grisi, travelled through Savoy and Switzerland, going to Chamonix and Zermatt.
[2] One of his best-known poems.

heavenly landscapes, a thousand shades which would be easier to express with a brush than with a pen. One realizes it is the skin of a star, and that the earth, seen from the moon, must shine like a golden globe. This change in colour always surprises lowland dwellers, and painters always dread such effects.

. . . When the bed of this ice torrent (the Glacier des Bois) becomes too steep, the ice mass breaks into slabs, leaning one against the other, looking like small white marble columns in Turkish cemeteries, which lean to right or left because of their weight; more or less deep or wide crevasses splitting the huge block and revealing the virgin snow in all its purity. The walls of those crevasses assume fantastic colours, the shades of an azure cave. An ideal blue, different from the blue of the sky or of water, ice-blue proper, an unknown tinge which is never seen on painters' palettes, touches up those splendid fissures and sometimes becomes an aquamarine green through gradations of surprising delicacy.

Les vacandes du lundi

JOHN RUSKIN

CLOUDS

June 25 (1849). . . . Out after dinner, rambling about Brévent with sketch-book in search of a view of the Aiguille du Plan; didn't find one, but found some wild strawberries, which were a consolation. The day had been fine, with scattered clouds; in the evening a most curious case of floating cap cloud, *hooding* the Mont Blanc summit without touching it, like gossamer blown upwards from a field; an awning of slender threads waving like weeds in the blue sky (as weeds in a brook current, I mean), and drawn out like floss silk as fine as snow. This cloud that does not *touch* the snow, but hovers over it at a certain height, following the convexity of the mountain, has always seemed most unaccountable to me.

Praeterita

GEORGES SONNIER

THE GLACIER

Then, at the very first peep of dawn, I discovered the glacier.
I mean the glacier of Tré-la-Tête. Through all the Alps I know no more

83

solitary or more forbidding glacier. And that was what I felt when I saw it in the wan light of early morning. It did not resemble at all what I expected. It looked like a gigantic dead beast, some dragon drowned for ever between desolate banks. The whole landscape was deeply inhuman and hostile, as if distorted by the light dripping from the dull sky. It was cold, and the cold permeated my whole being, gripping my heart and numbing my body. I felt terribly lost, miserable, a prey to blind but prodigious powers. And I felt terrified.

I had reached the very edge of the big grey glacier, the last of its frozen waves. I gazed at it in amazement; I had been expecting a shining armour, shot with light; I saw only a broken shell, with poisonous steel reflections.

It was just one step away, but I did not dare to make that step: it became a gaping chasm to me. Properly speaking, I was paralysed. My throat caught. I must repeat, I was terrified. And while the icy breath of that sterile universe was blowing into me, I was thinking of soft valleys and the warm rooms with drawn curtains – for it was early still – of wood fires and fresh milk – all that was pouring into me and calling me back. Neither my companion's reproofs, nor his taunts, nor his anger could conquer my terror. I stopped on the forbidden threshold and, while he stalked away on the glacier, having no patience with me, I began to walk down towards the valley: I had panicked and I ran away from that cursed bank.

Où règne la lumière

V. WINTER

MAX ALDEBERT

THE DOLENT IN WINTER[1]

The sun reached us fifty yards above the bergschrund, in the middle of the ice slope. Below my feet a giddy slope extended down to the vicar, tied to me by the rope, and towards the black depths of the crevasse. Above, the slope lost itself in the ice-glazed rock face which stretches to the Brêche de l'Amone.

I cut a step.

'All right?' inquired the vicar.

'All right,' I replied.

Below, an unstable step collapsed. I belayed the vicar at rope-length to help him across a tricky pitch. The staircase I had just cut up to the sky receded, on the almost perpendicular face, towards the flat glacier below.

I cut a last step and leant on a repulsive mixture of rocks and snow.

'A b. . . . shame!'

The vicar was coming up slowly, carefully, one step after another, the point of his ice-axe thrust into the ice.

The huge expanse of the Argentière Glacier lay at my feet and at the other end of my rope, belayed over my right shoulder, the vicar was coming up, full of confidence. My only thoughts were for the splendour of the world and the safety of my companion, as in a deep hymn.

The vicar enlarged a step which seemed too narrow to him.

> *Taille des marches dans le glace*
> *Taille des marches dans le nuit*
> *Taille des marches dans l'espace*
> *Taille des marches dans l'oubli.*

---

[1] The winter of 1940, when the author was with the Chasseurs Alpins in the Valley of Chamonix.

85

Mont Blanc

La corde est raide comme un mort
Où sont tes mains?

The vicar slid his knee up the slope to get his right foot into the step. I pulled at the rope which the cold had stiffened.

Où est la chaleur de la gorge,
Ton pouls qui bat?
Le vent ronfle comme une forge,
Où sont tes pas?

The vicar came up slowly, ten yards below me, widening a few steps with a sharp stroke of his ice-axe.

Taille des marches dans le glace,
Taille des marches dans le nuit,
Taille des marches dans l'espace,
Taille des marches dans l'oubli.

I belayed him against a sticky rock, my feet deeply buried in the snow.

Tu pleures, tu pleures, tu pleures
Ouvre les yeux.

The vicar emerged on the last of the hundred steps which I had cut from the bergschrund to my present nest.

Le Vertige est un escalier.

'O.K.,' said the vicar, leaning against me. 'It is steep!'
He was panting.
'It must have made you sweat, cutting all those steps!'
I answered, pulling off my gloves to blow on my fingers: 'I composed a poem.'
'Just like that, while taking in the rope? Well. . . !'
I looked at the staircase below us: 'Tonight, we shall have to go down that thing!'
Suddenly I felt cold. I added: 'Possibly tomorrow. We shall have to bivouac.'
We ate in the sun. It was very cold. The vicar and I, grabbing a sardine and a chunk of bread, looked at the huge expanse of the ice world.
We climbed very quickly over broken rocks, an overhanging slab and the big chimney of the Brêche de l'Amône. On the crumbling ridge of snow and insecure

rocks, where the wind blew fiercely into our faces, the vicar yelled, looking below him at green expanses far away:

'Switzerland!'

Snow, ice, rocks!

Rocks, snow and ice!

We went on along the frontier ridge, buffeted by the wind.

We stopped for a moment. The vicar drew his binoculars out of his rucksack and looked towards the Col Dolent:

'No gun,' he remarked.

And we pushed on. The sun was at its zenith and it was still cruelly cold.

Our orders were: to reach the triple frontier landmark, at 3751 metres, on the summit ridge of the Dolent, a little below the summit which is Swiss and Italian, and then come down.

But we turned round the gendarme, into a steep, ice slope on the French side, and emerged far beyond the rocks, on the ice frontier between Switzerland and Italy. The summit was somewhere about, within 100 metres. We waded into powdery snow, over a slope of steep stone and hard ice. On the left the gaping chasm of the north face, 1,000 metres of empty space, towards peaceful Swiss valleys. France was behind us.

Le royaume des hautes terres

GEORGES SONNIER

FROM WINTER INTO SPRING

The days were getting clearer, but colder too: the weather was frosty. Bare trees were holding up their crystal twigs to the sky. Over the valley swam long white wisps scarcely higher than the chalet; there was a keen haze, spun of icy needles. It lasted for weeks. At last, one day about the middle of January, the temperature grew milder, the distant prospects melted and the snow began to fall.

It snowed for twenty-one days, with short halts and delusive reprieves; twenty-one days during which, apart from a few hours when the visibility cleared a little, I saw nothing but a shifting curtain of snowflakes, and heard nothing on the smothered hills but the hushed rumble of avalanches.

The snow fell in masses. For more than a month no one came up to Colombaz. Even the village youths, who used to come sometimes on Sundays to ski on the big slope below the chalet, where they had built a jumping platform, abandoned such expeditions. Then I was the only one to use the snow-filled path. Every four or five days I had to go down to the village to collect a bare minimum. On the plateau the wind had formed drifts which blocked the way. The crucifix was buried, the bushes smothered. Sometimes, in spite of my skis, I sank knee-deep into the powdery layer, running at random over the slopes, blinded by white flakes. When climbing back, the wind had wiped out my track and I had some-times to struggle for hours to get back home. Each time the crossing of couloirs, constantly swept by avalanches, was a dangerous proposition. Heaps of snow had wiped out the path long before, and I tried awkwardly to hurry over the steep, slippery slope, struggling step after step through masses of powdery snow, which was sliding down over and round me, pushing me, overflowing me, trying to hurl me into the ravine. For the load I carried could well make me lose my balance. When I had passed the bad pitch I got my breath and started off again with renewed energy. A few yards higher, when I had passed the crucifix, I would see the chalet before me, peeping out of the mist.

The snow fell for twenty-one days, and at last, on the twenty-second day, the sun returned to a virgin world.

A secret world, frozen into an almost supernatural lack of motion. A wayward breeze, here and there, played delicately with shivering plumes. An overloaded branch shook itself free, rustling like silk. Buried under heaps of snow, the whole mountain seemed deeply conscious of its own perfection. This fragile perfection was a transient miracle and already dissolving from second to second, as the sun-light increased. That is how, during the war, I knew the solitary hills deserted by everybody, returned to their own animals, and to the deepest magic of their solitude, where nothing was to be seen but delicate and mysterious tracks, begin-ning nowhere and suddenly stopping, an unreadable writing which obeyed laws unknown to men, the living language of the snow. . . . Such were for me the hills of the solitary years, kept in their vastness as in the days before they were conquered. In the newly-born splendour of days, I drew my tracks over a virgin landscape, cut my way into a world which had been recreated for me. I owned the mountain.

Snowy skies, always new. The pale green skies of February dawns; jade skies. Intense midday skies, when everything burns and dissolves in flames. Deep blue night skies, shot with stars. I have known you all, through my solitary wanderings.

Shall I speak of wild animals – the friendly wild beasts I met, which had for-gotten men and often forgot to run away? Most of them had assumed the colour of the season – snow partridges, white hares, ermine-white weasels (one of them lived all the winter in a pile of wood, under the gallery of the chalet); herds of chamois rushing into a hollow and scampering away at breakneck speed, gallop-ing away with such grace that it seemed like one long graceful slide. I remember having seen within fifty paces a large fox – he was fiery red – playing with a hare, who was not a bit afraid, pretending to track him, while the hare was lazily run-

88

SOUSCRIPTION.

PREMIER VOYAGE

A LA CIME DE LA PLUS HAUTE MON-
TAGNE DE L'ANCIEN CONTINENT,

LE MONT-BLANC,

Par le Docteur MICHEL-GABRIEL PACCARD,
Médecin dans les Alpes de Chamonix.

Le 8 Août 1786.

LE Mont-Blanc, si renommé par les Voyageurs & les Savans, passé pour la plus haute montagne de l'ancien Continent; il est couvert d'un manteau de neige & de glace qui traïte jusqu'à sa base: des foules de Voyageurs viennent l'admirer toutes les années & parcourir les Glaciers qui en découlent: les tentatives des chasseurs de chamois les plus hardis pour atteindre sa cime, ont échoué jusqu'à présent: l'Auteur y est parvenu le 8 Août 1786. Plusieurs amateurs des montagnes désirant connoître les détails de ce nouveau Voyage; il en est même qui ont étendu leurs accueils jusqu'à solliciter une souscription pour former un prix qui fasse l'éloge & la récompense des Conquérans du Mont-Blanc: l'Auteur, pour mieux mériter ces accueils & pour

---

Ministère de la Guerre.

Division. Lettre de Service.

Bureau.

Napoléon, Empereur des Français,
Roi d'Italie, Protecteur de la Confédération du Rhin,
et Médiateur de la Confédération Suisse,

Ayant ... pour être
employé en cette qualité au ...

a fait choix de M. ...

Il est en conséquence ordonné aux Officiers généraux, aux Officiers d'État-major, à ceux de l'Artillerie et du Génie, aux Inspecteurs aux revues, aux Commissaires ordonnateurs et ordinaires des guerres, aux Commandans des Corps et à tous autres qu'il appartiendra, de le reconnaître en sadite qualité et faire reconnaître en ladite qualité par ceux étant à leurs ordres.

Fait à ... le ... Janvier 1814.

Le Ministre de la Guerre,

---

23 - Première page du prospectus du Dr Paccard.

23 - The first page of Dr Paccard's advertisement for his book.

24 - Diplôme de guide de 1814.

24 - Guide diploma, 1814.

25 - *Jacques Balmat.*

26 - *Richard Pococke.*

27 - *Dr M. G. Paccard.*

29 et 30
*Les souliers et le baromètre
de Saussure.*

28 - *H. B. de Saussure.*

29, 30
*Saussure's shoes.
and barometer.*

ning round his hunter, refusing to hurry. When the game was over, each went leisurely about his own business.

The delight of ski-ing! I drew my tracks across huge white expanses which I explored day after day, according to my own whims. Yet my daily exploration of the mountain taught me many things. For instance, I discovered that in winter it is warmer on the slopes than at the bottom of the valleys, so that at night the temperature, by a strange phenomenon, goes up while one ascends to a certain altitude, at least. By the end of the winter I no longer marvelled, when ski-ing down in the morning from Colombaz, where it was freezing no longer, to find ice in the village streets 300 metres below. That year the mountain taught me how wayward an avalanche can be, that it may well refrain from falling down a steep slope, but will start on the opposite side, though it is far less steep and there is nothing to warn you or explain why. Consequently the man who wanders through the Alps has to rely on his luck or a secret intuition as much as, and possibly more than, on experience. It taught many other things which I could only discover through close contact.

And the temperature was rising. A sort of tenderness was creeping into the cool air, with a portent of spring. There was something like the warble of a song in the light.

Winter had heaped successive layers of snow on my roof. Immensely long icicles were frozen to it: at the top end they were almost a foot wide and might well have stunned a man on falling. I had to hack them down. The thaw came and for one whole day the house was alive with long creaks and groans. Then, in the evening while I lay awake, I suddenly heard a rumble as if the world was coming to an end, and it made me jump up, rather pale in the face. It took me a few seconds to realize that it was not Mont Joly which had fallen down: it was merely that the roof had shaken off its tons of snow, which were now piled on the ground, window high. The house then stopped moaning.

The days were getting longer, the sun scorching. The last layer of snow was melting into the ground. The earth was discernible on the south slopes in irregular slabs which grew larger and larger and finally united. One could see last year's grass, yellow and frost-burned. Only the badly exposed *collieux* were still piled with thick heavy snow and shaky blocks, the remains of innumerable avalanches. At last, after a rainy morning, the whole rotten slope slid away in front of me, scraping the ground, tearing away some hundred yards of road, to roll down to the bottom of the valley where it stopped in a chaos of ice, broken trees and several metres of thick mud which dried up slowly, lying there until late in the summer. Thus the question of the *collieux* was settled. It might have been my own problem, in a totally different way, had I been on the slope a few minutes earlier. But I had been lucky that day.

Terre du ciel

GEORGES SONNIER

EARLY SNOW

Six o'clock in December. I opened my door: it had snowed all night. The sky was green over the hills. The weather was going to be fine.

Here the first winter snow was a festival which I wanted to celebrate in my own way. Here were my skis, my rucksack. I should be ready in a second.

I left when it was still dark. The village was asleep. All the paths had been wiped out. The hours of darkness had sculpted this crystal face for the world.

Snow wrapped itself round every shape, the reality of which was hidden though not suppressed. Through it I could not feel, though I could still imagine the hard-frozen ground, the soft moss, the sudden hard bite of rocks. Carried along by my impetus I climbed steadily, never looking back. Snow meant much more than a setting to me, it was an element in which I immersed myself. I met it again, and rediscovered it with delight: always the same and always new. The dawning day with the new birth. The air, hardly brushing it, wiped from my brow the weariness of late vigils. I forgot all that was not it. Freed from human ties, keeping away from the paths it had wiped out, I followed a route which led to it across a naked wasteland. This morning, everything was offered me. This newly fashioned universe was a great gift handed out to me.

Through the windless air a blue haze rose to connect the sky to the realm which was the earth. I hardly reached it when it closed round me with a soft, resistless sweep. It caressed and engulfed me. Above it, the slope had disappeared. I could not see it and yet it carried me. I was walking through the sky. My track was the thin thread which still tied me to those down below; strung across the virgin hill, it was the one human element, making me captive of my delight.

Through the swirling mist I pursued my motionless walk. My steps pressed forward, knowing where they were going. A black spot appeared and enlarged on the slope, making everything suddenly recover size, reality and poise. I reached it: it was the hut. I bent forward and grabbed the key, hidden behind a board: a little secret a few of us knew.

I entered. The room smelt of cold and neglect. Formerly, we used to climb up there sometimes, but no one came any longer. Years had elapsed. Where were my former companions?

I struck a match and set fire to a bundle of twigs ready in the stove. I had taken off my skis – a very old pair, of a kind no longer made. Together we have often raced over the hills, away from any beaten track. I fondled them with my hand: they were good, faithful tools.

The fire crackled and sparkled and a pungent smell filled the room while the cold retreated into distant corners. Out of my sack I produced some bread and a flask. I looked at the bread: it was dry and golden like a harvest day. How far you were from me, summers past or summers to come!

One does not cut bread: one breaks it, and the piece I put into my mouth yielded a strangely pleasant taste, made of the sun which ripened it. The wine had a green and pungent taste which also conjured up familiar things. Penetrating me, its stream became alive and part of myself.

I went towards the narrow window, opening over the white expanse. The haze was still there, but I knew where all my mountains were. Mont Blanc was there; also the Aiguilles and further on the Verte. Though invisible, all the familiar summits were coming to me across the distance.

The cloud was torn open, revealing a shred of sky. Where I had thought the Verte lay I descried, soaring into the sky, a summit I had not expected, the aspect of which was disconcerting. A moment passed and the shape I gazed at changed its form in a strange way. Mountains have many faces, which are recognized only through love. Once I climbed it, and for the space of a second I had trodden the tiny snow pyramid that is the summit. Then I went down. What remains of that moment but the mere remembrance? As the answer to my question, the cloud closed, wiping out the view.

It was time to leave. The fire had gone out, and I carefully closed the door of the deserted hut. The mist was lighter going down. The track I had drawn across the slope when coming up was enough to help me read it in its entirety, its drive, its scope, its tiniest secrets.

I let myself go. The world slowly gathered speed. The hut flew up in a smooth sweep. My track stamped its living language upon the huge and virgin landscape, just discovered and marked for the first and the last time. Little by little the air I displaced gathered life and caressed me. Across the intense silence time wavered, sank into dream and carried me away. The valley came up at last, reached me and stopped, with a silky rustling. I had found the road again. And here was the village. Someone was coming out and walking towards me. 'Good morning,' he said.

The sun had risen above the summits.

(Hitherto unpublished)

VI. ANIMALS

ST FRANCIS DE SALES

CHAMOIS[1]

I met God full of sweetness and tenderness even among the highest and most rigorous mountains, where many simple souls adored Him in full sincerity and truth, and where deer and chamois ran here and there among terrifying expanses of ice, to proclaim his praises. Not being devout enough, I understood but few words of their language, but I am sure they said very beautiful things.

Lettres

MARC-THÉODORE BOURRIT

COWS

We were about to reach the Allée Blanche; we were only separated from it by a mound named La Seigne. Mont Blanc and the westernmost of the big aiguilles were to be revealed to us, who were longing for discoveries. I wanted to shorten the distance and I went up alone, not expecting any incident; what could I have expected in places which only display empty and uninhabited nature? Imagine my astonishment when, reaching the mound, I saw myself surrounded by a herd of some seventy cows. I do not know whether I surprised them as much as they did me. Yet I do believe that they had already seen me and were ready to receive me as their enemy. Indeed my red coat and the umbrella unfurled above my head probably looked strange to them. However, they pretended to draw apart to let me pass and then closed again in a circle, which they tightened step by step. I

---

[1] It is obvious St Francis refers to Chamonix, though he does not name the place.

92

was then greatly frightened and had to use my stick to drive them away. I do not know what might have happened, if I had not been helped in good time by a shepherd who, from a nearby hillock, had seen the beginning of this ludicrous struggle. He ran towards me, shouting; his loud voice and threatening gestures impressed the enemy and I was set free.

Itinéraire de Genève, des Glacières de Savoie et de Chamonix

HORACE-BENEDICT DE SAUSSURE

CHAMOIS HUNTERS

Looking for crystals and shooting animals are the only forms of work which exclusively belong to men. Luckily, the former activity is far less practised than in former times; I say 'luckily' because it has killed many people. The desire to get rich quickly by finding a cave full of fine crystals had so many attractions that the hunters took the greatest risks and there was not a year during which men did not get killed, falling into the crevasses or down the precipices.

. . . Chamois hunting, possibly more dangerous than the quest for crystals, still occupies many mountaineers and nips in their prime men who would have been useful to their families. . . . Can you understand that it creates an unresistible passion? In the parish of Sixt there was a well-built, good-looking young man who had just married a charming wife. He actually said to me: 'My grandfather died hunting, so did my father, and I am so sure I shall die in the same way that this very sack, which I take with me when hunting, I call my winding sheet, for I know that I shall never have another. And yet, if you were to offer me a fortune, on condition that I gave up hunting, I could not accept it.' I made a few ascents in the Alps with this man; he was strikingly nimble and strong, but his rashness was greater still and I was told that two years later he lost his footing on the edge of a precipice and the destiny he had expected was fulfilled.

What can be the attraction of that kind of life? It is not greed, or, at least, conscious greed; for the finest chamois never brings more than twelve francs to the man who has killed it, even when the value of the meat is included; nowadays, when their number is very much reduced, the time one wastes in looking for one is worth far more than twelve francs. But the very danger, the alternating hope and fear, the constant agitation of the soul which those movements provoke, key the hunters up, as they do the gambler, the warrior, the sailor and even, to a certain degree, the Alpine naturalist, whose life somewhat resembles that of the chamois hunter.

Voyages dans les Alpes

EUGÈNE RAMBERT

GOATS

How lovely are the goats of Praz-de-Fort when, after they have been relieved of their milk, they leave in the morning for their daily journey! Within five minutes' walk of the village, when they have reached the *glariers* of the torrent, they stop, disperse and have their first breakfast; then, on entering the forest, they reform their column and trot off in a business-like way in the shade of the great fir-trees. Soon after, the leaders emerge at the foot of the Saleinaz glacier and cross the torrent by a bad bridge on which they must file one by one; then they leave the glacier on their right and climb the slope above, their pasture. It begins where the forest ends and extends to the snow line. In several places it is cut by rock walls, and access is so difficult that no other herds contest it. They climb more or less high, according to the season, but they always graze and climb to their hearts' content. They are not flat-country goats – sluggish, tame animals with a smell of stable about them and heavy udders dragging on the ground; they are mountain goats, clean, silky-haired, tough-haunched and light-footed, with small delicate heads, piercing eyes and straight little horns on their brows. Though well used to the mountains, they dread the rain. As soon as the rain starts, they take shelter under an overhanging rock or look for an under-ground hollow or the protection of a large tree. If they find inadequate shelter, they lean against a tree trunk or a rock, to have at least one side protected. Buffon wrote that goats don't mind the rain, but he is wrong. Few domestic animals resist the wet so little. Therefore, the goat-herd's first care when taking them to new pastures is to seek for caves and possible shelters. And if by any chance they have to submit to some heavy shower unprotected, their restless attitude or dull accept-ance betray what they think of the weather. They need the sun: then they can disperse over the mountainside, and they vie with each other in good grace, vivacity and capriciousness. They never remain close to one another, as sheep do. They scatter in little groups and the most headstrong go by themselves in quest of some distant adventure. They would seem to have a feeling for the picturesque. They know they are pretty, and they are constantly caught behaving in the most coquettish way and studying the attitude which suits them best. They have a genius for staging a group or a picture. Here stands a russet goat on the top of a rock, motionless, with her four feet together and leaning forward. What is she gazing at, so intent that she forgets the half-chewed tuft of grass which still hangs from her mouth? Actually there is another goat, a slender brown one, standing on a lower rock, erect on her hind legs and straining her neck, her head and her muzzle to snap the budding tip of an alder twig.

. . . Why do they need to climb so far? There is no reason whatever. A goat climbs because she likes it. They must know every accessible pitch, every alternative route, every projection of a cornice, every chimney, every ledge, every dangerous spot on their grazing ground. What the chamois does not need to study, because it has a genius for mountaineering in its blood, the goat assiduously learns every day. Contrary to the chamois, she was not born in a cave; she has not the chamois' breathing power nor its legs. But she is more inquisitive; she has a taste for discovery and a passion for what is new. When there is a choice between two routes, or between two tufts of grass, she selects the worst route and the more difficult tuft to reach; of all the animals domesticated by man, none has kept a freer temper, and a semi-independence which goes with an adventurous turn of mind.

Les Alpes Suisses (1866)

CHARLES NODIER

BLIND MAN'S DOG

It was the second time I approached the beautiful and melancholy vale of Chamonix, which I shall not see again.

It had been with renewed pleasure that I had visited again the graceful forests which surrounds the village of Les Bois. I had come to the small esplanade, daily invaded more deeply by the glaciers which are so majestically overhung by the finest *aiguilles* in the Alps, and which leads through an almost imperceptible slope to the picturesque source of the Arveyron. I wanted to gaze once more at its portico of blue crystal which changes every year, and derive some emotion out of that natural scenery. My tired heart needed it.

I had not gone thirty steps when I noticed with some surprise that Puck was no longer near me. Alas! You would not have got him away from his master, even with the tastiest macaroon, or the most delightful cracknel; he was somewhat slow in obeying my call, and I was beginning to get restless when my lovely Puck came back, looking slightly embarrassed and a little afraid, and yet with the caressing confidence of friendship, his body arched, his eyes wet and imploring, his head so very low that his ears were brushing the ground, like those of Zadig's dog. Puck, too, was a spaniel. Had you seen Puck in that attitude, you could not have looked angry.

I was not angry, but he ran away, then came back, and as the game continued I made towards the point which drew him until, when he was attracted by two perfectly equal sympathies – or if like me you prefer the phrase better, by two powers perfectly alike – he stood motionless.

On a stone bench sat a young man with the most pleasant face and the most touching aspect, clad in a sky-blue smock which looked like a sort of tunic, and holding a long shepherd's crook of laburnum wood, a strange costume which gave him some resemblance to the Greek shepherds painted by Poussin. His fair and heavy hair curled round his bare neck and hung over his shoulders. His features were sober without austerity. Though not depressed, his mouth expressed sadness rather than bitterness. Only his eyes had a strange aspect I could not account for. They were large and clear but fixed, lustreless and dead. There was no soul behind them. . . . I realized he was blind. . . .

'Did you lose your sight through an accident?' I asked.

'An accident which, alas, was my least misfortune. I was hardly two years old when an avalanche, falling from the heights near the Flégère, crushed our little house. My father, who was a mountain guide, had spent the evening in the Prieuré. You can understand his despair when he found his family under that dreadful heap! With his companions he succeeded in digging a hole through the snow and he crept into our hut, the roof of which was still supported by its fragile beams. The first thing he saw was my cradle; first he protected it against the constantly increasing danger, for the digging had loosened and brought down new masses, and our house was even more precarious. He went in to save my mother, who was unconscious, and he was seen by the light of the torches outside bringing her out in his arms, when suddenly everything collapsed. I was an orphan, and the next day it was seen that I was blind.

Les aveugles de Chamonix[1]

[1] A recollection of his journey to Chamonix in 1825.

4
THE MOUNTAIN

THOMAS BLAIKIE

EXPLORATION

September 1, 1775. In the morning we left Chamonix along with Gabriel Paccard,[1] directed our way straight towards Mont Blanc by what they call La Coudraz; here we came to a little lake where the water is exceeding clear upon the borders of ice; this is said to be 1,182 *toises* above the level of the sea. About this place I found many curious plants. . . . There is *Ranunculas Glacialis* and *Aconitifolius* upon the rocks of what they call the Aiguilles de Blaitière. . . . Here we scrambled up behind those Aiguilles which is calculated 1,680 *toises* high which makes 10,442 English feet; here it is only ice and rocks and nothing else to be seen, in some places it is entirely surrounded with those perpendicular rocks which are amazingly high; here as we was [sic] examining those solitary regions we was [sic] struck with the noise of a great quantity of ice or rather part of the mountain which fell down into this valley which with the echo of the rocks made a noise like thunder and seemed as if the whole mountains were going to fall about our ears. This is what they call in the country *les Avalanches* which happen continually. . . . Here we left those triste rocks as night was coming on and my companion told there might perhaps fall another avalanche so we descended by the Lake des Nantillons which is remarkably dismal surrounded with barren rocks hardly any verdure; from this we descended to the herds cottage called Chalet de Blaitière and as the people knew Mr Paccard we was well received. Staid there.

September 2nd. Left our lodgings early this morning and continued our march westward towards the bottom of Mont Blanc, until we arrived at the borders of this vast sea of ice called the Glaciére de Bossons; this is a vast extensive valley of ice of which Mont Blanc on the left hand is the head and looses itself in the skies to the right hand. Along the borders of this valley there is a great many larchs, and lower down the bottom of this glacier is surrounded with large spruce firs; one

[1] He was 18 and was studying medicine in Turin. He was back in Chamonix for the holidays.

99

thing which must be beautiful is the most part of those banks leaning towards the glaciers betwixt the larches, firs and the ice is covered with *Rhododendron feruginium* which the contrast of their fine scarlet flowers surrounding those white valleys must be enchanting but at this season they were in seed. Here we passed the ice to gain on the other side what they call the Montagne de la Côte; from the top of this you are opposite the middle of Mont Blanc; from hence the eye is fatigued with the view of this plain and the mountain which appears only a mass of snow as there is few rocks, betwixt you and the mountain but this desert mass of eternal snow. From hence we took our way higher up westward to what they call the Aiguille du Goûter which is exceeding high perpendicular rocks which towards the mountain support this bed of snow and ice which forms Mont Blanc and these glacières; here we are above every mark of vegetation. . . . Here I wanted to try to go higher but my companion almost tired out would go no further and as there was no plants to be got we agreed to return down to Chamonix; here is an exceeding good way to descend the ice by means of a stick with an iron pick at the end. You place behind and lean upon and, so slid down the steepest ice; arrived in the evening at Chamonix.

Diary of a Scotch Gardener

ANONYMOUS

AN ACCOUNT OF THE FIRST ASCENT

Mont Blanc in Savoy, near the glaciers of Chamonix, has been made famous by the journey of several scientists, among them M de Saussure; also by the accounts written by M Bourrit. This mountain is supposed to be the highest in our hemisphere; there the ice which has accumulated for thousands of years keeps increasing, to the point that gradually it swallows up the villages and fills neighbouring valleys. No traveller had yet succeeded in reaching the summit. This conquest has been made by M Paccard, a young doctor born in this valley, who studied in Paris. He slept in the ice valley and, followed by a man called Balmat, left the next day at four in the morning, after walking for some fourteen hours, and reached the summit of the mountain. Spectators who followed them with a telescope saw them on the highest summit. Those fearless travellers remained there for thirty-two minutes and descended in four hours by moonshine. A wish to know and observe, the noblest of all passions, helps man to attempt the most courageous things; this virtuous ambition brings out an infinitely sweet delight which draws no regret in its train, the aim being to enlighten other men by increasing the empire of science and multiplying observations.[1]

Journal polytype des Sciences et des Arts (Paris, September 15, 1786)

HORACE-BÉNÉDICT DE SAUSSURE

ACCOUNT OF PACCARD'S ASCENT[2]

We discussed the Doctor's ascent of Mont Blanc at length. He says that near the top he found large hailstones embedded in the snow; that fresh snow is far more fatiguing to the eyes than old snow, which has been the cause of more than one failure. I grasped his route perfectly. After crossing the glacier he left well to his left the chain of dark rocks[3] on which is my second cabin, and swerved towards the foot of the Dôme du Goûter, called the Gros Mont. He kept close to its foot, leaving it always on the right. After a long ascent he found himself on a great plain, or at least a very gently inclined snow-slope, and turning to the left, reached a kind of snowy bank planted between two lofty and perpendicular rocks that were bare of snow. He passed over the top of the left-hand rock, skirting the base of the summit of Mont Blanc and, having thus borne a good deal to the east, turned again southwards to climb the last slope, which is very steep and fairly hard. On the top the snow seemed loose. It was easy to plant the barometer as deeply as was desirable.

From the top it is possible to descend the gentle slope on the Val d'Aosta side and reach some rocks which rise in a sharp crest.[4] He looked there for a possible sleeping-place, but the wind was everywhere equally strong and cold. He found some loose stones on the snow at the foot of the last slope and higher up two little rocks that one sees from Chamonix, perhaps one hundred paces below the top.[5]

Four times the snow that covered the crevasses failed under their feet, and they saw the abyss below them, but they escaped a catastrophe by throwing themselves flat on their poles laid horizontally on the snow, and then, placing their two poles side by side, slid along them until they were across the crevasse. He thinks it would be an excellent idea to take a ladder. The place where they met the most crevasses was near the rocks on which my second hut stands. He told me he owed his success in part to the observations I made on the Buet on the

---

[1] The details and figures are accurate. It seems this is a first-hand account of the ascent, written on the spot, after an interview with Dr Paccard.

[2] August 22, 1786.　　　　[3] The Grands Mulets.　　　　[4] Mont Blanc de Courmayeur.

[5] La Tournette.

periodicity of fatigue and recovery. When they reached a considerable height he noticed that he was obliged to take breath and allow his strength to recover at about one hundred paces, and as they advanced further, at every fourteen paces. But after a rest his strength immediately revived, as I have noted too.

It was midday before they were opposite my second cabin, although they had started at 4 a.m. from the first; thus, if one were to start from the second, one would gain a great deal, and might reach the summit early in the day. A curious observation on sunburn and snow-blindness is that they did not come on till the next morning. They did not descend without a halt, as had been alleged. They stopped before midnight on the top of the Montagne de la Côte, and up to that point they did not suffer any inconvenience. But next morning, when at dawn they set out to return to the Priory, the Doctor could not see well enough to find his path and had to be led by the guide. He says it may prove one of the inconveniences of sleeping *en route* that it may lead to the eyes being weak on awakening. Anyhow, it would be a good idea if one were to take precautions against the brilliance of the sunlight. He confirmed the statement that the ink in his bottle was frozen in his pocket, and also some meat the guide had in his sack. He thinks his hand was frozen at a relatively moderate temperature because his skin glove had been wetted by having leant on the ice. His hand became black and insensible. He got rid of the blackness by rubbing it with snow. He adds that his fingertips are still numb. He changed gloves with Balmat, who had a pair of fur gloves; Balmat's hand also froze; it turned pale and was likewise cured by rubbing it with snow.

He agrees with Pierre and Jacques Balmat in thinking that the best time for ascents would be at the beginning of June, because then the crevasses are choked and the winter snows are firmer than those which fall in the summer months. The long days are another advantage. Distant objects were not clear; the accumulated vapour seemed to form and settle on the horizon. When they reached the plain which I have mentioned at the foot of Mont Blanc, they endured great fatigue from the fact that the surface was covered with a thin crust which alternately bore them and gave way under their tread. The guide told him he could not persevere unless he (Paccard) was prepared to take the lead from time to time and to break the snow, *and he did this all the way up to the top.* There they were exposed to a bitterly cold west wind which affected their breathing. They sought for temporary shelter below the final crest, but found the temperature insupportable. They could only withstand the cold by keeping continually in movement. He had a compass, and he believed that on the top its variations are different. I passed the rest of the evening in writing this.

Mss notes, published by D. W. Freshfield in his *Life of H. B. de Saussure*

The Mountain

HORACE-BÉNÉDICT DE SAUSSURE

HIS OWN ASCENT[1]

. . . Since for the last two hours I had had before my eyes almost all one can see from the summit, the arrival was no *coup de théâtre*. It did not even give me all the pleasure I might have imagined. My most lively and pleasant sensation was to feel myself at the end of my uncertainty; for the length of the struggle, the recollection and the still vivid impression of the exertion it had cost me, caused me a kind of irritation. At the moment that I trod the highest point of the snow that crowned the summit I trampled it with a feeling of anger rather than of pleasure. Besides, my object was not only to reach the highest point; I was obliged to make the observations and experiments which alone gave value to my venture, and I was very doubtful of being able to carry out more than a portion of what I had planned.

Still the grand spectacle I had under my eyes gave me great pleasure. A light haze, suspended in the lower layers of the atmosphere, hid, it is true, the more distant and low-lying objects, such as the plains of France and Lombardy.[2] But I did not greatly regret this loss; that which I came to see, and now recognized with the greatest clarity, was the order of the great ranges of which I had so long desired to ascertain the grouping. I could hardly believe my eyes; it seemed like a dream when I saw under my feet those majestic peaks, those formidable Aiguilles du Midi, d'Argentière,[3] du Géant, of which I had found even the bases so difficult and dangerous of approach. I grasped their connections, their relation and their structure, and a single glance dispersed the doubts which years of work had not sufficed to remove.

Voyages dans les Alpes

COUNT LAURENT-MARTIN DZIEDUSZCKI

AN ACCOUNT OF DE SAUSSURE'S ASCENT

It is not before Sallanches that one begins to identify the shape of Mont Blanc really clearly, and there also begins the exhaustion and dangers of a truly

[1] August 2, 1787.
[2] The plain of Lombardy cannot be seen from the top of Mont Blanc.
[3] The Aiguille Verte.

horrible road. One ascends hills where one finds nothing but torrents and the heaps of stones they have carried down. A few days before I arrived, a respectable old man, M Paccard, the Secretary of Chamonix,[1] had been drowned in one of these torrents, though he apparently knew the road well. On the 4th (of August), in the evening, I arrived Chamonix, having seen on my way the Glacier des Bossons, which is on the road. This day is illustrious and shall go down in the noteworthy History of the Glaciers as, on that very day, August 4, 1787, M de Saussure, who for twenty years had made so many unsuccessful attempts, was returning from the summit of Mont Blanc, the route up which had been known since last year, after the expedition of M Paccard, the Chamonix doctor and two guides who had gone up with him. Professor de Saussure had eighteen guides and his valet with him. On the 3rd, at midday, they had all been seen from Chamonix on the summit of Mont Blanc. All the bells had told the news to the inhabitants. M de Saussure was for four hours on the top, working at his observations, through which he made out that this frightful giant is 2,700 *toises* above sea-level. No man had ever been so high. It took M de Saussure three days and two nights going up and only nine hours down. When going up, four guides walked in front of him to open a path in the snow. Several were seen lying on the snow for four or five minutes to rest. M de Saussure had been for more than three weeks in Chamonix, waiting for propitious weather for his ascent. His wife and her two sisters were there with him, and had the pleasure of seeing him reach the top, through good glasses. On the summit of Mont Blanc there is nothing but ice and snow, but a little lower down one finds strange flowers and extraordinary stones. All the guides slept for two nights in a tent which M de Saussure carried with him.

Mss notes published by C. E. Engel in *La Suisse et ses amis*

DUCHESS OF DEVONSHIRE

DE SAUSSURE'S ASCENT[2]

How much we have been pleased here with M de Saussure, a great philosopher. He is a most interesting and amiable man – much attached to his wife – and has two sons and a beautiful daughter.

There is a very high mountain called Mont Blanc, covered with ice always and so high that nobody for many centuries has reached its top – a person got to the

---

[1] The Doctor's father.   [2] June 5, 1791. Letter to her daughter.

31 - *L'Aiguille de Blaitière.*   31 - *The Aiguille de Blaitière.*

32 - *Panorama
du Mont Blanc.*

32 - *The panorama
of Mont Blanc.*

Drawn on stone from a Sketch by J. Auldjo.

Drawn on stone from a Sketch by J. Auldjo.

Printed by C. Hullmandel.

33 *et* 34
Deux épis
de The As
of Mont B
de John A

33, 34
Two episo
from John
Ascent of
Mont Bla

36, 37 et 38 - *Acrobaties victoriennes.*
36, 37, 38 - *Victorian mountaineering.*

evasse   35 - *The Grande Crevasse*

39 - *Mme la Comtesse d'Angeville passe ses guides en revue* (1838).

39 - *The Countess d'Angeville inspecting her guides* (1838).

40 - *Le sommet du Mont Blanc,*

40 - *The summit of Mont Blanc.*

top and M de Saussure was desirous to go (though very dangerous), to try experiments on the air.

His wife, though she dreaded his going on account of the danger, had courage and love enough to tell him, as it had been done, so great a philosopher ought to try it. He went up. He was two days and so frozen with cold, though in July, that his victuals froze, and he was so weak he could not buckle his shoes. Often he was obliged to crawl over a ladder placed across the cracks in the ice hundreds of feet deep.

When he got to this height he saw underneath him all the snowy points of mountains and rivers of ice shining like diamonds – the whole country of Switzerland, Savoy and part of Piedmont, the lake of Geneva – and the sky appeared to him of deep Prussian blue – but what delighted him most was to distinguish, which he had the happiness of doing, his wife and sons at Chamonix where he had left them, waving a flag, which was the sign he agreed they should make if they saw him and knew he was safe.

I think the story is very affecting. He has given me two bits of granite from the rocks at the summit of Mont Blanc, which I shall preserve as great treasures, and he has given your dear grand-mama beautiful flowers.

From Iris Leveson-Gower, *The Face without a Frown: Georgiana,*
Duchess of Devonshire

ELIE-ASCENSION DE MONTGOLFIER

A STORM AT THE GRANDS-MULETS

I have already mentioned the fact that I often went chamois hunting, not to shoot but as a beater. Among the men who took me with them was an old man, nicknamed 'le Mont Blanc'.[1] He had been one of the guides and companions M de Saussure took with him when ascending the mountain, an ascent which cost him some 200 louis, and the man often told the story, showing me the route the caravan had followed. Seen from afar, the mountain did not look as difficult as old Mont Blanc made it out to be. I decided to make the journey alone. I got ready slowly, as it could not be denied that there would be obstacles on the way. Having provided myself with a hatchet, food for five days, and a kind of spur I could tie to my shoes to grip the ice, which had been given me by Father Mont Blanc, hiding my attempt from the world, but treasuring in my pocket the draft of his route, I

---

[1] Jacques Balmat du Mont Blanc. He was the only one to have been given that nickname. The climb took place about 1799.

set out one day at 2 a.m., and by 4 o'clock difficulties began. I repeated to myself: 'You are on the big cone of Mont Blanc. Just go up; you are sure to arrive.' But it was easier said than done. After endless efforts, I arrived at the Grand Mulet at ten at night, after twenty hours of the most exhausting ascent a tough child of fifteen or sixteen ever attempted. There was no doubt I was at the Grand Mulet; I had an accurate description of the place and I easily found the shelter mentioned by my old hunter. I withdrew into it and had a pleasant enough evening meal. During the night I was constantly awakened by the rumbling of avalanches falling from the nearby Aiguilles. Surrounded by snow, I felt that the weather was heavy: the south wind was blowing. At one in the morning a frightful storm burst: snow was whirling round me and thunder roaring under my feet. Nature was in regular combustion. Cramped with cold, I was wondering how I could creep from under the rock where I nestled, as the opening was getting narrower and narrower every minute.

Day broke at last, but that was not the end of the storm. The fresh snow which had fallen or had been swept down made walking impossible; I would have fallen into crevasses before having gone twenty paces upwards. Soon the weather got much colder, the snow surface became frozen, I attempted to sally out; the sun was shining but the cold was bitter. I was glad of it, thinking that now I could ascend Mont Blanc. I started up with an energy few grown men have displayed under similar circumstances. I climbed up for eight more hours, covering the necessary distance ten times, meeting with obstacles which compelled me to strike a new direction, or descend what I had just ascended. Finally, seeing that all my efforts were of no avail, having come across some insuperable obstacle which made me waste a whole hour to turn round it, I saw there was no chance of reaching the top before nightfall; or, if I could make it, there would be four hours of darkness to spend there, during which I might die of cold or from lack of air. I had already reached a height at which I could hardly walk more than twelve or fifteen paces without stopping to breathe. I was feeling oppressed; I was spitting blood and I had barely escaped being hurled down avalanche couloirs. To my regret, I had to give up and go down.

It was late, and it was not easy, as the snow was frozen no longer, under the rays of the setting July sun. I could only reach the Grand Mulet at nightfall and went back to my shelter. The weather had changed; instead of a north wind the south wind was blowing and a frightful storm broke; it raged until sunrise, and at that time the mountain was wrapped in a thick fog which would have made my descent not only dangerous but quite impossible. So I decided to accept the situation. At midday the fog lifted and a radiant sun lit the mountain, but the huge expanse of the plain was totally hidden. Soon I saw flashes of lightning coming towards me, and the thunder roared under my feet. I was basking in beautiful sunshine and watching a storm raging 400 metres below. Electrical commotion had a terrible effect on masses of snow poised over avalanche couloirs.

Their fall, together with the roar of the thunder was so striking and so majestic that I cannot remember having ever been more impressed. Heavy rain followed the storm, which poured all evening over the plain, while I was still basking in sunshine. While looking at the huge plain, which I compare to the waves of the sea at various stages of the tide, gaps were opening through the clouds, through which the sun shone. I then saw the valley verdure and even large inhabited centres – so many radiant islands in the middle of that wide ocean – but they did not last long. While some disappeared, others were opening.

I spent the whole evening musing and dreaming, all my fatigue of the days before clean forgotten. At nightfall I crept back under my rock and slept soundly, undisturbed. The next day, on awakening, the sun had risen. I gaily went down and reached the Priory of Chamonix in the evening and took shelter in Father Mont Blanc's barn. I had some food left, which I shared with him. I was careful not to mention my attempt at scaling Mont Blanc: he would have called me a pygmy trying to fight the giant of Europe. Two days later I was his beater while hunting chamois; on the way he told me that a man had been descried above the Grand Mulet, but he had probably perished, a telescope had failed to trace him later on the top of Mont Blanc. I was careful not to tell him that the man was really the child who was now playing the part of a dog.

Mss memoirs, published by C. E. Engel in *Le Mont Blanc, Route ancienne et voies nouvelles*

COUNT ANTOINE MALCZESKI

A NOTE ABOUT HIS ASCENT (1812)

This phrase ('the white feathers of stooping humility'), quite appropriate to the spirit of the Christian religion, may not be altogether irrelevant to the way in which the eye sees, from a great height, what pride or the spirit of Man did create, and also the beauty of Nature. When I ascended the summit of Mont Blanc, on which, for two hours, I experienced feelings I shall never feel again, when my eyes and thoughts overflowed with life, I lost sight of the realm of man and, from the place where I was, I could only descry white objects, those his power has been unable to alter. For instance, the lakes of Geneva, Neuchatel, Morat and Biel, were revealed to me looking like veils held out in the sunset, while houses and towns on their margins were but dark marks. Similarly, glaciers could be distinguished, while meadows, forests and even fairly high mountains, lying farther away, melted into a grey mist. There is nothing more wonderfully wild than the view from the top of Mont Blanc; but, as it is totally different from anything we know, we can only imagine it by fancying we are carried away by some good or evil spirit, when the god Chaos was creating the world. Any human work dies of its insignificance. Thousands of gigantic mountains, with granite summits and snowy shields, an almost black sky, thin air which makes breathing difficult and fevers one's pulse, all that impresses any mortal with a superhuman feeling. I am certain that, were there no other inconvenience but the terrible disproportion between this staggering mountain landscape and our puny imagination, no one could stand it for long. Let my recollection of the extraordinary impression I felt on this huge and solitary hill not be an incentive to any young traveller to try and attempt this expedition. Besides the very great difficulty and the danger of such an attempt, its full success depends very much on completely different circumstances. Three days of fine, totally cloudless weather, and a snow not too soft are almost more necessary than the most patient endurance and the strongest chest. To leave when such circumstances are not forthcoming would simply mean courting death, and it would be a most perilous stubbornness not to listen to the guides' advice. Everywhere in Switzerland and above all in Chamonix, those men are full of courage and commonsense.

Maria

RODOLPHE TOEPFFER

HOW TO DESCRIBE MONT BLANC[1]

You magnificent Monster, I wish there were someone to praise you! . . . Indeed, not a Delille, and even less a Hugo; this poet robs anything he describes of its soul, and only shows its shape, and that not even faithfully. There is nothing left but the colour, which is not even faithful, but always glaring and nothing but glaring. He is an illustrious dauber and not a painter. . . . I wish you had a genuine poet, a really truthful one who, filled with the sense of your majesty, dreading your deadly touch, a respectful observer of your habits, your instincts, and your destruction, and also aware of your lore in the valley at your feet, would put into his new, wildly inspired eclogues the thrill one feels when seeing you, the spell you cast on those who look at you, the charming, unexpected contrasts between your brutal rule and the fragile creatures you protect or tolerate; between your colossal slopes, which thrust other mountains aside in order to have more space, and that tiny flower which happily thrives in your shadow; between

[1] 1843.

the horrible creaking of your immense vertebra and those kids which carelessly nibble at a bush or drink the torrent under the gaping archway of your roaring mouth. The eclogue is a dying form of poem; the idyll fainted away under the insipid pastoral: why not attempt to revive them in the life-giving mountain air? Why are they not trying to recover where still exist the charm of simplicity, solitude and musing, which have vanished elsewhere, and get back into touch with Nature, an impossible task in other surroundings?

Nouveaux voyages en zig-zags

MARTIN BARRY

A LETTER TO MARKHAM SHERWILL[1]

(Edinburgh; August 12, 1836)

Respected Friend,

Thy letter was not received until long after its date because of my absence from Edinburgh, having been protracted unexpectedly without arrangements for the forwarding of letters, and an acknowledgement of it had been further delayed by a journey from which I have recently returned. To learn that my narrative had afforded satisfaction to one so much at home among the Alps was very gratifying to me indeed. I do not know of any person from whom the same expression of approval would have been more so. It was to James Marsden, a young gentleman studying medicine in this University that I was indebted for the perusal of thy narrative published in French, I think at Geneva, and bound up with an English copy of the excellent *Account of Chamonix*. When I saw him lately and told him I was about to write to thee, I think he wished a message of remembrance to be conveyed. I regret much not having seen this paper on the glaciers: They would I am sure have yielded information of which I should have been glad to avail myself.

Finding the Rochers du Nord[2] projecting just about as much as de Saussure had found them seven and forty years before, I concluded that snow did 'not upon the whole *deepen* on the *summit* of Mont Blanc' and on reflection it still appears to me that the conclusion was natural. As to the *form* of the extreme *apex*, that is of course, as I also stated, 'subject to frequent changes depending much on the direction of the wind while snow is falling'. I can readily conceive that Napoleon's cross, if it remained on the apex after it fell, might have influenced the *form* of

---

[1] Martin Barry was a Quaker. [2] The Rochers de l'Heureux Retour.

the latter in the manner thou hast described, but I do not understand in what was its *depth* could thereby have been increased.

The discovery of Saussure's ladder[1] was very interesting and important in connection with calculations as to the march of the glaciers. I stated that it *was said* they descended at the rate of a foot each day and was intending to offer an opinion myself on their velocity. I much regret not having had it in my power to quote thy experience of this subject. I found *Phyteuma hemispherica*, but it was much lower down than the Grand Mulet Roche – I think near Pierre à l'Echelle.

Again believe me, thy letter was very acceptable. I am respectfully thy friend,
Martin Barry.
Mss letter published by C. E. Engel in 'Markham Sherwill's Collection of Autographs' (*Alpine Journal*, 1938)

COUNTESS HENRIETTE D'ANGEVILLE

A LETTER TO MARKHAM SHERWILL

(Geneva, September 15, 1838)

. . . It is not necessary to come from the same country and to have met, to be on friendly terms; it is enough that we both made a long and dangerous journey at an interval of thirteen years to make me understand why you may like to have the information you ask for, and it is a real pleasure for me to supply you with it.

From the foot of the Mur de la Cote to the top I fell into a lethargic doze which compelled me to stop every ten or twelve paces, and required an unheard-of will-power to overcome. This semi-sleep, mastered by sheer effort, turned into a nervous state which pushed me on and up for a few paces, and then compelled me to halt again. As soon as I sat down, a deadly kind of sleep weighed, not only my eyes, but on all my limbs, and it is in such an alternation that I passed the last hours of the ascent, though the thought of giving up never entered my spirit. That is all the courage I displayed, and I deserved no praise at all, until the last fight, since I had covered seven-eighths of the route without feeling the tiniest bit of fright or of fatigue. As soon as I was on top, the resurrection was immediate. I recovered all my strength at once, the life which seemed to be about to forsake me, and all my intellectual power, which enabled me to enjoy that magnificent scene in all its grandeur! I do not know whether it was due to the happiness of triumph that I felt no more fatigue or depression during the

---

[1] Not on Mont Blanc but on the Mer de Glace.

remainder of the journey, though we waded for a four hours' traverse through two feet of *soft snow*. Here are the facts; try and find the cause.

Of course, I could give you a great many more documents by going over my recollections and adding facts to the fifty or sixty small pages of notes I made along the route and *on the very top of Mont Blanc*. But I must confess I am at present compiling the relation of my journey, and I would be very cross if you robbed it of its striking originality by writing about it with *too many details* in the book you are planning.

It is possible I may go to London to make an ascent *to the clouds* in Green's balloon and, when coming back, to go to the bottom of the sea in a diving bell. I would be greatly pleased to know your whereabouts for the next six months and both your addresses, so that, in case we might both be at the same time in either capital, I could let you know my arrival, as you may guess, Monsieur, my desire to know all my Mont Blanc brothers.

Mss letter published by C. E. Engel in 'Markham Sherwill's Collection of Autographs' (*Alpine Journal*, 1938)

VICTOR HUGO

DISINTERESTEDNESS

Mont Blanc, surrounded by a range of a hundred other hills, like birches round a tremendous oak, like Samson among the children of Amalec, or like the main stone erect in the centre of a cromlech, displays himself among the Alps he dwarfs by his size; and the lower mountains, the knitted brows of the world, the dark excrescences of the earth, shaped at Jehovah's feet, the crust broken open by Satan when he stood up, proud summits watered by the storm, admire him from the bottom of their hearts. 'Oh Greatness,' says the Dent du Géant; 'Oh Beauty !' echoes Monte Rosa. And all of them, the Matterhorn, the Combin, smoking Pilatus, which rings like a big horn, so deep is the tinkling of the bells of the homing herds on its flanks at sunset; Titlis, the powerful breath of which is the storm wind, Baken who drove Gessler away, and Rigi who hurls his hurricanes across the lake; Pelvoux, giddy with the scent of sweet-fragrant sage, Cenis who looks at the Isère and Albis, who sees the Vosges Morcle with its double tooth, the Dru as black as a hangman, the Ortler and the gigantic virgin, the Jungfrau, who allows only the stars to kiss her brow[1], Schwytz with its glaciers looking like pieces of white linen, the tall Mythen, the steeple in which hangs the bell

[1] It had been ascended for the first time in 1811.

111

named Aquilon – all of them, from lake and chalet, and from chasm to dale, all who roll clouds in the sky and rocks on moraines, with aiguilles or snowy peaks or majestic summits, gathered round the powerful mountain, raise to Mont Blanc a fantastic hymn.

'Here he is, the white shepherd of stormy mountains! He protects us all and towers above us! He is the radiant spell cast over space; his rocks are an epic and his dells a romance; he casts his dark silver over the silky gleam of Lake Leman; the ocean would be terrific at the foot of his huge precipices, and his blades of grass are prouder than our larches; he casts his light over us when the sun has set; when he is seen, leaning in the brown twilight, one may take him for Titan's fearful larva; he twines the blue Rhône to the golden-haired Arve; his summit, to weigh out has greater love, either his glance or daylight, stares straight at the sun, like the hawk. Night, when his huge figure stands erect, thinks that a new world is born on the horizon. He is splendid, displaying at the same time ice and grass. Archangels come to sharpen their swords on his summit. The Salève lies like a dog at his feet; a bleak spinner, he weaves rainy fogs; his pines are greener than all others and his snow is whiter; in one hand he grasps the dove Avalanche, and in the other the vast, ferocious Hurricane. He can unsheathe a blizzard like a sword, and lakes tremble under his mist. He dips the blazing saw of lightning into the massive darkness of night. Immensity stoops down to kiss his brow and takes him for her lover. He is crystal azure and diamond sea. His mane of icicles, worthy of the polar lion, spreads out like a terrifying cloak over his fierce shoulder. His precipices are too deep for chamois; on his sublime side, the twelve months are strung one above the other. He is higher, purer, grander than all of us and, were we men, we would insult him!

La légende des siecles

VICTOR HUGO

'BALMA'

Did he say: 'Winter, chasms and the storm watch over the king of mountains under his dais of fog; no man, so far, has been able to step on his head, which is almost beyond one's vision. I shall go! In my sublime daring, I shall besiege this icy fortress and those towers which touch the sky! On the snowy summit of this Hyperborean hill glory had planted an unknown palm which no eye but mine can descry?'

Did the humble shepherd in a dream hear voices calling to him from the air:

The Mountain

'Do not sleep! Let your soul soar up to the mountain brow! Let it guide your feet! Shepherd, let the earth admire you at this height. Go! the Divine spirit always dwelt on high places as in a temple. Go! there is no doubt that a vision awaits you on this new Sinaï where, like a new Moses, you climb to meet God?'

I do not know; but one day, at the hour when, still smothered in darkness, dawn had not yet touched the brow of the darkened Alps, he went. Mont Blanc was the first to be lit, standing like an active king who, while his whole camp and all his warriors still slumber, awakes in arms and over the darkened mountains raises his golden helmet. When he was seen, laden with his heavy sack, his bark ladder and stone hatchet,[1] shepherds and proud hunters surrounded him, asking where he was going. At first, as he pointed towards the clouds, it was not known whether he meant Mont Blanc or Heaven.[2] But, when he explained his magnanimous goal, they said: 'Brother, do you wish to reach the summit of the accursed mountain? What evil spirit takes your hand to lead you to your death? Stop! you are courting death! Storms and chasms bar the way.' He listened to their cries and resumed his way.

He passed the hill where the Bossons Glacier loosens its avalanches; the Peak of Chamois and the steps of the Malpas,[3] torrents, icicles pressed into pyramids, slippery granite slabs, wet meadows, and moss and rocks wearied his steps equally.

He went on up; flying over drifted snow, pushing back his crooked horn, the agile chamois hurried to his sheltering caves; stones, rolling under his uncertain foot, hitting the mountainside in endless fall, awakened echoes which had hitherto been silent.

He went on up; soon he was above the oaks and then above the larches which veil the very high mountains, black fir trees, clustering in deserted dales, then flowers covering bare rocks, running water, birds flying among clouds, grass under his feet and even noise in the air.

He went on up. The air grew thinner and failed him; heavy clouds hid the plain. The crimson brow of the mountain was gilded by lichen; his footsteps on the eternal ice were frightening from afar the strong-winged eagles which never need to raise their eyes, except to look at the sun!

Tout la lyre

[1] Those strange implements seem to be mentioned merely because the rhyme requires them.
[2] In point of fact, it was Paccard who found the route.
[3] A very strange route!

Mont Blanc

CHÊNEDOLLÉ

MONT BLANC[1]

So this is Mont Blanc, the monarch of mountains! His sceptre stands supreme above a score of hills that seem to crawl upon the plain, crushed by his magnitude.

Roaring tempests, on brazen wings, strike him ceaselessly, and never move him; the ageless head of Time has crowned him with a diadem of snow.

On his throne of rocks, made permanent by ages, he welcomes winter's shafts. His dais is the sky, his cloak the clouds and his belt the forests.

In his threatening hand he holds the avalanche, sister in wrath to the lightning. When the fiery sun sets the snow to fall, it comes down together with death.

Terror! Who can tell its ruins? Everything yields to its thunder, while old pines, chalets, huts and wild rocks alike roll down to the bottom of the ravine.

Poémes

PAUL VERNE

THE ROUTE TO AVOID AT ALL COSTS

When approaching the Petit Plateau, Edouard Ravanel suddenly stopped and turned towards us.

Indeed, a huge ice avalanche, falling from the Dôme du Goûter, had completely covered the route we had followed in the morning when traversing the Petit Plateau. Its mass was certainly no less than 500 cubic metres. Had it fallen while we were crossing, one more tragedy would doubtless have been added to a list of Mont Blanc casualties that was already too long.

Facing this new obstacle, we had either to find an alternative route or cross just below the avalanche. Considering how exhausted we were, the second choice was obviously the easier, but it involved great danger. A wall of ice, more than twenty metres high, partly severed from the Dôme du Goûter, to which it clung merely by an angle, overhung the route we were to follow. The huge sérac seemed to be precariously poised. When passing its foot, would not our progress, by moving the air, make it fall? Our guides discussed the situation. Each of them had a look through his telescope at the crack between the mountain and this

---

[1] 1820. This poem, written after Byron's *Song of the Second Spirit* in *Manfred*, is not printed here by mistake: it is meant to reveal the resemblance of Victor Hugo's lines to those of an extremely classical writer, whose style he despised.

threatening mass. The clear, sharp edges of the crack meant a recent cleft, obviously caused by the avalanche.

After a brief discussion, our guides, convinced there was no alternative, decided to risk crossing this dangerous pitch.

'We must walk very quickly, and even run,' they said. 'Then in five minutes we shall be safe. Well, gentlemen, a last effort!'

Racing for five minutes is not much, even for tired people; but we were completely exhausted, and running, even for so short a time, through a soft snow into which we sank to our knees, seemed perfectly impossible. Yet we made a supreme effort, and after toppling down three or four times, dragged by some and pushed by the others, we eventually reached a hillock of snow on which we collapsed, completely exhausted. We were out of danger.

It took some time to recuperate, and we sprawled over the snow with a satisfaction everybody understands. The greatest difficulties were now behind us and, if there were any danger left, we could face it without excessive fear.

Hoping to witness the fall of an avalanche, we halted for some time, but in vain. As it was getting late and it was not wise to linger in those icy solitudes, we decided to resume our route and by five had reached the Grands Mulets hut.

Quarantième ascension française au Mont Blanc (in *Le Docteur Ox*)

R. L. G. IRVING

THE HUTS

There are no fewer than seven huts where you may spend the night about half-way up the mountain; you have only to choose. First the Grands Mulets, perched on a rock between two great glaciers that join below it and pour down into the valley of Chamonix. Here you will normally have much company, and it is not easy to get away from evidence of previous occupation. As far as the Grand Plateau the routes from this hut are the same. There you may turn along its right edge and walk up to the Vallot hut and along the Bosses ridge; this is the usual route, on which any able-bodied man or woman can follow a leader, only do it in good weather and acclimatize yourself to height if you want to enjoy it. Or you may turn left across the end of the Grand Plateau and go up a broad white corridor to the Col de la Brenva, overlooking the Brenva Glacier; thence up a steep slope and a broad ridge to the top. Or, if you are an historically-minded person, you may cross the Plateau straight towards the summit and ascend the snowy shelf on the left which Saussure climbed; it must be more difficult to get on to than in his day. Lastly, if you have the mentality of some modern climbers and like dashing, direct ascents, what the Italians call a *direttissimo*, you may test your ice-manship, and your luck, by climbing straight up from the Plateau to the summit.

. . . The second hut, as we go round the mountain, is the Tête Rousse at the foot of the Aiguille du Goûter. The situation is very fine and you may wander about in slippers almost everywhere if you are disposed to solitude and contemplation. The route to Mont Blanc lies up a rib of the Aiguille and over the Dôme du Goûter to the Vallot hut and the Bosses ridge. It is the best route to choose if you want to climb Mont Blanc alone. I can strongly recommend this. The third hut is the Refuge Durier on the Col de Miage. You are not so likely to have company there. The route over the Aiguille de Bionnassay to the Dôme du Goûter and Mont Blanc is one of the grandest in the Alps; you must study the conditions, for there are generally big cornices on the narrow stretch descending from the Aiguille to the Dôme du Goûter; it is for a strong party. Fourthly, we come to the Rifugio Gonella, the former Cabane du Dôme, on the Aiguille's Grises on the Italian Miage Glacier. From there a fine and not often difficult route goes up to the Dôme du Goûter. . . . If alone you can avoid the Dôme Glacier altogether and climb up to the ridge straight above the hut and follow it all the way. Our fifth hut is the Sella hut, built at 11,000 feet on the great broad spur coming down from the Bosses ridge. The climb up it is long and cold, for the Brouillard Ridge keeps off the morning sun, but in my experience the serious climbing difficulties, if any, will be found on the way to the hut. If the season has been very fine and you are feeling up to the very big things, this is the best place to sleep before climbing up the long thin ribbon of snow or ice that leads to the small gap in the Brouillard ridge called the Col Emile Rey, and from there climbing that ridge to the point called the Mont Blanc de Courmayeur and thence walking along the highest promenade in the Alps to the summit 200 feet higher. Sixth on our list is the Gamba hut at under 9,000 feet between the steep broken cascades of ice known as the Brouillard and Fresnay Glaciers. All the routes from here are long and difficult; the most often taken is the magnificent Peuterey ridge. It is not a climb for the inexperienced; famous men in mountaineering history have spent a night on its fearfully exposed upper stretch and have survived, thanks to some forbearance of the weather. Seventhly and lastly, and best of all, is the Rifugio Torino on the Col du Géant. More routes start from here than from any other of the Mont Blanc huts, for it is the usual sleeping-place, rather than a bivouac, for the various climbs up the Brenva face. There is the fine route via the Col du Midi, Mont Blanc du Tacul and Mont Maudit to the summit of Mont Blanc; it is long and, if the snow is not in good condition, very tiring. Very difficult routes have been made in recent years up ridges that divide the dangerous furrows of the Brenva face. For those that are too long to be done in a day from the Col du Géant, parties bivouac under a big rock standing out from the lower precipices, called the Red Sentinel. A climber with a long record of fine guideless climbs has attributed the evident affection shown for the Sentinel by users of this route to the fact that 'it appeared to be the only safe place upon the whole face'. So impressed was he by the prominence accorded to it in the thrilling slides which illustrated Mr Smythe's account of the climb that he 'longed to nestle in its arms for safety and see the avalanches hurtling down on either side'. His only fear was: 'If ever I got there I might never have the courage to come away!'

Ten Great Mountains

A. W. MOORE

THE BRENVA ROUTE[1]

It was still dark when we started, but now, as our difficulties were commencing, there were signs of dawn. Gorgeous as had been the sunset, the sunrise was more gorgeous still, the gradations of colour over the eastern horizon before the appearance of the luminary being indescribably beautiful, while, as the sun rose, the great wall of precipices before us glowed again as its beams crept down them. This ice-fall certainly was worthy of Melchior's respect and admiration, for a grander and more broken one I have rarely seen, but when we fairly attacked it we got on with less difficulty than had been feared. Of course there was the usual up and down sort of work, but in spite of one or two checks, we progressed steadily, and finding ourselves more than half-way across, were about to indulge in a crow of exultation, when we came to what looked like a full stop. We had worked ourselves into a position from which there appeared, after several trials, to be no way of extrication except by returning in our footsteps, always a disheartening proceeding. We pottered about for some time without result, and then Melchior cast off the rope, and went alone to seek out a way, leaving us in rather a blank state of mind. We shivered miserably, but were finally rejoiced by a distant cry, which evidently meant 'come on'. The ground in front did not look promising, but following in Melchior's steps we gradually left the worst bit behind, and struck a broad causeway between two huge chasms which led us out of the labyrinth to where he was waiting for us.

One of the doubtful points in connection with our expedition was thus happily solved. The glacier was crossed, and all was plain sailing in front as far as the base of our buttress, which was not far above us. A smooth slope of snow between the foot of the cliffs on our left and the ice-fall offered an easy line of march, but we had ocular evidence of the propriety of keeping out of the way of the hanging glaciers already spoken of, as a large mass of ice from one in front fell before

[1] July 14, 1865.

118

our eyes, its débris rolling right across our path. At 5.30 we were at the base of the buttress. The rocks were approached by a steep slope of hard snow, intersected by the usual bergschrund. The latter gave us little trouble, and we were soon hard at work with the rocks. For nearly two hours we were engaged in a scramble which, though not difficult, was sufficiently severe to be interesting, some care being required in places where snow was lying. At first we kept straight up. . . .

The guides were in a hurry, so, cutting our halt shorter than would have been agreeable, we resumed our way at 7.55 and after a few steps up a slope at an angle of 50°, found ourselves on the crest of the buttress, and looking down upon and across the lower part of a glacier tributary to the Brenva beyond which towered the grand wall of the Mont Maudit. We turned sharp to the left along the ridge, Jakob leading, followed by Mr Walker, Horace Walker, Mathews, Melchior and myself last. We had anticipated that, assuming the possibility of gaining the ridge on which we were, there would be no serious difficulty in traversing it, and so much as we could see ahead, led us to hope that our anticipations would turn out correct. Before us lay a narrow but not steep arête of rock and snow combined, which appeared to terminate some distance in front in a sharp peak. We advanced cautiously, keeping rather below the top of the ridge, speculating with some curiosity on what lay beyond this peak. On reaching it, the apparent peak proved not to be a peak at all, but the extremity of the narrowest and most formidable ice arête I ever saw, which extended almost on a level for an uncomfortably long distance. Looking back by the light of our subsequent success, I have always considered it a providential circumstance that at this moment Jakob, and not Melchior, was leading the party. In saying this, I shall not for an instant be suspected on any imputation upon Melchior's courage. But in him that virtue is combined to perfection with the equally necessary one of prudence, while he shares the objection which nearly all guides have to taking upon themselves, without discussion, responsibility in position of doubt. Had he been in front, I believe that on seeing the nature of the work before us we should have halted and discussed the propriety of proceeding, and I believe further that, as the result of that discussion, our expedition would have then and there come to an end. Now in Jakob, with courage as faultless as Melchior's and physical powers even superior, the virtue of prudence is conspicuous chiefly from its absence, and on coming to this ugly place it never for an instant occurred to him that we might object to go on, or consider the object in view not worth the risk which must be inevitably run. He therefore went calmly on without as much as turning to see what we thought of it, while I do not suppose that it entered into the head of any one of us spontaneously to suggest a retreat.

On most arêtes, however narrow the actual crest may be, it is generally possible to get a certain amount of support by driving the pole into the slope below on either side. But this was not the case here. We were on the top of a wall, the ice on the right falling vertically (I use the word advisedly), and on the left nearly so. On neither side was it possible to obtain the slightest hold with the alpenstock. I believe also that an arête of pure ice is more often encountered in description than in reality, that term being generally applied to hard snow. But here, for once, we had the genuine article – blue ice, without a speck of snow on it. The space for walking was at first about the breadth of the top of an ordinary wall, in which Jakob cut holes for the feet. Being last in the line, I could see little of what was coming until I was close upon it, and was therefore considerably startled on seeing the men in front suddenly abandon the upright position, which in spite of the insecurity of the steps and difficulty in preserving a balance had been hitherto maintained, and sit down *à cheval*. The ridge had narrowed to a knife edge, and for a few yards it was utterly impossible to advance in any other way. The foremost men soon stood up again, but when I was about to follow their example, Melchior insisted emphatically on my not doing so, but remaining seated. Regular steps could no longer be cut, but Jakob, as he went along, simply sliced off the top of the ridge, making thus a slippery pathway, along which those behind crept, moving one foot carefully after the other. As for me, I worked myself along with my hands, in an attitude safer, perhaps, but considerably more uncomfortable, and, as I went, could not help occasionally speculating, with an odd feeling of amusement, as to what would be the result if any of the party should chance to slip over on either side – what the rest would do – whether throw themselves over on the other or not – and if so, what would happen then. Fortunately the occasion for the solution of this curious problem did not arise, and at 9.30 we reached the end of the arête. . . .

As we looked back along our perilous path, it was hard to repress a shudder, and I think the dominant feeling of every man was one of wonder how the passage had been effected without accident. One good result, however, was to banish from Melchior's mind the last traces of doubt as to our ultimate success, his reply to our anxious inquiry whether he thought we should get up being, 'We must, for we cannot go back.' . . .

At 9.40 we started up the slopes of névé which rose with ominous steepness in front of us, and for the next two hours and a half the work was rather monotonous. . . . The Corridor all the time was hidden, but we knew it to lie far away to our right and therefore worked generally in that direction. Two ridges of rock, running parallel to each other, but separated by a broad expanse of ice, crop out from the face of the slope. We passed underneath the first, and cut our way across to the second, and on reaching it, ascertained our exact position. On our right below was the upper part of the lateral glacier so often mentioned, beyond which was the wall of the Mont Maudit, the depression marking the head of the Corridor being apparently at the same level as we were. There was our goal in full view, but between us and it was a great gulf which there was no obvious way of crossing. Beneath the Corridor the glacier falls away very rapidly.

41 - *Le Col d'Anterne.*

41 - *The Col d'Anterne.*

42 - Mont Blanc seen from the Charmilles (Geneva).

42 - Le Mont Blanc vu des Charmilles, à Genève.

43 - *La Mer de Glace.*   43 - *The Mer de Glace.*

At the foot of the Mur de la Côte, the difference of level is but a few feet, but under the Mont Maudit a precipice of some 2,000 feet intervenes. It is, therefore, only practicable to pass from one to the other at the former point. Unfortunately, *we* were nearly opposite the Mont Maudit, and the glacier lay at a corresponding depth below us. From where we were standing it was not possible to descend on to it, nor, if it had been possible, would it have been profitable, as just above the point we must have struck was a great wall of ice running right across, and completely barring the way upwards.

Our position was, in fact, rather critical. Immediately over our heads the slope on which we were terminated in a great mass of broken séracs, which might come down with a run at any moment. It seemed improbable that any way out of our difficulties would be found in that quarter. But where else to look? There was no use in going to the left – to the right we *could* not go – and back we *would* not go. After careful scrutiny, Melchior thought it just possible that we might find a passage through these séracs on to the higher and more level portion of the glacier to the right of them, and there being obviously no chance of success in any other direction, we turned towards them. The ice here was steeper and harder than it had yet been. In spite of all Melchior's care the steps were painfully insecure, and we were glad to get a grip with one hand on the rocks alongside which we passed. The risk, too, of an avalanche was considerable, and it was a relief when we were so close under the séracs that a fall from above could not well hurt us. We passed close to a curious formation – a pinnacle of ice, in shape exactly like a man's head and neck. The neck in length and thinness was sadly out of proportion to the head, and was momentarily growing thinner so that it was a question of time how soon the two could part company. Melchior had steered with his usual discrimination, and was now attacking the séracs at the only point where they appeared to be at all practicable. Standing over the mouth of a crevasse, choked with débris, he endeavoured to lift himself on to its upper edge, which was about fifteen feet above. But to accomplish this seemed at first a task too great even for his agility, aided as he was by vigorous pushes *a tergo*. At last, by a marvellous exercise of skill and activity, he succeeded, pulled up Mr Walker and Horace Walker, and then cast a rope to reconnoitre, leaving them to assist Mathews, Jakob, and myself in the performance of a similar manoeuvre. We were all three still below, when a yell from Melchior sent a thrill through my veins. 'What is it?' said we to Mr Walker. A shouting communication took place between him and Melchior, and then came the answer, 'He says it is all right.'

That moment was worth living for. . . .

'Mont Blanc by the Brenva Route'

(The Alpine Journal, 1866)

A. E. W. MASON

THE BRENVA RIDGE

As they went along this ridge, Wallie Hine's courage rose. It was narrow but not steep, nor was it ice. It was either rock or snow in which steps could be kicked. He stepped out with a greater confidence. If this were all, the Brenva climb was a fraud, he exclaimed to himself in the vanity of his heart. Ahead of them a tall black tower stood up, hiding what lay beyond, and up towards this tower Garratt Skinner led quickly. He no longer spoke to his companions, he went forward, assured and inspiring assurance; he reached the tower, passed it and began to cut steps. His axe rang as it fell. It was ice into which he was cutting.

This was the first warning which Walter Hine received. But he paid no heed to it. He was intent upon setting his feet in the steps; he found the rope awkward to handle and keep tight; his attention was absorbed in observing his proper distance. Moreover, in front of him the stalwart figure of Garratt Skinner blocked his vision. He went forward. The snow on which he walked became hard ice, and instead of sloping upwards ran ahead almost in a horizontal line. Suddenly, how-ever, it narrowed; Hine became conscious of appalling depths on either side of him; it narrowed with extraordinary rapidity; half a dozen paces behind him he had been walking on a broad smooth path; now he walked on the width of the top of a garden wall. His knees began to shake; he halted; he reached out vainly into emptiness for some support on which his shaking hands might clutch. And then in front of him he saw Garratt Skinner sit down and bestride the wall. Over Garratt Skinner's head, he now saw the path by which he needs must go. He was on the famous ice-ridge; and nothing so formidable, so terrifying, had even entered into his dreams during his sleep upon the rocks where he had bivouacked. It thinned to a mere sharp edge, a line without breadth of cold blue ice, and it stretched away through the air for a great distance until it melted suddenly into the face of the mountain. On the left hand an almost vertical slope of ice dropped to depths which Hine did not dare to fathom with his eyes; on the right there was no slope at all; a wall of crumbling snow descended from the edge straight as a weighted one. On neither side could the point of the axe be driven in to preserve the balance. Walter Hine uttered a whimpering cry –

'I shall fall! I shall fall!'

Garratt Skinner, astride of the ridge, looked over his shoulder.

'Sit down,' he cried sharply. But Walter Hine dared not. He stood, all his courage gone, tottering on the narrow top of the wall, afraid to stoop, lest his knees should fail him altogether and his feet slip from beneath him. To bend down until his hands could rest upon the ice, and meanwhile to keep his feet – no he could not do it. He stood trembling, his face distorted with fear, and his body swaying a little from side to side. Garratt Skinner called sharply to Pierre Delouvain.

'Quick, Pierre.'

There was no time for Garratt Skinner to return; but he gathered himself together on the ridge, ready for a spring. Had Walter Hine toppled over, and swung down the length of the rope, as at any moment he might have done, Garratt Skinner was prepared. He would have jumped down the opposite side of the ice-arête, though how either he or Walter Hine could have regained the ridge he could not tell. Would any one of the party live to return to Courmayeur and tell the tale? But Garratt Skinner knew the risk he took, had counted it up long before ever he brought Walter Hine to Chamonix, and though it worth while. He did not falter now. All through the morning, indeed, he had been taking risks, risks of which Walter Hine did not dream; with so firm and yet so delicate a step he had moved from crack to crack, from ice-step up to ice-step; with so obedient a response of his muscles, he had drawn himself up over the rounded rocks from ledge to ledge. He shouted again to Pierre Delouvain, and at the same moment began carefully to work backwards along the ice-arête. Pierre, however, hurried; Walter Hine heard the guide's voice behind him, felt himself steadied by his hands. He stooped slowly down, knelt upon the wall, then bestrode it.

'Now, forward,' cried Skinner, and he pulled in the rope. 'Forward. We cannot go back!'

Hine clung to the ridge; behind him Pierre Delouvain sat down and held him about the waist. Slowly they worked themselves forward, while Garratt Skinner gathered in the rope in front. The wall narrowed as they advanced, became the merest edge which cut their hands as they clasped it. Hine closed his eyes, his head whirled, he was giddy, he felt sick. He stopped gripping the slope on both sides with his knees, clutching the sharp edge with the palms of his hands.

'I can't go on! I can't,' he cried, and he reeled like a novice on the back of a horse.

Garratt Skinner worked back to him.

'Put your arms about my waist, Wallie! Keep your eyes shut! You shan't fall.'

Walter Hine clung to him convulsively, Pierre Delouvain steadied Hine from behind, and thus they went slowly forward for a long while. Garratt Skinner gripped the edge with the palms of his hands – so narrow was the ridge – the fingers of one hand pointed down one slope, the fingers of the other down the opposite wall. Their legs dangled.

At last Walter Hine felt Garratt Skinner loosening his clasped fingers from about his waist. Garratt Skinner stood up, uncoiled the rope, chipped a step or two in the ice and went boldly forward. For a yard or two further Walter Hine straddled on, and then Garratt Skinner cried to him –

'Look up, Wallie. It's all over.'

Hine looked and saw Garratt Skinner standing upon a level space of snow in the side of the mountain. A moment later he himself was lying in the sun upon the level space. The famous ice-arête was behind them.

Running Water

GEORGE LEIGH-MALLORY

THE MONT MAUDIT ROUTE[1]

They lay at last on the broad welcome space of the Col de la Brenva. It was a place of safety and enjoyment, wide and comfortable. Such noble amplitude was due from Mont Blanc. The divine sculptor, as Gibbon might have observed, after laboriously carving a multitude of gigantic slopes, seemed in a moment of serene satisfaction to have designed a high imperial couch of purest snow. Here they must lie in delicious ease to stretch hard-worked muscles, to enjoy the high value of well-earned repose, and to drain the sunny cup of pleasure in contented peace. Much lay behind and beneath them. They had reached a brink of things – of all that lay, beyond sight, on the Brenva side falling into that steep Italian valley, and of the long slopes of snow and glacier stretching into France and into the lovely vale of Chamonix. Northwards lay all the spiky bed of aiguilles; to the south the smooth white dome. How near they were to fulfilling all their hopes! They had but to put out their hands and take the crown offered. This pause, it might seem, had been given them to taste beforehand, the final triumph in full confidence of anticipation; and to rejoice without restraint in the full measure of achievement. Any party that reaches the Col de la Brenva from Mont Maudit or still more from the Brenva Glacier must halt there with peculiar satisfaction. Perhaps, because thoughts of achievement would be scarce decent on the summit, one is presented with the opportunity of thinking them here. For his own part it was by no means wasted. . . .

They had halted on the col at 3.10 p.m. or a little later. Not too many hours remained to reach the summit and descend before dark. But enough, oh! yes, enough; they were all agreed on that point. If they kept going, the result was not in question. And what doubt they would keep on? The alternative, however, was suggested among them, the descent by the Corridor; a prospect clearly of ignoble ease, but quite seriously suggested on account of the weakest member. Shame couldn't allow him to accept such a proposal. They had trusted him so much! He

---

[1] It was the second ascent of that route. It was made in 1911 by R. L. G. Irving, George Mallory and H. E. G. Tyndale.

was proud to be there; he would be proud to the end. They must trust him for the rest.

. . . A breeze cool and bracing seemed to gather force as they plodded up the long slopes, more gentle now as they approached the final goal. He felt the wind about him with its old strange music. His thoughts became less conscious, less continuous. Rather than thinking or feeling he was simply listening – listening for distant voices scarcely articulate. . . . The solemn dome resting on those marvellous buttresses, fine and firm above all the chasms of ice, its towers and crags; a place where desire points and aspirations end; very, very high and lovely, long-suffering and wise. . . . *Experience* slowly and wonderfully filtered; at the last a purged remainder. . . . And what is that? What more than the infinite knowledge that it is all worth while – all one strives for? . . . How to get the best of it all? One must conquer, achieve, go to the top; one must know the end to be convinced that one can win in the end – to know there's no dream that mustn't be dared. . . . Is this the summit, crowning the day? How cool and quiet! We're not exultant; but delighted, joyful; soberly astonished. . . . Have we vanquished an enemy? None but ourselves. Have we gained success? That word means nothing here. Have we won a kingdom? No . . . and yes. We have achieved an ultimate satisfaction . . . fulfilled a destiny. . . . To struggle and to understand – never this last without the other; such is the law. . . . We've only been obeying an old law, then? Ah! but it's *the* law . . . and we under-stand – a little more. So ancient, wise, and terrible – and yet kind, we see them; with steps for children's feet.

GEOFFREY WINTHROP YOUNG

A ROCK CALLED LE PERE ETERNEL

Incomparable rock; the thought that framed
these mountains fashioned to a single stone;
brooding huge and alone
from a dark promontory of precipice,
projected on a moon of ordered spires
against the tumult of descending ice.
Some herdboy, watching by his brushwood fire
the shadow moving up the starlit range,
in a night vision named

Mont Blanc

its dim suggestion of a form divine:
figure, solitary and ultimate,
veiled till the slow discovery of change
reveals the mystery of things create,
the great designer in his own design

Collected Poems

BERNARD PIERRE

THE DIEDRE OF THE SORROWS[1]

Gaston [Rebuffat] went up first on the right, then back at the bottom of the *dièdre*, and the usual symphony of the hammering in of pitons could be heard: the clear, bell-like sound of the hammer striking the piton, the snap-ring locking with a click, the hard breathing of the leader.

Gaston was just below the first overhang and hammered in several pitons to get over it. The stirrups were hanging far out from the precipice. When he stepped into them, about to haul himself up, he was hanging over nothing at all.

A few grammes of metal . . . a nylon string some eight millimetres thick. How light is the life of a climber!

A swing of the rope carried Gaston to the top of the overhang. Then he stopped.

This time, after having climbed vertically for about two metres along the open corner, he drew away to go left. Flat on the rock, just below the overhang, he rested a bit. And then he sallied forth, hammering in a first and then a second piton: one more metre. His body was clinging to the overhang, which pushed him backwards; he tried to drive in a third piton. From lower down I was watching his struggle. I was grasping the ropes which held him in a precarious balance. I saw him groping blindly at the sun-swept rock. Right and left, his fingers were feeling for a crack they could not find.

Finally, after endless seconds, the piton was driven in. 'It is madness to do this kind of thing,' he shouted to me. He pulled himself up on to the top platform, was silent for a while and then, in a perfectly calm voice, as if it were mere climbing routine, he said: 'Now, you come up.'

When I was near him once more, the sun had set. Pulling out the pitons had required a great effort, yet I was at least belayed. Several times, when tearing out a piton or unhooking a ring, I fell off, like an awkward chough that knew not where to land.

[1] July 1949. The title is a pun on the title of the play *Deirdre of the Sorrows* by J. M. Synge. *Dièdre*: geom. a dihedron.

126

Having gathered up all our equipment, we traversed to the left. Some water dripping on the rock. It was a delightful harbour of coolness, the more so as we had been longing for it all day.

That rope-length was an easy walk which ended far too soon. We were now face to face with the key-pitch of the Ratti route, a big open corner that leaned out increasingly as it rose higher, with a roof at the top. On the right, the way out was hardly discernible. We stopped there, silent, our eyes glued to the rock. It was a formidable obstacle, out of all proportion to human strength and full of terror. The shadows of night were already prowling there, adding something quite weird to the black granite.

To reconnoitre the enemy was out of the question. We had to bivouac on the terrace where we stood. Fixed between the faces of the *dièdre*, it was luckily long and broad enough for the purpose. We might even lie down. While Gaston was preparing the site by throwing down blocks which crashed upon the Fresnay Glacier with a dull booming, I hammered in a belay piton, sorted out the ropes, lit the cooker and extracted the food from the sack. I moved as slowly as possible, in order to spin out the time.

We began to wait.

. . . Day broke at last and freed us. Round us the summits were catching the sun, but we were still captive in the wintry shadow, under the roof which was crushing us.

It was seven when the first piton rang. Gaston fixed himself in a crack, slightly to the right of the *dièdre*, and hammered in three pitons, then came back. It was too cold and he was blowing on his ice-cold fingers. It reminded him of the north face of the Matterhorn. He ate a few pieces of sugar and started again, getting back to the third piton, then into another crack further to the left.

He progressed very slowly, stopped for a short while, looked intently at the route and then said: 'I shall be short of pitons. I must get some of them back.' He came down again. The rope swung, he pulled out pitons, climbed back, and minutes passed in the process.

Having reached again his previous highest point, he fixed himself in the middle of the *dièdre*. He thought he saw two pitons which had been left by the Italians, and he was right. He tested them, fixed a stirrup for his left foot and, leaning on the right, hammered in three other pitons.

Before going all out for the last pitch he rested, sitting in the stirrups and hanging over the void. For a long time, now, the third rope, which we used to pull up the sacks, had not touched the face; it was swinging behind me, five or six metres away.

'Bernard, I'm off now. . . . Pull *this* rope.' The 20th, the 21st, the 22nd pitons were hammered in; thanks to the snap-rings, the stirrups and the ropes, the roof was overcome at last. It was almost midday. In this horrible *dièdre* the first man had taken five hours to climb some twenty-five metres.

Pulling the pitons out was hard work. I had only one stirrup out of four and the spaces between the pitons were far too long. The first were easy to pull out, but I soon had to drive in more pitons, to be able to pull out the rest! As they were slung through some half-dozen rings, the ropes were difficult to pull and got caught. I was badly belayed and I often lost my holds and revolved round and round, which twisted the ropes more tightly still. It was difficult to breathe and I was wasting time. Up there, precariously standing on a slanting ledge, Gaston was losing his temper. Finally, with cramped fingers I got to the roof, awkwardly dropping a large piton. I was longing for one thing only: to get out of that *dièdre*. A last effort, three more metres and I should be near Gaston. Then, like a runner who hands the token to his companion, I would hand him what I had pulled out of the rough granite wall.

At last I reached the final ledge. I was exhausted and I closed my eyes, silent for several minutes. Then I said, 'Gaston, that *dièdre*, let us call it the Dièdre of the Sorrows'.

From a book yet to be completed

5

FOR AND AGAINST
MOUNTAINEERING

MARC-THÉODORE BOURRIT

AN EARLY ATTEMPT ON THE AIGUILLE DU MIDI[1]

The sight of the Aiguilles from their feet is indeed delightful, but when one
reflects that from their summits the plains extending north, south and east can
be seen, how sad it is to think that they are inaccessible! What delight there
might be in the mere attempt to ascend them!

I felt all this as I gazed at them intently, and I thought I had found a route up.
Stung by hope, I courageously overcame many obstacles the rocks put in my
way; getting above the piled rubble, I finally reached the curve of the Aiguille
next to Mont Blanc.

The height I had reached was already quite satisfactory, but the view was
more or less the one we had enjoyed from the Brévent, and I was angered by the
huge curtain which hid from me the southern plains. I increased my efforts; I
climbed again with terrible exertion from rock to rock; like a small worm stuck
on a prickly plant, I followed the gully which produces such a fine effect from the
Brévent until the moment when, astonished at, and impressed by, the great height
I had reached, and even more by what was left for me to climb, I felt I had reached
my limits.

I then descended in great tremor and danger; stones fell under my feet and I
did not even dare to grab those huge masses which seemed to cling to nothing.
Yet I succeeded; I reached the bottom and rejoined my companions.

Description des Glacières de Savoie

[1] 1772.

Mont Blanc

JOHN RUSKIN

AGAINST MOUNTAINEERING[1]

You have despised nature; that is to say, all the deep and sacred sensations of natural scenery. The French revolutionists made stables of the cathedrals of France; you have made racecourses of the cathedrals of the earth. Your *one* conception of pleasure is to drive in railroad carriages round their aisles and eat off their altars. You have put a railroad bridge over the falls of Schaffhausen. You have tunnelled the cliffs of Lucerne by Tell's chapel; you have destroyed the Clarens shore of the Lake of Geneva . . . the Alps themselves, which your own poets used to love so reverently, you look upon as soaped poles in a bear-garden, which you set yourselves to climb, and slide down again, with 'shrieks of delight'. When you are past shrieking, having no human articulate voice to say you are glad with, you fill the quietude of their valleys with gunpowder blasts, and rush home, red with cutaneous eruption of conceit, and voluble with convulsive hiccough of self-satisfaction. I think nearly the two sorrowfullest spectacles I have ever seen in humanity, taking the deep inner significance of them, are the English mobs in the valley of Chamonix, amusing themselves with firing rusty howitzers; and the Swiss vintagers of Zurich expressing their Christian thanks for the gift of the vine, by assembling in knots in the 'towers of the vineyards' and slowly loading and firing horse-pistols from morning till evening. It is pitiful, to have dim conceptions of duty; more pitiful, it seems to me, to have conceptions like these, of mirth.

Sesame and Lilies

A passage referring to Alpine travellers will fall harshly on the reader's ear since it has been sorrowfully enforced by the deaths on Mont Cervin.[2] I leave it, nevertheless, as it stood, for I do not now write unadvisedly and think it wrong to cancel what has once been thoughtfully said; but it must not remain without a few added words. . . . It is not therefore strange, however much to be regretted, that while no gentleman boasts in other cases of his sagacity or of his courage – while no good soldier talks of the charge he led, nor any good sailor of the helm he held – every man among the Alps seems to lose his senses and modesty with the fall of the barometer, and returns from his Nephelo-coccygia brandishing his ice-axe in everybody's face. Whatever the Alpine Club have done, or may yet accomplish in a sincere thirst for mountain knowledge, and in happy sense of

---

[1] This scream of rage came after the ascent of the Aiguille Verte by Edward Whymper and a few days later by Charles Hudson.

[2] The accident on the Matterhorn, during the first ascent, when Charles Hudson, R. Hadow, Lord Francis Douglas and Michel Croz were killed.

youthful strength and play of animal spirit, they have done, and will do wisely and well; but whatever they are urged to by mere sting of competition and itch of praise, they will do, as all vain things must be done forever, foolishly and ill. It is a strange proof of that absence of any real national love of science . . . that no entire survey of the Alps has yet been made by properly qualified men; and that, except of the chain of Chamouni, no accurate maps exist, not any complete geological section even of that. But Mr Reilly's survey[1] of that central group, and the generally accurate information collected by the guide-book published by the Club, are honourable results of English adventure; and it is to be hoped that the continuance of such work will gradually put an end to the vulgar excitement which looked upon the granite of the Alps only as an unoccupied advertisement wall for chalking names upon. . . .

. . . It is indeed true that under the influence of the pride that gives poignancy to the sensations which others cannot share with . . . an ordinary traveller will usually observe and enjoy more on a difficult excursion than on an easy one; and more in objects to which he is unaccustomed than in those with which he is familiar. He will notice with extreme interest that snow is white on the top of a hill in June though he would have attached little importance to the same peculiarity in a wreath at the bottom of a hill in January. He will generally find more to admire in a cloud under his feet, than in one over his head. . . . Add to such grounds of delight the aid given to whatever is impressive in the scenery of the high Alps, by the absence of ludicrous or degrading concomitants; and it ceases to be surprising that Alpine excursionists should be greatly pleased, or that they should attribute their pleasure to some true and increased apprehension of the nobleness of the natural scenery. But no impression can be more false. The real beauty of the Alps is to be seen, and seen only, where all may see it, the child, the cripple and the man of grey hairs.

Sesame and Lilies (Preface to the second edition, 1865)

VIOLLET-LE-DUC

AGAINST MOUNTAINEERING

The man who gets to more than 2,000 metres above sea level thinks he is walking among solitudes where silence and the immobility of death reign for ever. Yet, it is not true; on those snow-covered plateaus, round those summits bare of any

---

[1] Adams-Reilly.

vegetable life, where the presence of a loved being is a very rare occurrence, nature is at work, as actively as at the bottom of the sea.

It is true that on mountains she gives no scope to animal life, and man feels isolated in the midst of a world which is not made for him.

In those vast high laboratories, man feels out of place. All that surrounds him seems to say: 'What are you doing here? Go back to your fields, your streams, your valleys; you are meant to live there; if you don't, do not complain if you meet with some mishap. In those high realms, we obey laws too exacting for you, puny being! Go and build dykes along rivers, dams to restrain running water; stone jetties on your beaches; pierce the feet of the mountains to get more easily from one valley to another: all this you may do. Here you are nothing, you can do nothing: leave us alone!' And yet, restless man, eager to know more, always wants to go higher, to see more of the dreadful phenomena which are worked out on those summits. His intelligence reveals to him the gigantic effort displayed in those laboratories, the easier aspects of which he can scarcely grasp after intense research.

Those who are wise or think they are, aimlessly repeat that it is madness to face such fatigue, to risk one's life to visit those deserts; a mysterious attraction draws us there and there are always men to undertake such pilgrimages towards the unknown. Many of them do it again and again, in spite of danger, fatigue, hunger or thirst. It is a passion similar to gambling.

One meets mountain-addicts in the Alps just as one sees professional gamblers in Baden or Monaco. Are they impelled by the love of science? No, they go up just because they like it.

When we meet them in the valley, they always look preoccupied; they browse in books which record altitudes; they ask for the best guides, look at the barometer, don mountaineers' clothes, get up in the middle of night to start. . . . When they have reached a summit, do they stop there? Are they impressed by the landscape which expands at their feet? No, they go down in haste, to do the same the next day on another peak.

I had many opportunities to observe those men suffering from a climbing sickness, and I must confess I am full of sympathy. They are in quest of the Unknown.

England produces the larger number of those ecstatic people. Sometimes, one of them is left at the bottom of a crevasse or falls from several hundred metres, like a gambler who commits suicide. One does not pity either.[1]

In France those altitude addicts are few, which is a pity. Apart from a few French scholars who made some new observations and added some new facts to geology, geodesy and meteorology, and who, thanks to some very remarkable

---

[1] Viollet-le-Duc was a bad climber. His ludicrous accident on the Schwartzberggletscher in 1870 is proof.

works, are duly praised the world over, there are very few amateur mountaineers among us, while England, Switzerland, America and Germany have thousands.

Le Mont Blanc

SIR LESLIE STEPHEN

LETTER TO ONE OF THE FIRST
FRENCH MOUNTAINEERS[1]

March 3, 1875

Dear M. Millot

You are really too grateful for the little thing I could do for you.

It is the Club which should thank you for the honour you paid us by desiring to become one of our members. Mme Millot should be elected by acclamations as soon as the principle of equal rights for women is accepted by the Alpine Club; and this principle is making headway very quickly in England, at present.

I hope our friend Loppé comes soon to England. I saw him in Courmayeur in September, when we visited together the crevasse where poor Fischer was killed with Mr Marshall. It was a very sad accident. Five minutes later, they would have been quite safe!

This year, I shan't be in the Alps until the end of August, probably in the Bernese Oberland. So, I am afraid we shan't meet. I wish you all good things and great prudence.

I am, my dear colleague

Yours very truly

Leslie Stephen

I hope you can attend some meetings of the Alpine Club. We are quite near Charing Cross, and you could easily lunch in Paris and dine with us.

[1] The original, in French, belongs to Mme Savine-Loppé, the painter Gabriel Loppé's granddaughter.

Mont Blanc

SIR HENRY PONSONBY TO MR GLADSTONE

QUEEN VICTORIA AND MOUNTAINEERING[1]

24th August, 1882

Dear Mr Gladstone,

The Queen commands me to ask you if you think she can say anything to mark her disapproval of the dangerous Alpine excursions which this year have occasioned so much loss of life.

Henry F. Ponsonby

MR GLADSTONE TO SIR HENRY PONSONBY

Iwerne Minster House
25th August, 1882

My Dear Sir H. Ponsonby,

I do not wonder that the Queen's sympathetic feelings have again been excited by the accidents so grave in character and so accumulated during recent weeks, on the Alps. But I doubt the possibility of any interference, even by Her Majesty, with a prospect of advantage. It may be questionable whether, upon the whole, mountain-climbing (and be it remembered that Snowdon has its victims as well as the Matterhorn) is more destructive than various other pursuits in the way of recreation which perhaps have no justification to plead so respectable as that which may be alleged on behalf of mountain expeditions. The question, however, is not one of wisdom or unwisdom; but viewing it, as you put it, upon its very definite and simple grounds, I see no room for action.

My attempt at yachting came to grief, and the chance of renewing it is small.

Yours sincerely,
W. E. Gladstone

[1] Extract from: *The Letters of Queen Victoria*, Second Series, Vol III. A Selection from Her Majesty's Correspondence and Journal between the Years 1862 and 1885, published by authority of His Majesty the King. Edited by George Earle Buckle. John Murray, 1928.

44 - *Le Mont Blanc*
vu des Grands Mulets.

44 - *Mont Blanc seen*
from the Grands Mulets.

45 - *Le chasseur de Chamois.*

45 - *Chamois hunters.*

46 - *Prospectus d'hôtel.*   46 - *Advertise*

...amonix hotel.

47 - Napoléon III au Montenvers.

47 - Napoleon III on the Montenvers.

48 - The Duke of Connaught at the Grands Mulets, 1868.

48 - Le Duc de Connaught aux Grands Mulets, 1868.

49 - *Sir John Herschell.*

50 - *John Tyndall.*

51 - *Sir Leslie Stephen.*

52 - *Edward Whymper.*

6
THE AIGUILLES

JOHN RUSKIN

THE AIGUILLE DE BLAITIERE

. . . The white shell-like mass beneath it is a small glacier, which in its beautifully curved outline, appears to sympathize with the sweep of the rocks beneath, rising and breaking like a wave at the feet of the remarkable horn or spur which supports it on the right. The base of the Aiguille itself is, as it were, washed by this glacier, or by the snow which covers it, till late in the season, as a cliff is by the sea; except that a narrow chasm of some 20 or 30 feet in depth and two or three feet wide, usually separates the rock from the ice, which is melted away by the heat reflected from the southern face of the Aiguille. The rock all along the base line is of the most magnificent compactness and hardness and rings under the hammer like a bell; yet when regarded from a little distance, it is seen to be distinctly inclined to separate into great flakes or sheets. . . . The pyramidal form of the Aiguille, as seen from this point is, however, entirely deceptive; the square rock which forms its apparent summit is not the real top but much in advance of it, and the slope on the right against the sky is a perspective line; while, on the other hand, the precipice in light above the three small horns at the narrowest part of the glacier, is considerably steeper than it appears to be, the cleavage of the flakes crossing it somewhat obliquely.

Modern Painters

EDWARD WHYMPER

THE FIRST ASCENT OF THE AIGUILLE VERTE[1]

We camped on the Couvercle under a great rock, and at 3.15 the next morning started for our Aiguille, leaving the porter in charge of the tent and the food. Two hours' walking over crisp snow brought us more than 4,000 feet up and

[1] June 28, 1865.

139

within about 1,600 feet from the summit. From no other direction can it be approached so closely with equal facility. Thence the mountain steepens. After his late severe piece of ice-work, Almer had a natural inclination for rocks; but the lower rocks of the final peak of the Aiguille Verte were not inviting, and he went on, looking for a way up them, until we arrived in front of a great snow couloir that led from the Glacier de Talèfre right up to the crest of the ridge connecting the summit of the Verte with the mountain called Les Droites. This is the route which I intended to be taken; but Almer pointed out that the gully narrowed in the lower part, and that, if stones fell, we should stand some chance of getting our heads broken; and so we went on still more to the east of the summit, to another and smaller couloir which ran up side by side with the great one. At 5.30 we crossed the schrund which protected the final peak, and a few minutes afterwards, saw the summit and the whole of the intervening route. 'Oh! Aiguille Verte, said my guide, stopping as he said it, you are dead, you are dead;' which being translated into plain English meant that he was cock-sure we should make its ascent.

Almer is a quiet man in all times. When climbing he is taciturn – and this is one of his great merits. A garrulous man is always a nuisance – and upon a mountainside he may be a danger, for actual climbing requires a man's whole attention. Added to this, talkative men are hindrances; they are usually thirsty, and thirsty men are a drag. . . .

At the top of the small gully, we crossed over the intervening rocks into the large one, and followed it so long as it was filled with snow. At last ice replaced snow and we turned over to the rocks upon the left. Charming rocks they were, granitic in texture, gritty, holding the nails well. At 9.45 we parted from them and completed the ascent by a litle ridge of snow which descended in the direction of the Aiguille du Moine. At 10.15 we stood on the summit, and devoured our bread and cheese with a good appetite.

I have already spoken of the disappointing nature of purely panoramic views. That seen from Mont Blanc itself is notoriously unsatisfactory. When you are upon that summit you look down upon the rest of Europe. There is nothing to look up to; all is below; there is not one point for the eye to rest upon. The man who is there is somewhat in the position of one who has attained all his desires – he has nothing to aspire to; his position must needs be unsatisfactory. Upon the summit of the Verte there is not that objection. You see valleys, villages, fields; you see mountains interminably rolling away, lakes resting in their hollows, you hear the tinkling of the sheep-bells as it rises through the clear mountain air, and the roar of the avalanches as they descend to the valleys; but above all there is the great white dome, with its sparkling glaciers that descend between buttresses which support them: with its brilliant snows, purer and yet purer the farther they are removed from this unclean world.

Even upon this mountaintop it was impossible to forget the world, for some vile wretch came to the Jardin and made hideous sounds by blowing through a horn. Whilst we were denouncing him, a change came over the weather; cumulus clouds gathered in all directions, and we started off in hot haste. Snow began to fall heavily before we were off the summit-rocks, our track was obscured and frequently lost, and everything became so sloppy and slippery that the descent took as long as the ascent. The schrund was recrossed at 3.15 p.m. and thence we raced down to the Couvercle, intending to have a carouse there; but as we rounded our rock a howl broke simultaneously from the three of us, for the porter had taken down the tent, and was in the act of moving off with it. 'Stop, there! What are you doing?' He observed that he had thought we were killed, or at least lost, and was going to Chamonix to communicate his ideas to the *guide-chef.* 'Unfasten the tent and get out the food.' Instead of doing so the porter fumbled in his pockets. 'Get out the food,' we roared losing all patience. 'Here it is,' said our worthy friend, producing a dirty piece of bread, about as big as a halfpenny roll. We three looked at the fluff-covered morsel; it was past a joke – he had devoured everything.

Scrambles amongst the Alps

A. F. MUMMERY

THE GREPON[1]

At 2 a.m. on the 18th of August, Simond gave me the unpleasant intelligence that the very name of Grépon had so frightened the porters that they had surreptitiously left their beds and fled to Chamonix. The difficulty appeared very serious. 2 a.m. is usually an inconvenient hour to charter porters, and Simond was quite sure that the C.P. was impassable from the Grépon side without a rope previously fixed. It appeared, then, likely that if we reached the gap leading to it we should have to retrace our steps all the way along the ridge. After much talk, Simond offered to lend us the herd-boy attached to the establishment, and also to wake and interview a one-eyed guide who was sleeping on the hotel, and who had been with M. Dunod on some of his unsuccessful attempts.

This guide, Gaspard Simond, proved willing, and with the herd-boy as second man we started gaily for the valley of stones. Each amateur member of the party was quite sure that the route taken along the detestable slopes of the stoneman ridge was far inferior to the line that such amateur had worked out and was

[1] Mummery's second ascent (August 18, 1892), with Pasteur, Hastings and Norman Collie, without guides.

prepared to lead us on; but I noticed that none the less we carefully kept to the herd-boy's lead, and for the first time we reached the moraine of the Nantillons Glacier without feeling the need of any serious bad language. Concealing our lanterns beneath a stone, we struck up the glacier just as the soft lights of morning were silhouetting the rugged limestone ridges of Sixt.

At this point Gaspard indulged in some very depressing statements. He told us that he had recently been up the Charmoz, and with true prophetic insight had devoted his time whilst there to an examination of the particular slab up which our route lay. This slab, he had been able to see, was coated with verglas and most ingenious defences of snow, rock and ice had been skilfully erected on the top; in short, it was simply courting defeat to go on with the attempt. It appeared to us, however, that these complicated defences were likely to be the products of our guide's imagination and were, perhaps, in part referable to an objection to carrying a heavy knapsack up to C.P. We therefore proceeded; but on reaching the top of the rocks known as the 'breakfasting station', Gaspard gave us further details; this very slab had, it appeared, fallen, crushing down to the glacier several years since, leaving a blank, unbroken wall, that could by no manner of means be ascended. We were struck dumb by this accumulation of difficulties; not only was the slab impassable by reason of the accumulated ice, but it was not even there! A state of affairs recalling to our minds the celebrated legal plans entered relatively to the cracked jar: We never had it. It was cracked when we had it. We returned it whole!'

Pasteur, however, by an interesting deductive argument, reached an equally gloomy conclusion. . . . He suggested we should tell the porters to halt at the foot of the couloir till we got to the col, and, if we found that we could not storm the Grépon ridge, we would shout to the guides and they could then deposit the baggage and return as fast as they liked. This suggestion was duly accepted by the party – indeed, a telescopic examination of the peak had not enabled me to trace my old route – for the excellent reason, that it is not visible from this point of view. This and the wide prevalence of a rumour that a great crag really had fallen from this part of the mountain, led me to fear that it might be all too true, and that the peak was closed for ever from this side . . . and it was only when I climbed round a crag on the Charmoz side of the col that I recovered my bearings and recognized the cleft up which we had to go.

Possibly the knowledge that I was going to try to lead up to it made it look worse than it really was, but for the moment I was startled by its steepness. With the exception of two steps where the rock sets back slightly . . . the whole is absolutely perpendicular. In this estimate I exclude a preliminary section of seven or eight feet, which bulges out and overhangs in a most painful manner. On the other hand, it was distinctly more broken than I had expected, and the longer we looked, the better we liked it, till with fair hopes of success I climbed down to the foot of the crack, scrambled on to Hastings's shoulders, and tackled the toughest bit of rock climbing I have ever attempted. For the first twenty feet or so the climber is to some extent protected by the rope, which can be hitched round a great splinter close to the col; beyond that point the rope is simply worn as an ornament, though doubtless it supplies one's companions with pleasing sensations whenever a slip seems imminent. About half-way up is an excellent step on which one can take breath. When I say excellent, I only mean relatively to the rest of the crack, not that it is suitable for lunch, or even that one can balance on it without holding on; indeed, on the first occasion that I ascended, my meditations at that point were rudely interrupted by my foot slipping on the shelving rock and I was launched into thin air. Wiser by this memory, I hung on with my fingers as well as the absence of anything to hang on to would permit, and then, having somewhat regained my wind, began the second half of the ascent. This section was, by the general consent of the party, voted the hardest. There is really very little hold for the hands, and nothing at all for the feet, the climber proceeding chiefly by a pious reliance on Providence, eked out at intervals by loose stones wedged with a doubtful, wobbling sort of semi-security into the crack. Above, the need for piety is replaced by excellent handholds on the right, though the gasping and exhausted climber still finds it difficult to propel his weight upwards. Ledges then become more numerous, and at length one's arms and head hang down the Grépon side of the slab, whilst one's legs are still struggling with the concluding difficulties on the other side. At this juncture wild cheers broke from the party below, and awoke in me the dread that the porters would regard them as the wished-for signal and fly incontinently to Chamonix. In the intervals of gasping for breath I suggested these fears to my companions, and a silence, as of death, instantly showed their appreciations of the danger.

. . . We then scrambled up the gully and through the 'Kanones Loch', and with our hopes rising at every advance, we followed my old route to the top of the great gap. Here we fixed a hundred feet of rope, and the party went down one by one. As I was descending last, having just passed a perfectly smooth and precipitous section of the cliff relying exclusively on the rope, I rested a moment on a trifling irregularity in the rock. When I essayed to continue the descent, the rope came to me as I pulled. With a great effort I succeeded in keeping my balance on the insecure footing where I had been resting, but for a moment I felt supremely uncomfortable. The rope was apparently quite loose above, and there appeared to be no means of climbing down the rock to the gap without its aid. However, after about ten feet of it had been hauled in, no more would come, and it resisted the united efforts of my companions in the gap. Collie also managed to see an apparently possible line of descent, and skilfully coached by him, keeping the rope in my hand merely as a *dernier ressort* I succeeded in reaching the welcome security of Hasting's grip and was landed in the gap.

So far as I could see, the rope had slipped off the top of the tower on to the

Nantillons face, and caught in a hitch some ten feet down. . . . As it was still doubtful whether we could scale the final peak, and thus get down on to the C.P. route, this was not an impossible contingency, and we hastened forward to see the question at rest.

This final peak had nearly baffled Burgener and Venetz and we scarcely hoped to be able to climb it by fair means. We determined, in consequence, to try and win the summit by throwing a rope over the top. It is true Burgener and I failed singularly in so doing, but on this occasion we had a light rope with us, far better adapted for that purpose than the ordinary Alpine Club rope we had used in 1881. Collie, on the way along the ridge, selected two excellent stones where-with to weigh the rope and give it some chance of facing the furious gale. With much discomfort to himself and grave damage to the pockets of his coat, he conveyed these murderous weapons through various difficulties to the very foot of the final climb.

The preparations for a preliminary assault by fair and legitimate methods were in progress, when Pasteur joyfully shouted that we had already joined the C.P. route and could ascend by a perfectly simple and fairly easy line. The crack by which Venetz had climbed, is not the only one leading to the top. To the right, and rather on the Nantillons face, is a second cleft, precipitous at the bottom, where a friend can conveniently give you a shoulder, but quite practicable above. . . . Pasteur gave me a shoulder and in a few minutes we all crowded round the ice-axe and its fluttering flag.

The wind was howling across the ridge with such fury that we could only crouch under one of the stones, and we soon determined to go down to warmer quarters. We scrambled off the summit, and, sheltering under its lee, rejoiced in victory and lunch. Pasteur, who had been previously on this side of the mountain, now took the lead. He slipped a spare rope through a piton left by M. Dunod, and we all quickly slid down to a broad shelf. When I say all, however, I must except Hastings, who unluckily inserted his foot into a tempting crack, and found that no effort could subsequently release it. All hands heaved on the rope, but it was of no avail, and he bid fair – save for the dearth of eagles – to rival Prometheus. Someone at last suggested that he should take off his boot. The idea was hailed with approval, and we all shouted and yelled the advice. When, however, one is supported on a steep, not to say perpendicular slab by one foot jammed in a crack some twelve inches from the surface, it is a problem of no slight complexity to unlace and remove an offending boot. The task was, however, accomplished; but then a second difficulty arose; what was to be done with it? Happily, a pocket was discovered large enough to contain the property, and the ledge was soon reached in safety.

My Climbs in the Alps and Caucasus

ARMAND CHARLET

AN ASCENT OF THE GREPON

In the afternoon, M. Tézenas and Georges [Armand Charlet's brother] met me.
. . . The weather was still doubtful, but both Georges and I decided to go either
to the Charmoz or the Grépon. As for M. Tézenas, he did not care. Provided it
was a tough climb, he was happy; he was not much interested in the view.

Very early (far too early), we left the hotel, so that we were still using the
lantern when we reached the Rognon des Nantillon. There was just one party
behind us on the glacier. It was a Greek climber, I think, with Arthur Ravanel,
Ravanel-le-Rouge's son, and a Taugwalder from Zermatt; they were to traverse
the Grands Charmoz. We did not officially state where we were going but I knew
it perfectly well.

I was not feeling quite happy about this warm early morning. I was vainly
scanning the view on the Brévent or the Prarion for an encouraging sign, but
everything looked rather hostile, including the Y-shaped couloir down which
stones were hissing. At the top of the couloir, I took to the right without hesitat-
ing, and an ice-glazed open chimney gave me plenty of trouble before reaching the
broad terrace on the Col Charmoz-Grépon. M. Tézenas, who had strong principles,
stretched himself on the platform, his head lower than his feet: according to
him, it was the best way to relax.

Now we were about to start working in earnest. When I scrambled up the
easy ledges and platforms leading to the small gap at the foot of the Mummery
Crack, our *monchu* said to Georges:

'Do you know where Armand Charlet is taking us?'

'Well, I have some idea we are in for the Grépon. Don't bother,' answered my
brother.

I am not going to describe the most celebrated bit of rock climbing in the Alps:
it is far too well-known, and it could be nicknamed 'the Wall of Sighs and Wails'.
A fresh breeze was blowing up the couloir, licking the rocks round us with a swish
which is the ominous portent of a storm. The first part of the crack was not quite
free of snow and I had to traverse sideways across the steep slab; the rock was
deadly cold. While I was scrambling up the second part of the crack, snow began
to fall, but not much, and soon it was just a thin snowy drizzle.

From the highest point on the Grands Charmoz, Arthur's party was watching
us, expecting to see us retreat on account of the bad weather; but they did not
know us well, apparently.

Then M. Tézenas came up to me, quite enthusiastic about that tough bit of
climbing. At that moment, Ravanel shouted to us that he was abandoning the
traverse.

'What about us?' asked our patron.

'What about us? We go on, double quick!' shouted Georges from below, and in accordance to his words, he shot up the Mummery Crack with two sacks on his back.

I took this opportunity to say: 'Besides, one never goes down this way; it is not done.'

M. Tézenas asked nothing better than to go on; he trusted both of us to the utmost. There is nothing more pleasant for a guide than such trust. I am quite sure that it actually increases the leader's capabilities. Strange as it is, I have noticed this fairly often, and the reverse, too. Some of my failures came more from that sort of thing than from some temporary lack of enterprise on my part. Our trio had a sort of special gift at creating close-fitting parties, both physically and morally. We did not need so much to overcome the Grépon, even in bad weather.

When I came out at the foot of the Rateau de Chêvre there was a lull in the storm, but we kept on at the same speed: had not Georges said 'double quick'? The double rope was wet and we had some trouble when pulling it down after the Grand Gendarme, but any mountaineer knows that this always happens when the weather is foul. At one moment we were going at such a speed that we did not see the Letter-Box, that very characteristic pitch where, during the whole length of a rope, one is completely hidden inside the mountain. We had gone round it and only realized our mistake when we came to its gaping hole on the other side.

Sitting together on the summit rock, we were surprised that it was already over. For a few minutes we could see the Mer de Glace and the Couvercle; I was hoping to see the Verte, but a very light snow started to fall again, just to finish soaking the ropes. Once more there was trouble in getting the double rope down after the Dunod Chimney: a volley of oaths (but in our Chamonix vernacular they are tamer and much more picturesque), joint efforts, a violent pull, coaxing pulls, and so on. How many ropes have been caught in rocks since the beginning of mountaineering! Our rope suddenly came down, when we were about to abandon it. Guides and mountaineers, let me tell you that sooner or later you will have to fight against evil gremlins who shamelessly hold back the best set of double ropes. When all fair means have proved of no avail, try praying to the mountain gremlin: all the evil spirits will be eliminated and your rope will slip down; but it is the only way. . . .

Still threatened by bad weather, we raced down to the Montenvers. M. Tézenas, who had been perfect during the whole ascent, was just a bit tired. . . . This traverse of the Grépon has left me an unexpected impression: less difficult than what I feared, but so varied that even now I think it is unique.

Ma vocation alpine

The Aiguilles

EARLY MORNING

Above us the snow-covered mountains had not yet been touched by the sun. In spite of the late hour, they still displayed this dull, slumbering aspect things assume early in the morning, which I always connect with endless hours spent in station waiting-rooms when a connection has been missed, or with the written part of the *bachot*. The bleak setting of an execution, the sort of weather which makes you turn up your collar and long for a cup of steaming chocolate and a warm bed.

In the grey light of dawn, I was looking at my group of friends, alike in their clothing of the monkish Bonneval cloth, enlivened with the clashing tones of their mufflers, red, yellow, green and purple. Who are they, those companions of mine in our perilous endeavour? I know nothing of their lives, and they know nothing of mine. I know that their speech is full of symbols, and that this mountain they are constantly referring to provides them with neutral ground and an alibi. I understand their enthusiasm or their irony when they relate the various episodes of a fight in which their lives were at stake. I also know those who are almost silent, haughty, well beyond enthusiasm, as a matter of principle. When questioned, they answer in a most matter-of-fact way. They climb because they like it and it is a simple necessity. But I have caught the glint in their eyes.

'As we have to mark the way, we go first,' said Tom, and turning to me: 'You begin!' he said.

Yet this way of drawing lots, if it was proof that we completely trusted one another, had left the Aiguille out of our discussion completely, and, as a sort of joke, but really because I did not care to tackle the first slab, which was gaunt and ice-glazed, I answered: 'No, *you* begin; we are still too far from the summit, where you promised to let me go first.'

Tom was stopped by unscalable rocks, and Lagarde, scrambling up a slab, passed us.

Like gossamer strung between the leaves of a rose bush, the light thread of remembrance is entwined with apparently slight but precise details: an emotion, a smell, the taste of tea (not the amber-coloured tea one sips, together with small mouthfuls of cake, but a suspicious tea, neither hot nor cold, scarcely sweetened), a friend's word or gesture. Now, when I remember some words spoken by Lagarde, I still conjure up the aspect of the place, the black rocks we were scaling in the shade, the weird yellow stone steeples soaring before us, right in the sun, and the majestic expanse of the Argentière Glacier, stretched like a lake into which a thousand ice streams were flowing, the sources of which were on the high ridges, at the feet of granite spires. I was sitting on a little snow-covered

147

rock, blowing on my fingers to warm them, when my friend said, smiling that arch transparent smile children are given on English postcards: 'What is the matter with your fingers? Do you want my gloves? I am warm.'

Soon I descried the top ridge, as erratic as a mane shaken by a wind from the sea, the living and expressive crowning of a huge iced slab, extending like a powerful brow. This upthrust of stone stood between us and the sun, like a screen against which the rays of pale light crashed, the diverging branches of which, catching here and there a spot of snow or a shining arête, threw over the summit a veil of mineral glow which gave it a sort of cloudlike halo.

La Pointe Lagarde

RENE CHABOD

WHY I CLIMBED THE GRANDES JORASSES[1]

I began the struggle for the north face of the Jorasses in 1932 with my friend Gabriel Boccalatte (who was killed in 1938 on the Aiguille du Triolet). One day, while we were studying the face, I asked him: if we were certain that nobody would ever hear of our having conquered it, should we try to scale it? Neither of us dared to reply. On the one hand, there was our passion for mountaineering for the sake of the mountains, but on the other we were urged towards this terrible face by pride, by team spirit, by our wish to succeed before others, as we were representatives of western and Italian mountaineering. As for myself, I was also spurred on by the Aostan aspect of the question: being a native of the Val d'Aosta, I wanted to be among the first on the top of a mountain which is half-French, half-Aostan.

In 1935, I wrote: 'I must say that I don't feel very enthusiastic, because I do not like to endanger my old skin merely for a mountain – even *that* mountain – but my friend Gervasutti had made up his mind, so I must go with him. Am I a victim of friendship? Exactly so, a victim of friendship and also of the foolish ambition to make a first climb. Now that the first climb has been accomplished by others and we have been forestalled, I am committed to make the second, so as not to lose face!' In a word, I was for it. I had wanted to tackle the face as a climber from the Val d'Aosta. I was bound by promise to Gervasutti, so there was no backing out.

Of course, I did not exactly start in a suicidal frame of mind. In our 1934 climb, when we gave up the attempt from lack of daring, we had discovered that it was

[1] From a letter written to C. E. Engel in 1947.

quite possible to come down. So that on our second attempt we were for doing everything within our power, but we knew that we could come down if we failed. We found the conditions so bad – mainly on account of the awful weather – that we had to go on at all costs, to the very limit of our capacities. But had the weather been good, the face would not have been as difficult as we thought. Of course, I speak of the 1935 route, leading to the Pointe Croz, not to the Eperon Walker, which I have not done.

Our mistake was that we had been too timorous in 1934: had we gone on, we should have conquered with less danger than during our second attempt in 1935. Owing to our rate of progress in 1934 we should have reached the top before the blizzard in which Peters and Haringer were caught. In 1935 we ran great risks on account of the weather, but I must repeat that we did not attack in a suicidal frame of mind. Personally, I did not then think that one is justified in taking enormous risks for a second climb and I just went because I was committed.

Now that the climb is done, I think I ought to have answered 'yes' to the question I put to Boccalatte, for I experienced some of my finest mountain impressions when climbing the Jorasses: it is a wonderful, unforgettable climb. And I thank my sense of duty, of friendship, of personal dignity which conquered the sinking feeling I had in the Leschaux hut when I heard that we had been defeated by the Germans.

EDOUARD FRENDO

THE CENTRAL SPUR OF THE GRANDES JORASSES[1]

At five a milk-like light, filtering through the mist, heralded in the day.

I put the meta tablets on the heater meticulously, to brew the re-invigorating Nescafé, of which we had dreamt all through the night. It was all we could swallow. Our wish to finish the climb before the beginning of a storm, the longing to see how it would end, and our exhaustion, took away our appetite.

To keep one of them more or less dry, we decided to use only one of our fifty-metre ropes, so that we had only about twenty metres between us: we were soon going to regret it.

When we got up to leave our bivouac at six, we were so cold still that we kept our big rubber hoods on. Rebuffat, deadly cold, was as stiff as our frozen rope; so,

[1] July 16, 1945.

as my effort in dealing with our morning cooking had put some warmth into me, I went first.

At first my injuries of the day before were less painful than what I expected, but I soon realized that I had been too optimistic about my strength. As soon as I got into the red chimney above the gully, I had to stop. I was hoping I could scale it or cut steps. Alas! scaling was out of the question: it was far too open to afford any hold for feet kept flat against those smooth, wet slabs. It was also impossible to use the back of the chimney, as it was covered with a thin coat of ice-glaze. Between them a few thin scales of rock could be detected at close view, brittle and sharp, which seemed to be safer than the night before because of the night frost. That was a piece of luck, as they are the only means up.

I suddenly noticed that my fingers hurt so much that I could not use them, and I had to give up. I came down to Rebuffat, who took the lead, with his usual look, full of resignation.

With his back against the overhang on the right, his feet groped for some hold on the wet slabs on the left; he was held by a few insecure pitons, and went up slowly. The very bad condition of the dripping mountain and the rotten rocks compelled him to drive in one nail after the other. None of these was perfectly safe, for their shafts cracked the rock as they were driven in. 'Perhaps one will be safe,' said Rebuffat, who showed no sign of nervousness.

At the start of this third day on the mountain, I deeply admired my young companion, who kept up the struggle, a tremendous trial for body and mind, and I was furious at myself because I was unable to help him more on account of my stupid injuries.

Out of the mist, which became thicker, a thin ice-cold drizzle was falling, and we were wet through. We hoped there would be no storm before we were out of trouble! The knowledge that our safety was conditioned by our exertion gave us the strength to continue, and to do so properly.

With my nose against the back of the ice-glazed *dièdre* and practically hidden beneath the two rucksacks that hung on a nail above my head, shielding me, I patiently bore the assault of the stones and icicles that Gaston hacked down, and of the missiles that fell from the last ridge, over which the wind was blowing, together with drops of melted snow collected by that wretched gully. We clung to a fragile ladder, in a very precarious situation, and I was thinking of Samivel's cartoon: 'I do wish I were elsewhere. . . .' But from the bottom of my well I saw no way out except by the top.

Rebuffat went on with his meticulous line of shaky pitons. Then suddenly I heard a resounding note. I drew my head out of my shelter and saw that my leader had succeeded in moving out of the back of the chimney to reach the slabs on the left, which were safer; five more metres and he would reach a convenient resting place which he had detected on the left. Unfortunately, our short rope did not allow him more than a metre. He had to stop. He did not mind. He put both his feet into stirrups, hammered in one more piton, meant for me, and asked me to come up. We would have to have a relay on our stirrups. Well, it would be just one more acrobatic feat among many others.

Our one hammer-ice-axe was lowered to me with the utmost care. The stiff rope was then pulled up, together with a sack which was hooked up on a piton. Then I got myself hauled up, together with the other sack, to save time. All along the chimney the pitons were so insecure that a single hammer-tap on the edge was enough to loosen them. Soon the sacks, ropes, stirrups and climbers were hanging to the two God-sent nails, and Gaston left them as soon as I arrived to get a little higher, on the more comfortable resting place he had seen.

From there, through the mist, we finally realized it might be possible to escape out of our grim couloir-chimney. . . . From the snow platform where we had landed we looked once more for the celebrated ledge we should follow, 'hanging with our fingers', an ordeal I dreaded on account of their injured state. At first sight it seemed to begin right there, but we noticed there was a larger ledge a little higher up.

We climbed up a short distance. For once curiosity looked like a major virtue, as we discovered a perfectly comfortable ledge, not at all the kind to creep along, holding by one's fingers, and at the end of it we found one of Cassin's pitons. We were therefore on the right route, yet we did not wholly understand.

Or perhaps we did. We realized that the end was in sight. I saw it quite near, and, without going any deeper into the problem of the mysterious ledge, I moved quickly to its eastern end. A wet and overhanging black rock, not too repellent, barred the way to easy couloirs we could detect on the west side of the summit ridge.

Without taking off my sack, I started tackling the overhang. As I was hampered by my woollen gloves, I pulled them off with my teeth, and in spite of the pain I grabbed the tough granite holds with my injured fingers. The tiny quartz pebbles cut cruelly into my flesh, which started bleeding again, but it did not matter. Overhang, slabs, ice: they suddenly all looked so easy! The summit was in sight. We were soon to reach the end of our trouble. I had just to keep my jaws clenched for a short while. . . . I bit into my gloves hard enough to cut them.

I got to a good platform in a hollow and Rebuffat came up to me.

Now, suddenly, brutally, exhaustion overwhelmed us. We dropped heavily upon the stones, weighed down under our sacks which now seemed unbearably heavy. Now that we realized that our difficulties were over, the nervous strength which had sustained us so far gave way. A huge and happy fatigue fell on us and we felt an irresistible longing to lie down and sleep.

La face nord des Grandes Jorasses

ANDERL HECKMAIR

THE WALKER SPUR OF THE GRANDES JORASSES[1]

Sunday, August 5th, as early as daybreak, we knew that the bad weather had been driven away. This fourth day dawned bright and chilly. As soon as we were out of our sleeping bags, our clothes and shoes were frozen. When we handled our crampons, our hands stuck to the steel. The early sunlight was already falling upon the surrounding summits, but our grim faces remained in the icy shadow. When we reached the top of the ridge and were in the sun at last, a raging mountain gale deprived us of the warmth we had hoped for and drove long wisps of powdery snow into our faces. We were compelled to pull off our gloves, stiff with ice, each time we had to overcome a moderately difficult pitch. Our stiff white fingers had lost all feeling: it was as if we were tapping bits of wood against a stone. Realizing the danger, I kept my limbs moving to restore the circulation to my fingers and toes. We struggled on in this way for six endless hours. Finally, we got below the last cornice, several metres thick, just below the summit ridge. I looked anxiously for a possible belay to overcome the last obstacle. Suddenly, I discovered in a crack an old rusty piton, tightly stuck. The click of the spring-ring echoed my yell of triumph. Heaving myself over the cornice, I landed on the summit.

To commemorate their triumph, the first two parties to climb the spur had fixed this symbolical piton. Yet for us, it was no mere symbol. The overhanging cliff, covered with fresh snow, required a strong belay, and our stiffened hands could not have done the trick.

The howling wind prevented us from hearing each other. Only by pulling at the ropes could I make my companion understand that he could come up in his turn. His head showed above the arête at last, in the sun. We were too moved to speak, but we embraced. Then we slid down a few metres on the easy, snow-covered summit slope. The cold was too intense to allow us even to think of resting there, and we immediately started down to warmer levels.

From the ridge connecting the Pointe Whymper to the Pointe Walker there is an ice couloir opening down the south face. At first we thought it looked good, and Hermann, on his rubber soles, started down first while, with my crampon-shod boots, I belayed him round an ice bulge.

'Be careful we don't start sliding down; face the mountain and kick good steps.'

We went down together, very gingerly. Suddenly, my companion slipped, dragging me with him. Such a slip is not dangerous when it ends in a hollow at the bottom of a gentle slope. This was the case, and happily, except for a somersault of a few yards over an ice bulge, everything ended well. An avalanche of

[1] 1951

powder snow kept us company down those 200 yards, which ended just above a deep crevasse. In spite of the care I took, a crampon spike tore my trousers and penetrated my knee. Yet I was on my feet at once, while Hermann sprawled in the snow ten yards below. I called to him, feeling worried, but he was only having a rest and rose, rather disgusted. The scratch on my knee bled freely, but it was only a flesh wound and a quick dressing was all that was needed. We shortened the rope between us and went down with even greater care, to avoid further mishaps.

Les trois derniers problemes alpins

JOHN MOORE

AN EARLY ATTEMPT ON THE DRU[1]

From the highest part of the Montenvers we had all the following objects under our eyes: the valley of ice, the Aiguilles, Mont Blanc with the snowy mountains below,[2] finely contrasted with the Brévent and the green hills on the opposite side of Chamonix, and the sun in full splendour showing all of them to the greatest advantage. The whole formed a scene both sublime and beautiful, far beyond my powers of description. . . .

While we remained contemplating this scene, some of the company observed that from the top of one of the Aiguilles the prospect would be still more magnificent, as the eye would stretch over the Brévent and beyond Geneva, all the way to Mount Jura, and comprehend the Pays du Valais and many other mountains and valleys.

This excited the ambition of the Duke of Hamilton. He sprang up and made towards the Aiguille du Dru, which is the highest of the four needles. Though he leapt over the ice with the elasticity of a young chamois, it was a considerable time before he arrived at the foot of the Aiguilles: for people are greatly deceived about distance in those snowy regions.

'Should he get nearer to the top,' asked Mr G, looking after Hamilton eagerly, 'he will swear we have seen nothing: but I will try to go up as high as he can; I am not fond of seeing people above me.' So saying, he sprang after him.

In a short time we saw them both scrambling up the rock: the Duke had gained a considerable height when he was suddenly stopped by a fragment of rock which was perfectly impracticable (for his impetuosity had prevented him from choosing the easiest way), so Mr G overtook him.

[1] In 1772. [2] Needless to say, Mont Blanc is not seen from Montenvers.

Here they had time to breathe and cool a little. The one being determined not to be surpassed, the other thought the exploit not worth the effort, since the honour had to be divided. So, like two rival powers, who have exhausted their strength by a fruitless contest, they returned, fatigued, to the place whence they had started.

A View of society and manners in Switzerland

HORACE-BENEDICT DE SAUSSURE

THE DRU

Among the mountains which surround the Glacier des Bois, the one which first draws the visitor's eye is a big granite obelisk, facing Montenvers; indeed, its rounded and slender shape makes it look more like a needle than an obelisk; its sides are polished like those of a building of elaborate architecture, and one only notices a few protruding rocks and straight neat cracks. If, as I have said, some of those peaks can be compared to artichokes made of large, pyramidal slabs, this cone is the centre of one of them.

It is quite inaccessible from anywhere, so that one is compelled to observe it through a telescope. That is what I did in 1776 with Sir William Hamilton,[1] who had carried with him a big achromatic telescope for just that purpose. We saw that this elongated cone, the point of which is broken, is topped by several big rocks in an irregular heap. Below them, the upper part of the needle seemed to be an accumulation of big horizontal steps, made of rectangular fragments, like a piece of masonry. There were some ten or twelve such steps. Below, and to the bottom, one could see no other step, and most of the cracks which divide the huge granite block look irregular and cut to face sideways.

Voyages dans les Alpes

C. T. DENT

THE FIRST ASCENT OF THE DRU[2]

We followed the couloir running up from the head of the glacier, keeping well to the left to a little below the col. At this point it became necessary to cross the

[1] Saussure knew him well, had travelled with him in Italy and stayed in his palace in Naples.
[2] In 1875, after many attempts.

154

couloir, and for that purpose we employed the long ladder which we had placed in position the day before. Right glad we were to see the rickety old structure, albeit it creaked and groaned dismally under our weight, and ran its splinters into our persons at all points of contact. Yet there was a certain companionship about this same weather-beaten ladder, and I felt as if it was almost a hardship that it could not share more in our promising success. Next we fastened a double rope, about 20 feet in length, and swung ourselves down a rough cleft, as if we were barrels of split peas going into a ship's hold. Up again, and the excitement waxed stronger as we neared the doubtful part. Then Alexander (Burgener) lay flat on his stomach, and wriggled round a projecting rock, disappearing suddenly from view. We followed, progressing like the skates down the panes of glass in an aquarium tank and found ourselves huddled together on a little ledge. An overhanging rock compelled us to assume the anomalous attitude enforced on the occupant of a little-ease dungeon. What next? An eager look up, and part of the doubt was solved. There was a way – but such a way! A narrow flat couloir, its angle plastered with ice from top to bottom, invited, or forbade, further progress. Above, a pendulous mass of great icicles, black and long like a bunch of elephants' trunks, crowned the gully. We tucked ourselves away on one side, and the guides performed the best feat of rock climbing I can imagine possible. Unroped they worked up, hacking out the ice, their backs and elbows against one sloping wall and their feet against the other. The masses of ice dashing down, harder and harder as they ascended, showed how they were working. Suddenly a slip above – a shout – a crash of falling ice. Then a brief pause, broken after a few minutes by a triumphant yell from above, and the end of a rope dangled down close to us. Using this latter aid considerably, we mounted and found the top of the couloir blocked up by a great overhanging boulder, dripping still where the icicles had just been broken off. 'Come on,' said voices from above. 'Up you go,' said a voice from below. I leaned as far back as I could, and felt for a hand-hold. There was none. Then right, then left – still none. So I smiled feebly, and said: 'Wait a minute.' Thereupon, of course, they pulled with a will, and struggling and kicking like a spider irritated with tobacco smoke, I topped the rock gracefully. How the first man did it, is, and always will be, a mystery to me. Then we learned a great mass of ice had broken away under Maurer's feet while in the couloir, and that he must have fallen had not Alexander pinned him to the rock with one hand. From the number of times that this escape was described to me during the next day or two I am inclined to think it was a near thing. 'The worst is over,' said Alexander. I was glad to hear it, but, looking upwards, had my doubts. The higher we went, the bigger the rocks seemed to be. Still, there was a way, and it was not so unlike what I had often pictured.

Another rough scramble, and we stood on a comparatively extensive ledge. Already we had climbed more than half of the only part of the mountain as to the nature of which we were uncertain. A few steps on, and Burgener grasped me suddenly by the arm. 'Do you see the great red rock up yonder?' he whispered, hoarse with excitement; 'in ten minutes we shall be there, and on the arête – and then –' I felt that nothing could stop us now; but a feverish anxiety to see what was beyond, to look on to the last slope, which we knew must be easy, impelled us on, and we worked harder than ever to overcome the last few obstacles. The ten minutes expanded into something like thirty before we really reached the rock.

Of a sudden the mountain seemed to change its form. For hours we had been climbing the hard dry rocks. Now there appeared to vanish, and – blessed sight – snow lay thick, half hiding, half revealing the last slope of the arête. A glance showed that we had not misjudged. Even the cautious Maurer admitted that as far as he could see all was well; but he added: 'Up above there, possibly –' And now, with the prize almost within our grasp, a strange desire to halt and hang back came on. Alexander tapped the rock with his axe, and let out his pent-up excitement in a comprehensive anathema of Chamonix guides. Already we could anticipate the half-sad feeling with which we should touch the top itself. The feeling soon gave way. 'Forward,' we cried, and the axe crashed through the layers of snow into hard blue ice beneath. A dozen steps, and then a bit of rock scrambling; then more steps along the south side of the ridge – some more rocks, and we topped the first eminence. Better and better it looked as we went on. 'See there!' cried Alexander, suddenly: 'The actual top.' There was no mistaking the two huge stones we had so often looked at from below. A few feet below them, and on our left, was one of those strange arches formed by a great transverse boulder, and through the hole we saw blue sky. On again, while I could hardly stand still in the great steps the leader hacked out. A short troublesome bit of snow-work followed, where the heaped-up cornice had fallen back from the final rock. Then Hartley courteously allowed me to unrope and pass him, and in a second I clutched at the last broken rocks, and hauled myself up on to the flat sloping summit. There for a moment I stood alone, gazing down on Chamonix. The dream of five years was accomplished. The Dru was climbed.

Alpine Journal, 1878

GUIDO GERVASUTTI

THE NORTH FACE OF THE DRU[1]

A week after our first attempt, we again left the Montenvers at 1 a.m. and by 5 o'clock we were at the foot of the snow slope. There we realised that we had

[1] August 1937.

made a big mistake in reducing our ice and snow equipment to one ice-axe, and no crampons. A week ago the slope had been covered with a thin layer of snow which had enabled our lightweight boots to get a grip, but this layer had now disappeared leaving bare ice. So we were forced to cut steps the whole way up the slope, which meant a considerable expenditure of energy, and above all a loss of time which resulted in a most uncomfortable bivouac after the climb. Our advice to parties repeating this route is to take crampons, one ice-axe being quite enough in any case.

At 7.30 we reached the rocks where we allowed ourselves a brief rest, and left again at 8 o'clock, two hours behind schedule. At first we climbed on easy rocks then, bearing to the right, up some rather tiring verglas-coated chimneys and cracks; an exposed traverse brought us out beneath the Niche. By a difficult crack which widened into a couloir-chimney we gained the sloping névé which covers the lower part of the Niche. We crossed this at its narrowest, going up obliquely from left to right, and making for the steep ridge separating the north and west faces. We continued up this ridge until it merged into the vertical wall, and it is here that the hardest climbing occurs. There is a succession of cracks with rounded edges, reached by a leftwards traverse, which slash the smooth walls for 130 feet or so, where the difficulties are continuous. However, enough pitons had been left in on the first and second ascents to lessen the original severity. I even managed to avoid using two or three of them. All the same, the climbing here is of absolutely first-class standard, and extremely tiring. Afterwards some easier sections alternate with some short very hard pitches where one has to throw in every ounce. However, the climb has one general feature: there are plenty of ledges everywhere which allow one to belay and to rest comfortably, and this makes it a very safe climb. When, towards the end, the angle of the wall relents, the ascent ceases to be a pure rock climb, and alternates between bands of steep ice and broken rock; as there was a good deal of verglas we had to proceed with the utmost caution. Darkness overtook us when we were still battling with the final slopes; we despaired of reaching the summit and looked for a bivouac site under the terminal arête.

It was 9 p.m. when we came to a curious grotto of crystal, not more than a yard high, its bed formed of absolutely pure green ice. It was splendid to look at, but the prospect of spending a whole night there was quite definitely repellent. We were little more than a hundred feet from the summit, but it was pitch dark and it would have been risky to go on. So we resigned ourselves to the unpleasant prospect of a long vigil sitting on bare ice, on which we spread the ropes and our sacks. To add to the icy cold of our couch, a draught blew up from the back of the grotto. We tried in vain to sleep. . . .

In the morning, when we made up our minds to get out of our bivouac, we saw a gleam of light at the back of the grotto where the draught came from. Much intrigued, I crawled on all fours towards the narrowing depths of the cave, and managed to wriggle along the crack. Suddenly, to my surprise I came out on to the vast terraces of the south face of the mountain, in the full light of the sun which was climbing up above the Aiguille de Leschaux! Had we discovered this tunnel the evening before we would have had a more comfortable bivouac. Lucien passed the sacks through to me and then followed himself, and after warming ourselves a bit in the sun we carried on to the summit.

Gervasutti's Climbs (translated by Nea Morin and Janet Adam Smith)

GASTON REBUFFAT

THE NORTH FACE OF THE DRU

However, with the fine weather back like a gift from heaven, there was nothing for it but to embrace it with open arms; here we were, in shirtsleeves, at a most unorthodox hour, on the north face of the Drus. It really was fine that August afternoon. The face was in the shade, but the soft air around seemed redolent with gaiety in the place of the cold and severity of the early hours. There was a strange charm here, as if the mountain were about to give up its secrets, on this afternoon bright with all the beauty of autumn.

We had to climb fast, in fact very fast indeed, if I was to attend the guides' festival at Chamonix the next morning. This fact added zest to the whole day. To go fast merely for the sake of going fast usually seems senseless, but on this occasion it was quite different; we *had* only these few hours to climb the two 2,500 feet of this face. But René had not exaggerated when he said that he was a quick mover; he kept on my heels the whole time. At about 3 p.m. we arrived at the Niche, printed like a giant's thumb-mark in the clay of our mountain. We stopped to look at it, and also at the west face which soared like a stone waterspout from the moraine direct to the sky.

'In ten years' time that will be climbed,' I said to René.[1]

We ate a few dates, some currants and an orange – fruits of the sun in the chill north face – and went on. We found ourselves climbing with ease and pleasure. Our movements were linked in smooth rhythm, like water flowing from a spring. All skills have this effect on a well-trained body: they remove the sense of difficulty and leave only the pleasure of a task prepared and well performed. As children we used to climb trees, and perhaps that instinct was with us still. If we had been suddenly stopped and asked the question 'Why do you climb moun-

[1] The first ascent of the west face was made in 1952 by Guido Magnone, L. Bernardini, M. Laine and A. Dagory. See page 160.

tains?' I feel sure that we would have answered on that day: 'That's what we are made for.' We have the instinct for it, the love of rocks and the necessary skill, so that we can climb without being worried by the technical problems. Thus the whole climb was pure joy, for, while superficially watching over the actual ascent, the spirit had leisure to wander happily. It was an exquisite afternoon; no incident marred the day.

The breeze that fanned us was cool and gentle. The sun, hidden behind the west face, spared us the overpowering heat of its direct rays, but we were cheered by its nearness. Down below, the Montenvers train continued to rattle along, the torrent to run its course, the waterfall to break over the jagged cliff edge. Close at hand the rock had a good rocky smell, its roughness bit firmly into our rubber soles and our fingertips. It was all very nice and very reassuring, like the shade of an oak-tree; we felt as if the world was made for us, this corner of the planet on which we knew peace.

I climbed first, because of my position as guide, but René's job was as vital as mine. Almost the whole time we climbed together, without stopping, both in order to go faster and because we each had confidence in the other. . . .

Now at last we were on the face together, and as we climbed I became aware of a special source of happiness. I could not define it; at first it seemed to come from the climb, and yet the song which rose to my lips had surely some other origin. True, there were tinglings of the atmosphere and the earth around us, the taste of air and the gold of sunshine on our mountain; but all that could be no more than a fragrance. The real truth was that we were two men in a realm of rock, both climbing towards the same star. René's pleasure lay in bringing off a nine-year-old plan, mine in helping him to do so. I felt happy to be on the Dru, but my happiness, here as elsewhere, lay in my task of leading a companion. For where would a guide be without his companion? Whatever the weather, no matter what the climbing difficulties, my need was to play the same tune as he, for that is the best gift that our mountains can give us. One man of the two as he climbs to the summit is doing his job. The other is on holiday; and the cream of their combined effort is their friendship.

Starlight and Storm

Mont Blanc

GUIDO MAGNONE

THE FIRST ASCENT OF THE WEST
FACE OF THE DRU[1]

Lucien had just come out above the last overhang which cut this length of rope, and debouched under the immense roofs which barred the face.

It was the key pitch: it was here that we would be beaten or victorious.

He stood up on a small platform, hoping with all his might that he would not be deceived. These famous roofs did not present a very comfortable appearance.

His gaze raked the face above his head, looking for a weak spot in this superb architecture. Suddenly, a leap of the heart, a whistle of stupefaction: just at the intersection of the two most formidable overhangs, a breach opened up. Lucien no longer saw anything but this enormous gash.

'Good God, it can't be: we can get through like a letter through a letter box.'

Down below, we were burning with impatience.

'What's going on?' cried Adrien. 'What can you see?'

Lucien was in no hurry to reply. He continued to examine the passage and analyse the difficulties, foreseeing each movement and making quite sure; and at last he announced:

'I think we'll get through.'

We shared out the load which Lucien had abandoned. Marcel started off and I soon followed. It certainly called for some exertion. Lucien was decidedly in form!

The efforts we had to expend on this passage belied the apparent ease with which it was so surely and swiftly overcome. The chimney was extremely steep, intersected by wicked little overhangs. With my legs extended, I pushed violently away from the lower supports, while my fingers clutched at weak projections. I came out at the summit completely out of breath, my heart pounding fit to burst. When we had all four regrouped, we could smile again. Just above, that ardently longed-for breach opened the way for us into an attractive couloir.

Ah! how easy it all seemed now, compared to our previous difficulties.

To be sure, our rucksacks were heavy enough, but the certainty of having the summit within our grasp gave us wings. The key pitch was crossed in no time at all. It seemed ridiculous to us, that key pitch. The passage of which we had spoken so respectfully for years, and which had scared us so, was one of the easiest of the whole course: a fine detached blade, very obliging, on which we could set foot . . . one energetic heave, and it was all over.

We were across the *dièdre* which followed in no time. Hands took hold of good,

[1] July 18, 1952.

sound, solid rock, feet clambered wide apart up a series of little notches most conveniently placed.

This delicate climb was an agreeable change from athletic heaving and the tedious manipulation of the hammer.

One good length farther on, the exiguousness of the shelves made the relay purely theoretical. Lucien fixed it according to his fancy, and we were obliged to dispose ourselves around this point he had chosen, with our legs wide apart and the 'cow's tail'[1] well secured by a snap-link at belt level.

Below, Adrien waited at a loose end until Marcel had set off, before climbing up beside me.

'Look!' he let out suddenly. 'What odd choughs!'

My eyes followed the direction in which he was pointing, a thousand metres lower down. Two small, tawny blobs were wheeling above the moraine. They came up at an amazing speed, growing larger under our eyes. It was a pair of royal eagles with white-barred wings. Side by side they soared, without a movement, at a strong upward angle, and in a few seconds they were on a level with us.

They went on rising, passed the summit of the Drus, and disappeared in the direction of the Verte.

My attention, momentarily distracted, returned to Marcel. He had emerged from the *dièdre* and was now ready to attack a vertical slab. The holds were thinning out. Very much reduced in size, they distinctly resembled the characteristic finger holds of Fontainebleau – familiar terrain where every whim was permissible. But here it was better not to play about too much with our style of climbing over a gulf which it was advisable not to contemplate.

'Look out!'

Two metallic clinks rang like a tuning-fork in my ears. A piton whistled past, skimming my head. Instinctively I watched its fall. I saw it flash once or twice, and then, without touching the wall, it disappeared, swallowed up in the depths. I waited for the little metallic sound, but however hard I strained my ears I heard nothing.

'Well, old man, I don't think we'd care to go the same way,' said Adry in a low voice, with a little smile.

We remained motionless for a few seconds, our gaze held downwards. If we should 'unstick', all the records for free fall would certainly be broken. I turned away with a faint shudder.

For the first time in three days we saw the sun. Towards noon the first rays crossed the arête on our right and brought us a little warmth. The weather gradually turned fine. Now we climbed calmly, we were so sure of the whole affair. As we had been climbing for more than four hours already, we must be pretty high.

Pressed to the side of the Dru, it was hard to judge our position. I remembered

---

[1] Short rope buckle securing the climber directly to the piton.

then the bearings we had fixed to measure our progress. The day when we should see the swimming-pool over the Montenvers, the day when we should see the Potinière . . . then our hopes would be on the verge of fulfilment.

That day had come, for I turned round and all Chamonix lay spread out before me.

At the same moment, as though some confirmation were necessary, Lucien's voice came to us.

'Here it is, boys, it's finished! Here's the way out!'

Adry had hardly heard these words before he seized his rucksack, unfastened the bottle which he had been lugging about with four litres of water in since this morning, and vindictively emptied it to the last drop. His gesture was almost a symbol. From here on, we would no longer be thirsty.

The west face finished here. Above, the face flattened out, slowly changed direction, and was lost in the North face. To the left, less than twenty metres away, was an inviting platform.

The way to it was quite an arduous one. Lucien, wedged in an overhanging chimney, struggled furiously with all four limbs; he made his way inch by inch under the twisting overhang.

Finally he succeeded in ramming his fist into the bottom of a fissure and, clinging to this single hold for a brief instant, entirely suspended over a formidable gulf, he searched for a point of support, while his feet scraped madly against the rock.

But we were blasé, and it was with tranquil indifference that we watched Lucien in the process of forcing the passage.

His fingers hesitated, clutched, then seized the secure hold for which they were searching. Instinctively he got a good grip there and tested its quality. Then, with a flick of his hips and a ferocious shudder, he pulled with all his might and, with a sonorous grunt, was over the top of the overhang.

A few seconds later, his silhouette rose on the ledge of the north face. We were soon beside him.

The West Face (translated by J. F. Burke)

WALTER BONATTI

THE SOUTH-WEST PILLAR OF THE DRU

I had almost described a full circle since the morning and had at last come near to those blessed broken and easy rocks which seemed to continue for at least another hundred and fifty feet, but then . . . more roofs and overhangs, very fractured but also very marked. I braced myself to repeat the traverse in the opposite direction for the usual operations of recovering the sack and the pitons. At first the motion contrary to the direction of the swings I had just carried out disconcerted me but in the end, I don't know how, I managed to reach the famous bunch of pitons. A stirrup slipped unexpectedly out of my hands; my eyes refused to follow its fall and it was some seconds before I heard it bouncing down the face. Then for the third time I braced myself for those rappels. The rope and the rocks around me were spotted with blood. My poor hands were almost in ribbons, the pads of my fingers gripped the rock with open flesh, but the work they had to do was such that it made me insensible to pain. By the end of the third series of swings it was almost nightfall and I hastened upward in the hope of finding at least some narrow little ledge on which to pass my fifth night. I found one about fifty feet higher up. When I went down again to recover the pitons it was pitch dark.

At first the bivouac seemed even more dramatic than on the previous night, but suddenly I heard very distant shouts and I saw faint lights moving. They were my friends from the Charpoua hut, who were making signals and looking for me. I replied at once with what little breath I had left and in order that they might see me I lit a little torch made from a piece of paper. They saw me and it even seemed to me that I understood that they would come to meet me the next day (by an optical illusion they thought that I was already descending along the ridge of the normal route).

The mere presence of my friends, even though far away from me, was of no material use to me but it gave me a wonderful sense of power which made me feel that I was certain to reach the summit of the Dru and return to that life which during those days had little by little become so distant, so remote that it seemed as if it no longer had anything to do with me, but belonged to some imaginary person of whom I had only heard tell. As far as I was concerned nothing had changed materially from a few minutes before; the pain in my hands was still acute, I was burning with thirst and the dark shadow of the roofs above my head was just as repellent, yet within me the whole situation had changed and I was able to look at things in a very different way than I had been able to during the past few days. Only now did I feel that I had a true measure of comparison to help me to understand the intensity of all that I had lived through. The mountain, its rocks, the void, had become so alive as to make them seem, little by little, a part of myself, as if I formed a single body with them. Now, however, as if at an awakening, I was able to dissociate myself from these sensations and to reconcile them with reality. I even seemed able to toy with the idea of having always lived on this mountain, with the sole aim of suffering and of climbing ever upward towards an eternally unattainable summit.

For the first time I felt that victory over the south-west pillar of the Dru was in my hands, that I had surmounted the almost impossible barrier which had separated me from my true self and in the exaltation of the moment I felt a great longing to weep and to sing.

On the Heights, translated by Lovett Edwards.

7
ACCIDENTS

MARK TWAIN

ONE OF THE WORST ALPINE TRAGEDIES

On September 5, 1870, a caravan of eleven persons departed from Chamonix to make the ascent of Mont Blanc. Three of the party were tourists, Messrs Randall and Bean, Americans, and Mr George Corkindale, a Scottish gentleman, and there were three guides and five porters. The cabin of the Grands Mulets was reached that day; the ascent was resumed early the next morning, September 6th. The day was fine and clear and the movements of the party were observed through the telescopes of Chamonix; at two o'clock in the afternoon they were seen to reach the summit. A few minutes later they were making the first steps of the descent; then a cloud closed round them and hid them from view.

Eight hours passed, the cloud still remained, night came and no one returned to the Grands Mulets; Sylvain Couttet, keeper of the cabin there, suspected a misfortune, and sent down to the valley for help. A detachment of guides went up, and by the time they had made the tedious trip and reached the cabin, a raging storm had set in. They had to wait. Nothing could be attempted in such a tempest.

The wild storm lasted *more than a week*; but on the 17th Couttet with several guides left the cabin and succeeded in making the ascent. In the snowy wastes near the summit, they came upon five bodies, lying upon their sides in a reposeful attitude; which suggested that possibly they had fallen asleep there while exhausted with fatigue and hunger, and benumbed with cold, and never knew when death stole upon them; Couttet moved a few steps farther and discovered five more bodies. The eleventh corpse – that of a porter – was not found although diligent search was made for it![1]

In the pocket of Mr Bean, one of the Americans, was found a notebook in which he had pencilled some sentences which admit us in flesh and spirit, as it were, in the presence of these men during their last hours of life, and to the grisly horrors which their fading vision looked upon and their failing consciousness took cognizance of.

---

[1] In point of fact, only five bodies were recovered. The others probably disappeared into the Brenva Glacier.

'*Tuesday, September 6.* I have made the ascent of Mont Blanc with ten persons: eight guides and Mr Corkindale and Mr Randall. We reached the summit at half-past two. Immediately after quitting it, we were enveloped in clouds of snow, which afforded but poor shelter, and I was ill all night.

Sept. 7 – Morning. The cold is excessive; the snow falls heavily and without interruption. The guides take no rest.

Evening. My dear Hessie, we have been two days on Mont Blanc in the midst of a terrible hurricane of snow; we have lost our way and are in a hole scooped in the snow at an altitude of 15,500 feet; I have no longer any hope of descending.'

They had wandered around and around in that blinding snowstorm, hopelessly lost in a space only a hundred yards square, and when cold and fatigue vanquished them at last they scooped their cave and lay down there to die by inches, unaware that five steps more would have brought them into the right path. They were so near to life and safety as that and did not suspect it. The thought of this gives the sharpest pangs that this tragic story conveys.

A Tramp Abroad

GEORGES SONNIER

A RESCUE

I think of this other solitary climber, who, when coming back from an expedition on the Aletsch Glacier,[1] broke through a snow bridge and fell into a crevasse. The hole was bottomless. By great luck, he fell on a snow bridge some twenty feet below the surface and was only slightly injured.

He was alive. Alive, but alone, abandoned, lost at the bottom of an ice hole, above which he saw but a narrow stretch of blue sky and, at night, a few faint twinkling stars.

He was there for eight days and seven nights, eating only a little chocolate which he melted over the flame of a candle and diluted with the glacier water that dripped over him. With this tiny flame he also tried to thaw his hands and feet, slowly becoming frozen by the endless night of the glacier depths.

Eight days and seven nights! No search party had found anything. Everybody thought he was dead, even his friends, even his mother. Only his father, for no reason whatever, was still hoping; but he had been abandoned. For living people, this living man was but a name and a shadow. In spirit, a tombstone had been planted above him.

[1] It actually happened on the Glacier des Nantillons.

56 - *La Dent du Géant.*   56 - *The Dent du Géant.*

57
*Brouillards
d'hiver.*

57
Winter mist.

58 - *La vue du Col des Montets.*   58 - *The view from the Col des Montets.*

59 - *Le glacier des Pèlerins.*   59 - *The Glacier des Pèlerins.*

And yet, obstinately, he persisted in living. His ice-axe had become stuck in the broken snow-bridge. With a frightful exertion he managed to climb up to within one metre of it; a single metre from light, freedom, warmth and life. But that one last metre was beyond him. His strength gave way and he fell back.

He tried again seven times and always in vain. Clutching at the ice with his bleeding hands, which were now without sensation, he crept up the terrible, steel-coloured wall, and finally dropped back into the night of his ice prison. He was exhausted and had to abandon his attempts. Then, on the evening of the fourth day, the ice-axe fell beside him. It was useless now, for he no longer had the strength to use it.

Sometimes he heard parties passing above him. He heard words, songs, laughter, and he shouted in vain. The edges of the crevasse were formed in such a way that they magnified the sounds that came from outside, while shutting in those which might come from below. So the prisoner's voice was captive too, and was lost in the useless echoes of the dead galleries of his underground world.

I can picture to myself the wounded man, fighting against so much cruelty, against the exquisite torture of the mountain; abandoned by everything, left at the gate of the next world and yet fighting, still fighting in the shadows, trying to grasp his ebbing strength in his exhausted hands, keeping the last gleam of sanity in a mind verging on madness. I can picture to myself his hopeful dawns, the endless days of forlorn hope, the fearful nights. And I admire him for his dogged fight for life, when it would have been so easy to slip into the last torpor of the snow, or gently into the open depths. There is no word to describe such courage. It was more than courage; it was saintliness.

And yet he was saved at last by a miracle – a lesser miracle than that of his dogged protracted fight. Passing near the crevasse, a guide noticed the broken bridge, drew near and saw the prisoner. That very night he was brought down to the valley, half his body frozen and his burnt eyes full of shadow.

Où règne la lumière

WILFRID NOYCE

AN ACCIDENT ON THE VERTE

It seemed to him that he saw the Alps again, as he had last seen them seven years ago, on the day when he gave up serious mountaineering. It was a morning warm and glorious, and he was with Halliday, the rope-mate and genius of his early ventures. Halliday had been older, cynical perhaps, devoted to John the more.

They were coming down the snow gully called the Whymper Couloir. They were late, for they had done a long climb through darkness and dawn up the other side, and were now descending snow steps which the sun had softened. The quicker down, the better; but the quicker you went, on this mushy apology for snow, the more likely must be the chance slip. And, the slip once made, though the angle was not very high, there could be no stopping. Half-way down, a passage leftward brought them to another, smaller gully that slid smooth and direct down to the sun-flecked, crinkled table-cloth of glacier below. But beyond this gully, left again and looking straight into blinding sun they could see a black skyline of rock rib which promised clear safety. Between it and them, dirty froth-snow lay dull and glitterless, the steps of a previous party already decaying. But slightly above, a band of yellow slab showed in places, a nick which the pick point should flake through to the rock below. The rock rib itself, once reached, might take time to descend, but it would certainly 'go'. The sun was high, throats dry for drink; windproofs, thin against the morning cold, clung now to the wrist with sweat.

'Better take the high road,' Halliday said.

'With those steps there? We'll be down in ten minutes.'

'You may be down in shorter time, on that snow.'

'Do you honestly mean. . . ?'

'You're the leader now. Just as you wish. You choose between descent and death.' Halliday, unconcerned, was peeling off his zip sweater. He seemed to be interested in nothing but preventing the cigarette ash from falling between the folds.

'Well, I saw the snow. Only for God's sake let's be careful, do it facing in.'

'And Tim Proctor and Barnaby behind?'

'They can do which they like. Damn it, we're not their nannies.'

'As you wish.'

Again indifferent.

They continued cautiously, on a zig-zag line that the old tracks had left. Slowly, but in half-an-hour, at ten-thirty as he remembered still, they were not far above the great overtilted crevasse or 'bergschrund' that marked the slope's end neatly, as with a pencil ruling. Then suddenly . . . two grey rucksacks, no they were bodies with rucksacks too, came rolling faster, faster, from somewhere above. They had lost sight of the others, had not thought of them even. At their own level, and ten yards across the slope, the bundles struck a black rock mass projecting from the yellowy evenness. A confused human noise, blood mixed with the snow, the bodies, all limbs, now like marionettes with no cohesion to them, careered on, one rucksack torn away, ice-axes slithering by with a hiss of their own. Aghast, he and Halliday were watching the bergschrund. The bodies seemed to hesitate, then like divers to take the plunge – across. They lay, two sad little semaphore dummies, on the heaped mounds below.

John had been the first to speak. 'My God, Oh God! what has happened to them?'

'They just didn't take the intelligent route,' Halliday's voice was toneless, insensible, and John had hated it.

'They took *our* route, *my* route!'

'As you rightly remarked, we're not their nannies. Still, it might have been safer if they hadn't.'

They climbed down to the two. Tim's face was black; black blood oozed from his nostrils. At the crown of his fair head was a strange dark dent and his legs were twisted unnaturally. He was very clearly dead. Barnaby's face too was discoloured, lips swollen, negroid almost and unrecognizable. But he was groaning, and they hurried to cut away the rucksack that held him contorted. Then they saw that his eyes were sightless, glazed; the groan changed to a rattle that ended in a sigh. He, too, was dead.

For about an hour John had sat, in the warm sun of the August forenoon. The bottom of the Whymper Couloir is a good viewpoint. Opposite, the grim square bulk of the Grandes Jorasses is softened by the twin soaring ridges. The north face, already a huge shadow, rises in one mottled sweep from the warm Leschaux Glacier. Thence the eye wanders fascinated along the great frontier crest, to the Dent du Géant and beyond. This John had been examining already with pleasure, while he rested; but now somehow, it was different. Something had gone for ever. The hills were the same hills, placid and yellow under the morning sun, yet they were different too, heartless and savage and treacherous. They had betrayed him, and killed his friends. Perhaps he had betrayed himself, perhaps *he* had killed them. In this thought he found his bitterest pain.

The Gods are Angry

WALTER BONATTI

THE FRESNAY PILLAR

The slow and exhausting descent of the glacier began. We refused to accept our bad luck. The snow was still very deep. Not even in winter climbs could I recall having met with so much. We left behind us not a trail but a burrow. Fortunately the mists were beginning to rise and visibility gradually improved. That made it possible for us to enter safely the labyrinth of crevasses which led to the Col de l'Innominata, the last serious difficulty on our way to safety. But the deep snow so slowed down our advance that we despaired of being able to reach the base of the col while there was still daylight.

I felt faint with fatigue, physical suffering and cold, but refused to give up.

Our file grew longer. Oggioni was stumbling every few steps, at the end of his tether. He was without a rucksack, which he had handed over to Gallieni. Sometimes he was last man, sometimes last but one. We groped our way on to the glacier in complete disorder, drunk with fatigue. We were roped together, but each went his own way without heeding anything. I realised that in such conditions it would be very hard for us to reach the foot of the Col de l'Innominata in daylight. Gallieni, behind me, seemed the least exhausted. I decided to unrope myself and him in order to go ahead as quickly as we could and prepare the couloir of the Innominata; otherwise our companions would no longer be able to climb it. This task would have to be completed by nightfall.

Our companions followed in our tracks. Meanwhile I attacked the terrible ice which had encrusted the Col de l'Innominata. Guillaume had remained behind. Within half an hour it would be dark and we were still struggling to reach the col. Now we were again all roped together; myself, Gallieni, Oggioni, Mazeaud and Kohlman. Our only hope was to reach the rescue parties while we still had a little strength left. They alone might be able to save those left behind. It was pitch dark when I reached the Col de l'Innominata. It was Saturday evening, after nine o'clock, and we had been out for six days. The powdery snow driven by the wind had begun again and in the west we could see the flashes of an approaching thunderstorm. There was nowhere to fix a piton to anchor the rope which supported my four companions and I had to hold it on my shoulders. I urged them to hurry. But the operation was very long and desperate. Orders mingled with cries of pain and desperation. Behind Gallieni, Oggioni seemed unable to grip the rock. Gallieni tried to help him in every way he could, supported in his turn by the rope which I held on my shoulders. The two Frenchmen down at the end of the rope were shouting and raving.

It was chaos. Three hours passed and we were still at the same point. I could not move. Every so often there were tugs at the rope which nearly pulled me into space. The pain of the rope and the cold made me feel faint. But if I collapsed it meant the end for everyone. In all those three hours Oggioni had not been able to move. All encouragement was in vain. Now and then he would reply with a wail; he seemed to be in a sort of trance. He was attached by a karabiner to a piton, and would have to free himself from it to give us a chance of hauling him up. But he hadn't the strength and he was so exhausted that perhaps he was incapable of thinking. I would have liked to go down to him but that was impossible since I had to keep the rope, which was holding him as well as Gallieni, firmly on my shoulders. At last, not being able to do anything else, Gallieni made sure that Oggioni was firmly fixed to the piton, undid the rope that bound him to Oggioni and the Frenchmen and came up to join me and was thus able to carry on rapidly towards the rescue parties. Oggioni remained roped to the strong Mazeaud, to whom I shouted to wait and look after the others who would soon be rescued. . . .

In this way we covered the last 1,200 feet which still divided us from the Gamba hut. It was pitch dark. We only managed to find it because I knew this area as well as my own house. Gallieni followed me unhurt. We circled the hut, hammering on the windows with our fists. We had just reached the door when we heard heavy steps inside and a hand raised the latch. The door burst open; we saw the interior of the hut dimly lit by a small lamp. It was full of sleeping men. We stepped over several bodies without recognizing anyone. Then suddenly one of the men leapt to his feet and shouted: 'Walter, is that you?' and there was a rush of people and we were suffocated by embraces.

'Be quick!' I shouted. 'There's one man still out there! The others are on the Innominata! Be quick!' It was three o'clock on Sunday morning. The storm was still raging. We stretched out on the table in the middle of the hut and the others took the frozen crampons from our feet, undressed us and gave us dry clothes and warm drinks. I fell into a heavy stupor. When I awoke about three hours had gone by. The bodies of my companions had been found, except Vielle. They told me that Oggioni was dead and I was filled with uncontrollable grief. Dear Mazeaud, the only one of them to be found alive, embraced me and wept with me.

On the Heights

8

MEN OF THE MOUNTAINS

60 - *Vue depuis l'Index.*

60 - *The view from the foot of the Index.*

61 - *L'arête Midi-Plan.*

61 - *The Midi-Plan ridge.*

62 - *La face sud du Mont Blanc.*

62 - *The south face of Mont Blanc.*

AN EIGHTEENTH-CENTURY GUIDE

In July 1788 . . . I decided to visit the celebrated Savoy glaciers and a Genevese friend was kind enough to come with me. I shall not describe the journey: to make it interesting, I should imitate the excited, sublime unintelligible style which any traveller must assume nowadays, when he has done about two leagues and is endowed with a sensitive soul. I should write about ecstasy, embraces, thrills, and I must say that such words though they have become somewhat trite, are still unfamiliar to me. I have seen Mont Blanc, the Mer de Glace, the Arveyron spring; I gazed silently for a long time at these terrible snow-covered rocks, those icy summits which pierce the clouds, the broad river, called a sea, of which the motionless waves still seem angry. This huge canopy out of which a milky torrent springs, trundling blocks of ice through heaps of broken rock. I was struck with terror and filled with gloom: I thought I had seen the fearful image of a sunless world, given up to the god of storms. When looking at those terrifying beauties, I thanked the Almighty for having made them so scarce; I longed for the moment to go down, to recross the delightful valley of Magland. I had promised myself to soothe there my sorrowful eyes, travelling very slowly across this smiling landscape.

. . . Such were the ideas I conceived at Chamonix as I walked down the Montenvers from the Mer de Glace. After an exhausting two-hour walk, I came to the spring beside which I had rested in the morning. I wanted to rest again; though I do not like torrents much, I am very fond of springs. Besides, I was deadly tired. I asked my good and honest guide – whose name was François Paccard – to sit beside me, and we started a most interesting gossip about the habits, the temper and the way of living of the Chamonix people. Good Paccard greatly interested me with his description of those simple customs I was delighted to hear about, if only to regret their disappearance; suddenly, a lovely little girl came and offered me a basket of cherries. I accepted it and paid for it. When she was a little way off, Paccard remarked, laughing: 'Ten years ago, on this very spot, one of our young country girls had a very bad time, after having offered some fruit to a visitor.' I immediately requested Paccard to tell me the story. . . . We were both sitting against a fir tree, eating our cherries, and Paccard began his tale: 'I must tell you, Sir, that ten years ago our valley was not as well known as it is now. Travellers did not bring us their gold *louis* in order to look at our frozen snow and pick up our pebbles. We were poor, ignorant of evil and our wives and daughters, busy with household chores, were even more ignorant than us. I tell you that to begin with, so that you can forgive Claudine's sin. The poor child was so simple that she was easy to deceive. . . .'

Claudine

RODOLPHE TOEPFFER

NINETEENTH CENTURY GUIDES

Though we did not need a guide to go to St Gervais, nevertheless we engaged Jean Payot for the whole length of our tour round Mont Blanc. It would have been silly, for reasons of mere thrift, to dispense with the advantage of a Chamonix guide, for one can always rely on the fact that the guide is experienced, most helpful, not a braggart, well mannered and well spoken and perfectly aware of his responsibilities as a member of a body which keenly upholds its good reputation. We were told that, during this very summer, sixty men of the valley had been accepted as guides, and all of them had had to display their knowledge of local requirements before experts. This organization, besides providing travellers with the guarantees they are entitled to expect from those who offer to guide them through difficult Alpine paths had rid them of the unauthorized guides who used to pester them on the road a day or two before they reached the Priory.

Chamonix guides, who keep alive the traditions of those of de Saussure's time, as well cultured, tactful and good mannered, are nice travelling companions as well as good guides, and a man must be very lacking in curiosity or unpleasantly haughty to feel bored in their company. Knowing all about mountains, being good and sensible talkers, and having a good store of stories to relate, and being observant to begin with, there is no end to the interesting things one can get out of them, and we were among those who thought that six francs a day was cheap, if only in return for their conversation. As soon as we had procured Jean Payot, questions showered on him from twenty-two sides, so that during the first hour he really did not know whom to answer first. Meanwhile, he drew our attention to the fact that Mont Blanc was veiled, not by a cloud, as we had thought at first, but by snow blown off by a gale into shapeless and confused wisps.

Nouveaux voyages en zigzags

LIONEL TERRAY

TWENTIETH CENTURY GUIDES

On one of my six ascents of the south ridge of the Noire I had just finished the delicate and exposed traverse which constitutes the escape from the big groove on the fifth tower. My client had done brilliantly as far as there, and although the traverse was long thought to be grade VI, I was pretty sure he would be able to do it without the complicated rope tactics (called by guides a 'télépherique') necessary to protect him simultaneously from before and behind. I called out to him to start across. He was so impressed with the smoothness and exposure of the pitch, however, that he hesitated, fearing to fall into an irretrievable position under an overhang if he slipped. Each time he made a few tentative inches he would shrink back quickly to his starting-point.

Knowing that he could do it quite well if only he could overcome his fear, I tried every trick I knew; technical explanation, coaxing, raillery, finally even curses, but all to no avail. He just stood there, hanging on to his belay piton, his eyes full of mute supplication. This performance went on for more than half an hour. The sky was clouding over and I wanted to avoid a bivouac. Reversing the pitch to install the 'télépherique' struck me as both a long and a delicate process, but I was just about getting resigned to it when in a thoughtless moment of inspiration I shouted out:

'If you don't hurry up and do it we won't be friends any more. I'll never speak to you again.'

The result could not have been more miraculous if I had played the magic flute to him! I had no sooner finished speaking than, to my immense surprise and pleasure, he launched out on the traverse with the energy of despair, and in a few moments stood at my side.

On the first direct ascent of the Arête du Tronchey I was held up for some time by an enormous overhang. Finally, by turning on the high voltage for a few feet and also applying every bit of technique I possessed, I got over it. The difficulties now decreased, the summit was not far distant, and success seemed within our grasp. Unfortunately, although my client M. Gourdain was an excellent climber, he had never done anything as extreme as this. Despite valiant efforts he was unable to get any higher, and the friction of the rope through the numerous karabiners was so great that I could not hoist him. It looked as though we were beaten within sight of victory and would have to make our way painfully back down the ridge, which had cost us more than a day to climb.

It all seemed too futile, and I desperately sought a solution. By scouting along a ledge to my right I discovered that the overhang gave out into a smooth but not quite vertical slab. If I could just get my client across to there it seemed probable that I could then haul him up the fifty feet or so that separated us. After all kinds of strange manoeuvres I succeeded in getting the rope clear of the karabiners, which I deliberately abandoned, and threw it back down to Gourdain. Unfortunately he was unable to reach the slab, but, noticing a little ledge directly below me, I called down to him to pendulum across to it on the rope. This meant a twenty-five foot swing in mid-air, and not many people would have faced up to it. However, he courageously let himself go, and a moment later he was on the ledge. This manoeuvre was irreversible, the ledge being lower than the point of departure. Gourdain's bridges were now burnt, and he had to be got up to me at all costs.

The slab turned out to be extremely severe, and after his efforts to climb the overhang Gourdain's arms gave out completely. I was in an awkward position on a narrow ledge, ill-placed for haulage, and could not bring my force to bear properly. Neither could I see any way of getting down from where I was. Unless I could find some rapid solution, the outlook was tragic indeed. At this precise moment a technique for rescuing wounded men from crevasses came into my head, and with the aid of a few pitons and karabiners I rigged up a sort of pulley. Thanks to the mechanical advantage thus obtained Gourdain was soon at my side.

On another occasion I was doing the south-east ridge of Mont Maudit with one of my oldest clients, then about fifty-eight. The mountain was in poor condition and our progress had been proportionately slow. In the early afternoon, as we approached the neighbourhood of the summit, the storm broke. Needles of flame stood on the pompoms of our woollen hats and I felt the old familiar panic which the presence of lightning always inspires in me. After a few minutes the storm passed over, but the mountain remained enveloped in cloud. Before long a violent wind sprang up, whipping the snow into our faces and plastering our goggles. We started down in an absolute blizzard.

Now the ordinary route, which we were descending, consists of huge, steep snow slopes, interrupted here and there by ice walls and bars of seracs. Even in fine weather the route is hard to pick out on such featureless ground. This state of affairs being exacerbated by the cloud and the driving snow, it taxed all my local knowledge to find the way. Unfortunately my companion had bad eyesight, and with his goggles all plastered up he was practically blind. As is proper in descent he was going down first, but I soon realized that even when I shouted instructions to him he had lost the power to move steadily in a given direction; instead he was zig-zagging all over the place.

However we had to get moving if we were not to be frozen to death. The only solution seemed to be for me to go first, keeping my client on a short rope. By a cruel stroke of fate the slope, which was quite steep, was packed with the ice bulging through in places. The cramponning was delicate in such conditions, and an exhausted and half-blinded client seemed likely to slip at any moment. The reader can imagine my state of mind throughout this descent, peering through the thick cloud to seek the way and at the same time trying to keep an eye on my second lest he should suddenly shoot into me from behind and knock me over with the twenty spikes of his crampons.

In point of fact I have only had about a score of clients in my whole career who were really competent, and no more than three or four who could follow anywhere I could lead. One of these, a German-Swiss, gave me an unusual and amusing experience. Normally he never climbed with a guide, but as his friend had been injured he engaged me in order not to waste the end of his holiday. We set out for the Mer de Glace face of the Grépon, a well-known classic which is, in fact, quite long and difficult. Going up to the little Tour Rouge hut the evening before, already about a quarter of the way up the face, I had quickly noticed his astonishing facility.

In the morning I set a brisk pace from the outset, and since my client appeared to have no difficulty in keeping up I soon pulled out all the stops. Every so often I would turn round to see how he was getting on, and always he would be just behind me, smiling and not even out of breath. Once or twice, for form's sake, I asked:

'All right? Not too fast?'

And each time he replied:

'No, no. It's going fine.'

Now and again he would pause for a moment to take a quick photograph, manipulating the camera with extraordinary dexterity. As the going got harder and we had to climb pitch by pitch the pace hardly slowed up at all. By the time I had turned round at the top of the pitch he would already be some way up it, climbing like a squirrel, and a few seconds later he would rejoin me. We reached the summit three and a half hours after leaving the hut, an hour and a half sooner than my fondest hopes, including halts for some twenty-odd photographs.

It was 8.30 a.m. I felt in tremendous form, my client was climbing like an aeroplane, and we had plenty of time to do another ascent. I suggested traversing the west face of the Blaitière to the foot of the south ridge of the Fou, then rounding off the day by doing the ridge. It was an unconventional and even rather far-fetched idea, but it struck me as amusing and it would make a wonderful gallop. To my vast disappointment, my Switzer replied mildly:

'Oh! No, monsieur Terray, I'm not at all interested in ideas of that sort. I've never climbed as fast as that before, and I found it great fun, but that's enough for one day. What I like about mountaineering is being in touch with nature and looking at the scenery. Anyway, the weather's perfect, and since you're engaged for the day we'll just stay here until noon.'

Conquistadors of the Useless

9
HUMOUR

MME VICTOR HUGO

UNCONSCIOUS HUMOUR[1]

There was still the Mer du Glace to visit . . . M. Victor Hugo's guide, new to his profession, got on to the wrong path and landed him on an ice promontory between two cracks, which each step brought nearer. Soon the promontory became so narrow that the guide grew anxious, but did not dare to confess his mistake; so he pushed on, saying that it would soon get broader. It became narrower still and was but a thin edge between two chasms. The guide grabbed M. Victor Hugo's hand and said: 'Have no fear!' But he was very pale. A little further on, one of the chasms ended and the narrow edge ran up against a plateau. There was no room to walk abreast; the guide had only one foot on the level, and walked with the other on the slippery slope. Yet the young mountaineer did not falter and supported the traveller's weight with the staunchness of a statue. They reached the plateau, but that danger was not over. The plateau to which the ridge abutted was about five or six feet higher and very steep.

'Let go my hand,' said the guide. 'Lean on your stick and shut your eyes, so as not to get giddy.'

He scrambled up the ice wall, and after a few seconds, which seemed several quarter-hours to M. Victor Hugo, he lent down, held out both his hands and swiftly pulled M. Hugo up.

The plateau was familiar and the guide had no trouble in finding his way. Besides, from afar M. Victor Hugo saw Messrs Nodier and Gué, who were anxiously looking for him. M. Nodier's guide, seeing where the other was coming from, understood what had happened and began scolding him severely. . . . The young Swiss, who had been so firm when facing danger, was less strong when reproved, and heavy tears fell from his eyes. . . .

M. Victor Hugo's guide had to produce his book; he was quite out of countenance and trembling when M. Hugo handed it back to him, though he beamed with joy when he read: 'I strongly recommend Michel Devouassoud, who saved my life.'

Victor Hugo raconté par un témoin de sa vie

---

[1] Mme Victor Hugo accompanied her husband, the Nodiers and their other friends during the 1825 expedition to Chamonix.

Mont Blanc

EUGENE LABICHE

M. PERRICHON AND THE MER DE GLACE

PERRICHON (*enters, most excited*): Quick! Water! Smelling salts! Vinegar! (*He leads Daniel to a chair.*)

EVERYBODY: What is the matter?

PERRICHON: Something horrible! Make him drink! Chafe his brow!

DANIEL: Thank you! . . . I feel better.

ARMAND: What happened?

DANIEL: Were it not for M. Perrichon's courage. . . .

PERRICHON (*quickly*): No! Not you! Don't speak! It is frightful! We were on the Mer de Glace . . . Mont Blanc, in his quiet majesty, was gazing at us. . . .

DANIEL (*aside*): Theramene's relation.[1]

MME PERRICHON: Can't you hurry a bit?

HENRIETTE: Papa!

PERRICHON: Now, *do* listen! For five minutes we had been following a steep path, winding between two ice crevasses! I was walking ahead.

MME PERRICHON: How very dangerous!

PERRICHON: Suddenly, I heard something sliding down behind me. I turned round; M. Daniel had just disappeared into one of those bottomless chasms, the mere sight of which makes one shudder. . . .

MME PERRICHON (*exasperated*): My dear!

PERRICHON: Then, heeding nothing, I, though I have a daughter, dashed forward.

MME PERRICHON and HENRIETTE: Good Lord!

PERRICHON: From the brink of the chasm I held out my stick to him. . . . He grabbed it. I pulled. . . . He pulled. . . . We pulled and, after a tremendous fight, I dragged him out of this cave of death and brought him back to a place where he could gaze at the sun, our heavenly father. (*Produces a handkerchief and wipes his brow.*)

HENRIETTE: Oh Papa!

MME PERRICHON: My dear!

PERRICHON (*kissing his wife and daughter*): Yes, darlings, a beautiful story. . . .

ARMAND (*to Daniel*): How do you feel?

[1] The long and rather dull account of Hippolytus' death in Racine's *Phèdre*. Mont Blanc is not visible from Montenvers.

186

DANIEL (*in a whisper*): I am all right; don't worry (*He stands up*). M. Perrichon, you have just restored a son to his mother. . . .

PERRICHON (*with great dignity*): It is true.

DANIEL: A brother to his sister.

PERRICHON: And a man to humanity.

DANIEL: Words are too trite to thank you.

PERRICHON: You are right.

DANIEL: Nothing but my heart. . . . I say, my heart. . . .

PERRICHON: M. Daniel. . . . No, allow me to call you Daniel!

DANIEL: With the greatest pleasure! (*Aside.*) Now, it is my turn.

PERRICHON (*deeply moved*): Daniel, my friend, my child. . . . Your hand (*he grabs his hand*). I owe you the sweetest impressions of my life. Without me, you would now be a shapeless and hideous thing, buried under heaps of snow. You owe me everything (*with immense dignity*), I shall never forget it.

DANIEL: Neither shall I!

PERRICHON (*to Armand, wiping his eyes*): Ah, young man! . . . You can't realize the pleasure one feels when saving a life.

HENRIETTE: He does, papa! Just a moment ago. . . .

PERRICHON (*suddenly remembering that Armand had rescued him a short time ago*): Oh, yes, of course! Innkeeper, bring me the visitors' book.

MME PERRICHON: Why?

PERRICHON: Before leaving this place, I want to immortalize what has just taken place.

INNKEEPER: Here is the book, Sir.

PERRICHON: Thank you. . . . Who has written that?

ALL: What?

PERRICHON: 'I want to suggest to M. Perrichon that, as the *Mère de Glace* had no children, the E he provides her with makes grammar shudder with shame.' Signed: The Major.

HENRIETTE (*to her father in a whisper*): Yes, of course, papa! *Mer* has no E at the end.

PERRICHON: I knew that. I am going to answer that gentleman (*He writes.*) 'The Major is a dirty fool.' Signed: Perrichon.

THE GUIDE (*coming in*): The carriage has arrived.

Le Voyage de M. Perrichon

Mont Blanc

ALPHONSE DAUDET

CROSSING A CREVASSE

Leaning over the abyss, which the shadows represented as bottomless, he watched through the damp vapour the movements of the little lantern by which the guides below were preparing the way. Tartarin, none too easy himself, warmed his own courage by exhorting his friend: 'Come now, Gonzague, *bou*!' and then in a lower voice coaxed him to honour, invoked the banner, Tarascon, the Club....

'Ah! *vaï*, the Club indeed! . . . I don't belong to it,' replied the other, cynically.

Then Tartarin explained to him where to set his feet, and assured him that nothing was easier.

'For you, perhaps, but not for me. . . .'

'But you said you had a habit of it. . . .'

'*Bé*! yes! habit, of course . . . which habit? I have so many . . . habit of smoking, sleeping. . . .'

'And lying especially,' interrupted the president.

'Exaggerating – come now!' said Bompard, not the least annoyed.

However, after much hesitation, the threat of leaving him there all alone decided him to go slowly, deliberately, down that terrible miller's ladder. . . . The going up was more difficult, for the other face was nearly perpendicular, smoothe as marble and higher than King Réné's tower at Tarascon. From below, the winking light of the guides going up, looked like a glow-worm on the march. He was forced to follow, however, for the snow beneath his feet was not solid, and gurgling sounds of circulating water heard round a fissure told of more than could be seen at the foot of that wall of ice, of depths that were sending upward the chilling breath of subterranean abysses.

'Go gently, Gonzague, for fear of falling. . . .'

That phrase, which Tartarin uttered with tender intonations, almost supplicating, borrowed a solemn signification from the respective positions of the ascensionists, clinging with feet and hands one above the other to the wall, bound by the rope and the similarity of their movements, so that the fall or the awkwardness of one put all in danger. And what danger! *coquin de sort!* It sufficed to hear fragments of the ice-wall bounding and dashing downward with the echo of their fall to imagine the open jaws of the monster watching there below to snap you up at the least false step.

But what is this? . . . Lo, the tall Swede, next above Tartarin, has stopped and touches with his iron heels the cap of the P.C.A. In vain the guides called: 'Forward! . . .' And the president: 'Go on, young man! . . .' He did not stir.

188

Stretched at full length, clinging to the ice with careless hand, the Swede leaned down, the glimmering dawn touching his scanty beard and giving light to the singular expression of his dilated eyes, while he made a sign to Tartarin: –

'What a fall, hey? if one let go. . . .'

'*Outre!* I should say so . . . you would drag us all down. . . . Go on!'

The other remained motionless.

'A fine chance to be done with life, to return into chaos through the bowels of the earth, and roll from fissure to fissure like that bit of ice which I kick with my foot. . . .' And he leaned over frightfully to watch the fragment bounding downward and echoing endlessly in the blackness.

'Take care! . . .' cried Tartarin, livid with terror. Then, desperately clinging to the oozing wall, he resumed, with hot ardour, his argument of the night before in favour of existence. 'There's good in it. . . . What the deuce! . . . At your age, a fine young fellow like you. . . . Don't you believe in love, *qué!*'

No, the Swede did not believe in it. Ideal love is a poet's lie; the other, only a need he had never felt. . . .

'*Bé!* yes! *bé!* yes! . . . It is true poets lie, they always say more than there is; but for all that, she is nice, the *femellan* – that's what they call women in our parts. Besides, there's children, pretty little darlings that look like us.'

'Children! a source of grief. Ever since she had them my mother has done nothing but weep.'

'Listen, Otto, you know me, my good friend. . . .'

And with all the valorous ardour of his soul Tartarin exhausted himself to revive and rub to life at that distance this victim of Schopenhauer and of Hartmann, two rascals he'd like to catch at the corner of a wood, *coquin de sort!* and make them pay for all the harm they had done to youth. . . .

Represent to yourselves during this discussion the high wall of freezing, glaucous, streaming ice touched by a pallid ray of light, and that string of human beings glued to it in echelon, with ill-omened rumblings rising from the yawning depth, together with the curses of the guides and their threats to detach and abandon the travellers. Tartarin, seeing that no argument could convince the madman to clear off his vertigo of death, suggested to him the idea of throwing himself from the highest peak of the Mont Blanc.

. . . That indeed! *that* would be worth doing, up there! A fine end among the elements. . . . But here, at the bottom of a cave. . . . Ah! *vaï*, what a blunder! . . . And he put such tone into his words, brusque and yet persuasive, such conviction, that the Swede allowed himself to be conquered, and there they were, at last, one by one, at the top of that terrible *roture*.

They were now unroped, and a halt was called for a bite and sup. It was daylight; a cold wan light among a circle of peaks and shafts, over-topped by the Mont Blanc, still thousands of feet above them. The guides were apart, gesticulating and consulting, with many shakings of the head. Seated on the white ground,

189

heavy and huddled up, their round backs in their brown jackets, they looked like marmots getting ready to hibernate.

Tartarin on the Alps

10
WAR IN THE ALPS

63 - *La montée des Bosses.*   63 - *Going up the Bosses ridge.*

65 - Christ in the Snow.

65 - Le Christ dans la neige.

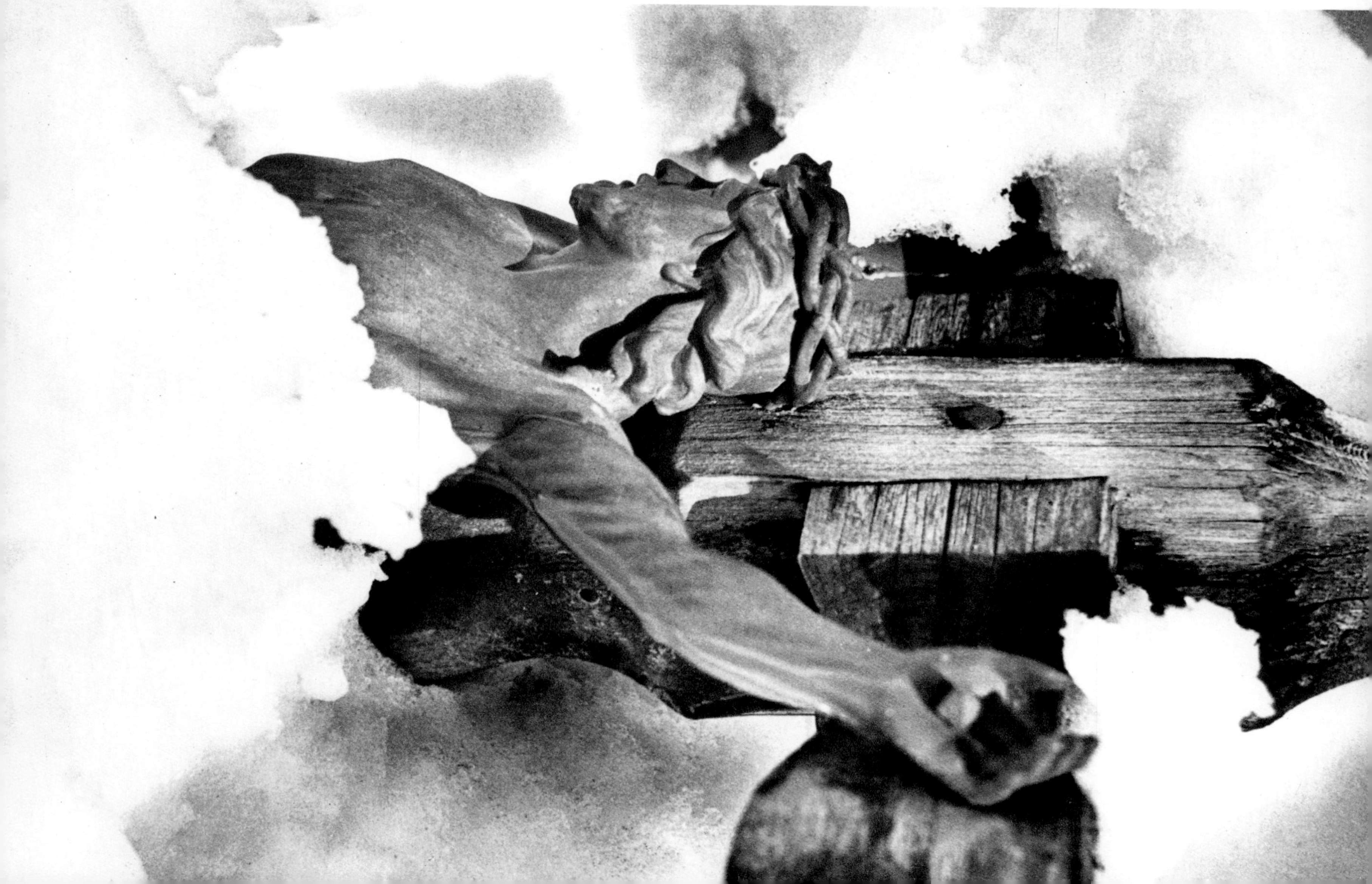

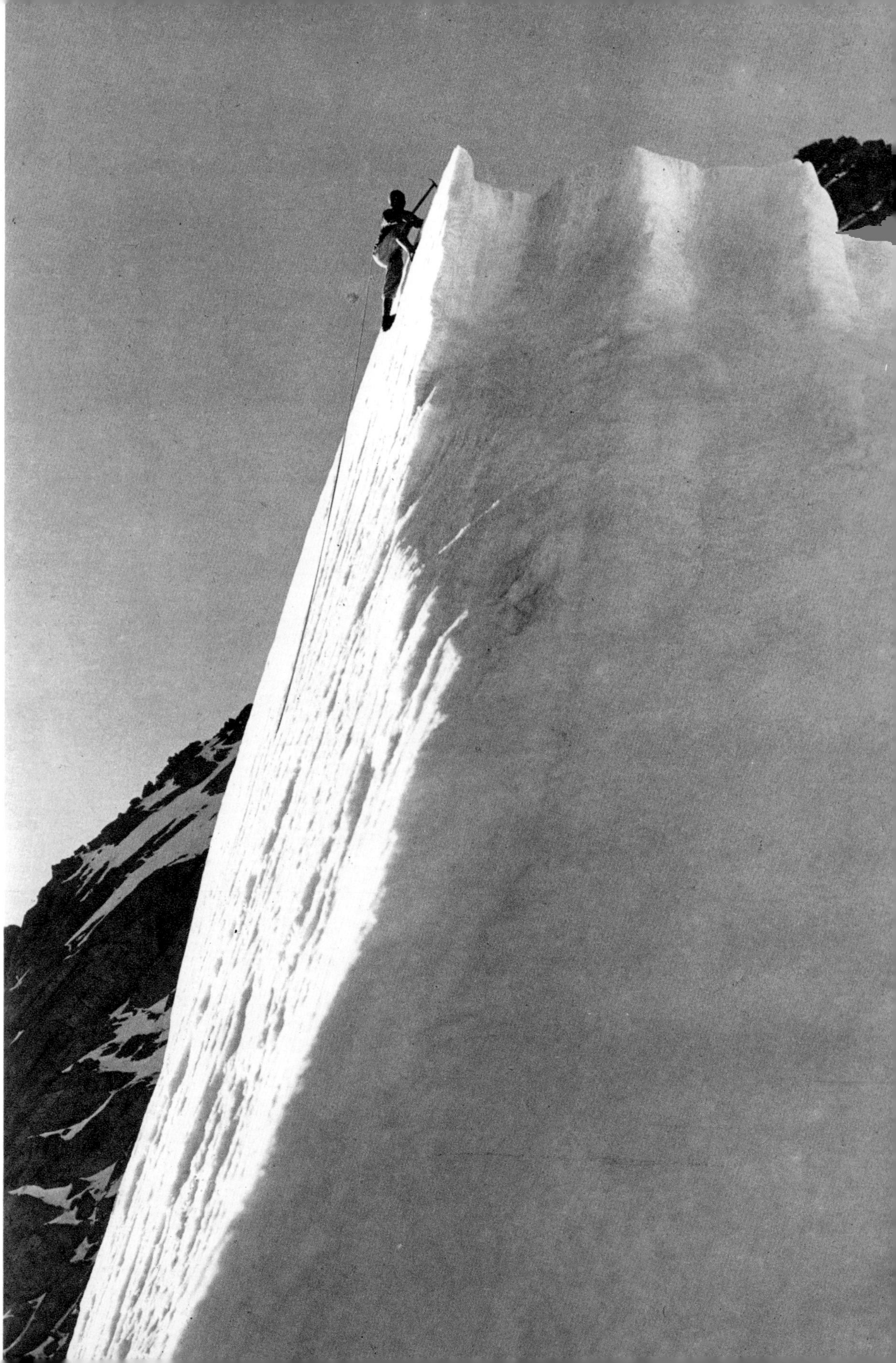

67 - A steep pitch.

67 - A pic.

68 - *Ecole alpine italienne au col du Géant. Photo C.-E. Engel.*

68 - *An Italian mountaineering school on the Col du Géant.*

69 - *De gauche à droite : Lady Hunt, Sir John Hunt, Basil Goodfellow, C.-E. Engel, Gaston Rebuffat, Mme Rebuffat. Photo Bernard Pierre.*

69 - *From left to right : Lady Hunt; Sir John Hunt; Basil Goodfellow, C.-E. Engel, Gaston Rebuffat, Mme Rebuffat.*

ABBÉ DESNOUES

ESCAPE INTO THE VALAIS[1]

This mountain is marvellous. It is 2,400 *toises* high and requires twenty-one hours to reach its summit; it is two leagues long. It is covered with snow in all seasons. Above its summit one descries in some places ice needles which, when reflecting the rays of the sun, look like so many transparent crystals. We rode along it all through the afternoon of Monday, September 25th. The plains or meadows we crossed at the foot of that mountain are almost untilled, producing only buck-wheat and betoking a poor country. The inhabitants look very pleasant, ploughing the little fields near their houses. I could not better describe those houses than by saying that they looked like our windmills, only much larger, but are protected by wooden piles, made of beams which raise them three feet above the ground, so that the snow has room enough to spread below the floor. . . . Innocence and candour show on the faces of those good people. . . . When the water is high the strength of the main torrent is so great that under my windows I saw scores of stones, as big as the quarter of a wine cask, being carried away as easily as if they had been grains of sand. I would like to describe some ice mountains which are called glaciers, and which attract visitors from very far away, but I only saw their lower end, though they are more than a mile long. (Better look them up in the book called the *Délices de la Suisse.*[2])

On reaching Chamonix, the first thing we did was to hire a mule for each of us, the one animal which can get through the forest on the Tête Noire, also part of those Alps, like Mont Blanc. The price seemed high to us: one could scarcely get one for nine francs. It was impossible to rest at all during the night, so great was the number of priests who came into the inn between the evening and 6 a.m., when our mules were brought us.

How many mishaps did I escape during that Tuesday, September 26th, in that procession of mules along narrow roads or paths, can only be realized by seeing for oneself. I did not know there was active hatred between the mules of one house and those of another. I had hardly got on the one I had been given, which

[1] 1792.
[2] By Abraham Stanyan, who was the English Ambassador to Switzerland. It was published in 1714.

happened to be the tallest and the worst tempered, than one of them wanted to display its hatred towards mine in passing. It drew near and kicked my mule in the ribs; thanks be to God, my leg sustained only a slight injury which, soon made worse by a bad twist, did not prevent me from following my companions, and healed without any nursing.

Our minds at least were free from trouble, since we were sure that we need fear French no more.[1] We happily reached the point which separates Savoy from the Valais, a country allied to the Swiss, with the Bishop of Sion as sovereign lord. A very thick rock wall is pierced by a narrow gate, looking like the mouth of an oven; it is guarded by the inhabitants of the country, who take turns each fortnight to watch over their frontiers. Seeing our passports, which made clear that we were exiled priests, they welcomed us with open arms, and to help them to remember us we gave them a few coins, which they looked at with interest, in order to drink our healths. From then on our mules clambered up their well-known paths over the Tete Noire, on which fir-trees are so thick that one scarcely sees the sun except at intervals.

We rode for four hours. Rain and mist overwhelmed us, as we were among, or even above, the clouds which bordered the precipices; the fog was so thick when we came out of the forest that we could scarcely see the path. Our mules walked on, and they brought us to Trient at the moment when, from some neighbouring parts, came a procession praying for the good weather that was needed for haymaking.

What a hamlet is Trient! Is it even worth that name? There are just two houses there. One is called the inn, and it has but one room, which was full of priests, lords and emigrants. All of them were soaked, for the rain was teeming down as if there had been a storm. We could be admitted only to the other house, which belonged to a peasant. . . . Sitting on a bench in a row, we tried to dry our very wet legs. That was not all: we tried to eat and there was no bread left in the place. . . . Finally, they found some cakes, kneaded with milk, with which we got some salted butter and white wine, the best I drank on my journey. We dined with a good appetite. We were so hungry that we could have eaten roots.

Mon emigration

[1] The French troops with Montesquieu had invaded Savoy.

War in the Alps

MARC-THÉODORE BOURRIT

REFUGEES IN CHAMONIX[1]

People of all classes, loaded with cloaks and other most necessary things, marchionesses, countesses carrying the babies they were nursing, priests like the venerable Bishop of Nîmes,[2] eighty years old, officers and a crowd of other people, old or young, some of them provided with money, others practically penniless. . . .

Mules carried a basket on either side in which were young girls, covered with a veil so that they would be spared the sight of the horrible rocks and precipices along the road, while their mothers staggered on foot, stumbling at each step and raising their hands towards Heaven to pray for help. What a sight! All those refugees who once had travelled from town to country in comfortable carriages!

Description des cols et passages des Alpes

COMTE DE RAMBUTEAU

WINTER FLIGHT[3]

First I had decided we should leave Sion on December 24th for St Maurice and Geneva, but I was made aware that our little company would need at least three days for this very exposed journey; while, if I went alone, I could still use a coach and do it in twenty-four hours. I could not remain deaf to the entreaties of eight hundred French people who were cut off from everywhere, so that, without money and resources, we had to get across some fifty leagues of snowy mountains and impossible paths in the dead of winter, risking a rebellious population or the enemy. I decided to act as guide and leader of the troop, certain that, if I were to face the worst of fatigue, I would at least win their confidence, as I was facing it with them.

From Martigny, where I gathered all my people, I sent letters to the mayors and vicars of Vallorcine, Le Tour, Argentière, Chamonix, requesting them to come and meet us. We left on December 25th at midday, with a fine sun. I had

[1] In 1792, Bourrit heard of the invasion of Savoy and hurried to Chamonix to see what had happened and to help.

[2] Mgr de Courton de Balore. Actually, he was not quite so old.

[3] In December 1813, the Austrians had reached Lausanne, and they were to enter Geneva on December 31.

had a double ration of bread and wine handed round to encourage them, and had so well divided my own cellar among them that I had to beg here and there for one or two glasses of Spanish wine for myself.

Two women wanted to share our peril: the wife of a customs collector, whose strength gave way if not her courage, and had to be left behind with the vicar of Vallorcine, and the tax man's daughter, who refused to part from her elderly father. In man's apparel, she followed us cheerfully, sustained by her youth (she was twenty), her vigour, her energy and our help, and she arrived hale and hearty at the end of this six days' expedition.

The snow was so thick that we found five feet of it at Trient and the Col de Balme.[1] We arrived at Trient at midnight, behind our guides holding torches; we followed them in single file, since no one could ride. I had even alighted from my mule. The gendarmes brought up the rear and, to help young soldiers who were less inured to fatigue and were overcome by the weight of their weapons, food and ammunition, I had organized a group of guides who came last to help those who lagged behind, and they had agreed not to be paid until the end of the journey and only if nobody was missing. Our night in the fifteen or twenty huts in Trient was rather unpleasant; snow came up to roof level, so that we constantly dreaded to see them collapse under the weight of the horses which were parked above. Outside, the temperature was 12° below zero.

The next day, on arriving at Vallorcine, it was a most encouraging sight to see the vicars of the neighbouring parishes coming to meet us with all their parishioners, to cut open the road. In the morning they had climbed into their pulpits and had said to their congregations: 'My children, we are here to pray to God, but there is no prayer more agreeable to Him than helping our brothers. A troop is now coming towards us across the snow. Let us go towards them to help them.' How great was their assistance in that plain called the 'Val des Morts' between Vallorcine and Argentière, where we found eighteen feet of snow! In spite of the track they had opened, we sank waist deep into it and walked between dazzling white walls, six feet high. 'Were the wind to start blowing,' the vicar of L Tour told me, 'no one would escape alive.'

I do not know what would have happened without those good people, and yet they refused all payment, like those in the villages where we spent the night in their touching hospitality, so that I had to leave in the church coffers a token of our gratitude. On the evening of the second day we reached Chamonix, quite exhausted.

Mémoires

---

[1] He possibly means the Col de la Forclaz, since they did not use the Col de Balme.

War in the Alps

KENNETH GRINLING

INSCRIPTION IN THE VISITORS' BOOK OF THE SALEINAZ HUT[1]

October 13, 1943. Escaping from the threat of a concentration camp I arrive from France over the Col du Chardonnet after an eight days' approach (all on foot). Itinerary: Left Bourg d'Oisans (Isère), October 6. October 7, Col du Glandon; October 8, Col de la Madeleine; October 9, Col de la Longe (above Arêches); October 10, Col de Goly and Col de Voza; October 11, Valley of Chamonix; October 12, left by night for the Col du Chardonnet. All worked out very well; eight days of magnificent weather. I will pay one franc by check as soon as I have cashed some money.

Kenneth Grinling, CAF-NZ Alpine Club (English passport)

PS. June 23, 1945. I could not suspect then that October 14, 1943, was my last day of freedom and, as soon as I reached the valley, I would be rigorously imprisoned for five months!

JACQUES BOELL

THE HIGHEST BATTLE IN THE WORLD[2]

. . . While Rachel and his men were fighting against exhaustion to save their lives, let us go back two hours to follow the third reconnaissance group. It was only four men strong, their quality making up for their deficient numbers, for they were among the best of the S.E.S.[3]: an energetic and wilful NCO, Jaquet, a good specialist in automatic weapons, Frossard, and two hearty, courageous *chasseurs*, Charlet and Buffet.

Following their companions' tracks, ten minutes behind, the four men progressed, groping their way along the silent Vallée Blanche. As in a nightmare, in that compact night, they felt as if they were walking over nothingness into nothingness.

[1] The original is in French.
[2] February 1945. The Germans were trying to capture the teleferic station above Chamonix. The little group of Alpins was commanded by Lieutenant Rachel.
[3] S.E.S. — Section d'Eclaireurs Skieurs (Ski Scouts).

They reached the Col du Rognon, where they were to settle, while the others were even more adventurous. Frossard, helped by Charlet, started stamping an area of snow firm in order to plant his machine-gun; the sergeant, listening intently, was probing the night, ready to answer his chief's call at once.

Suddenly, on the slope below the col, gunfire started, crackling all over the place and even quite close at hand. Was it from our own men? No; for there were tracer bullets, of which we had none, and wild shouting, which was not our habit. They were left in no doubt.

Could they just fire into the group at random? No; the risk of hitting some of our own men was too great. Jacquet hesitated and then came to a decision. The orders were to hold out on that line; so they were to hold out, but not in the open. Two hundred metres away on the right the last buttresses of a ridge descending from Mont Blanc du Tacul came to an end; they were to get there and stay there, helping the rest of the S.E.S. as much as possible.

He imparted his plan to his companions in a few brief words. No sooner said than done. In those fine granite rocks above the Combe du Géant they felt that the four of them could hold out against a whole battalion! Yet in the black hollow at their feet the gunfire was as confused as ever; it would only be at day-break – not far off, now – that they could do something.

It was seven and dawn suddenly rushed upon the battlefield. Rachel and his scouts had still a hundred metres to go before the last slopes of the Aiguille du Midi.

Now the machine-guns made up viciously for wasted time; they fired band after band at the poor wretches who were running zig-zag through the clattering bullets. Happily the goal was near. Some jumped into the bergschrund, others hurried behind rocks, all of them unhurt; they started planting their machine-gun at once.

Now they would fight to the death.

The Germans, who could have wiped out the French party, had failed in their attempt, but they did not abandon their original plan. Regrouping behind the Rognon, they organized an impressive attack towards the Col du Midi, which they tried to overrun north and south. Could the twelve men who held it with-hold the shock? Showers of bullets swept the plateau, clattering on the rocks, turning the hut and the landing platform of the teleferic into sieves.

Suddenly, the forgotten guests came into action, the tiny Jacquet group, perched on their Tacul ridge, silent until then. In the early morning light they could at last make out who was who among the white ghosts crowded on the plateau, and who they were to shoot at. Identification was made easier by the Germans themselves, who, unaware of their presence, were shouting orders at the tops of their voices. Box after box, they emptied their guns into the figures scattered over the Vallée Blanche, some of whom collapsed, obviously hit.

But the *Feldgrau* soon detected the eagle's nest from which the deadly salvoes had been fired, and they were not long replying. One of their machine-guns started to sweep the Tacul ledge, but Jacquet's team continued firing. A few *Gebirgsjäger*, first-class mountaineers, climbed towards our men, who could not see them, up a steep rock precipice.

Suddenly, Frossard and Buffet, busy with the machine-gun had the unpleasant surprise of seeing, emerging from the abyss, three Austrian Alpine soldiers, who rushed upon them yelling. Luckily, as it was a matter of seconds, their reaction was swift and they stopped the onrush with revolvers; three men fell backwards over the edge, their arms stretched out.

There was no time to spare! Now, fearing no immediate danger, Jacquet was able to do some useful work. His gun was going to be most valuable as, spurred on by Captain Singel who, running far ahead of his men, was encouraging them by his shouts, the German skiers began to threaten the col dangerously.

A new burst of fire clattered from the Tacul ridge and the Austrian officer fell dead, a bullet through the heart.

As a wave on the beach, ending its course, slackens, seems to remain motionless for a second, hesitates and draws back, the German line, deprived of its leader, lightened its pressure and started to organize a retreat. Now, for our men, the battle was won.

At that very moment, a small French reconnaissance plane, piloted by Captain Guénon, a specialist in mountain flying, flew very low over the Vallée Blanche and a the right moment started dispersing with grenades the German groups that were coming up to help.

A wave of enthusiasm swept over the defenders of the col, despite their exhaustion. The enemy were making off in a hurry; but before leaving, in spite of the showers of bullets, a huge German reached Singel's dead body, bent over him, heaved him up on his back and skied straight off towards the Col du Rognon and the Glacier du Géant. Gottfried had refused to leave his officer, even after his death.

Now the sun had risen behind the crests and the mountain was pink, a portent of good weather; after this agonizing night, full of pain, fatigue and gunfire, a victorious dawn was climbing the sky. Forgetting their exhaustion for a moment, Rachel and his men rushed, on foot or on ski, towards the retreating Germans.

A few scouts of the very active Borgeat section had just arrived by the teleferic, a most welcome reinforcement.

Yet because of their small numbers and their exhaustion, the pursuit could not go much further than the outskirts of the Glacier du Géant. It could not get to the retreating German team, which had already reached the Flambeaux; but the pursuers were able to capture two *Gebirgsjäger* hidden in a crevasse, identify nine dead Germans, including Captain Singel, whose body, after all, had not been carried any further than the Combe Maudite, and be present at the death of our only fatally wounded man, who had disappeared in the fray.

Braz, a tall student with an open, smiling face, had been hit during the night by one of the numerous showers of bullets fired at the surrounded French party. Badly wounded and caught by the shouting enemy, he suffered agonizing pain, being still alive and captive.

He was filled with joy when his fleeing captors left him and, soon after he had been found by his companions, he breathed his last in their arms, expressing his gladness at being among them: 'I prefer dying this way to being a prisoner.'

Section d'Eclaireurs Skieurs au combat

11
THE MESSAGE

DÉODAT DE DOLOMIEU

THE PEACE OF NATURE[1]

To forget the fateful aspect of my country, I have visited the glaciers of Mont
Blanc and, when seeing those majestic masses, those huge rocks and the eternal
snow, for a short while I have been able to forget the cruelty of men and the vile
passions which move them.

Lettres

WILLIAM WORDSWORTH

THE VALLEY OF CHAMONIX

Well might a stranger look with bounding heart
Down on a green recess, the first I saw
Of those deep haunts, an aboriginal vale,
Quiet and lorded over and possessed
By naked huts, wood-built, and sown like tents
Or Indian cabins over the fresh lawns
And by the riverside.
    That very day,
From a bare ridge we also first beheld
Unveiled the summit of Mont Blanc, and grieved
To have a soulless image on the eye
That had usurped upon a living thought
That never more could be. The wondrous Vale
Of Chamonix stretched far below, and soon
With its dumb cataracts and streams of ice,
A motionless array of mighty waves,

[1] To the Chevalier de Fay, September 7, 1795.

Five rivers broad and vast made rich amends,
And reconciled us to realities.
There small birds warble from the leafy trees,
The eagle soars high in the element,
There doth the reaper bind the yellow sheaf,
The maiden spread the haycock in the sun,
While Winter like a well-tamed lion walks,
Descending from the mountain to make sport
Among the cottages by beds of flowers.
　　　What'er in this wide circuit we beheld,
Or heard, was fitted to our unripe state
Of intellect and heart. With such a book
Before our eyes, we could not choose but read
Lessons of genuine brotherhood, the plain
And universal reason of mankind,
The truths of young and old.

The Prelude, Book VI

S. T. COLERIDGE

HYMN BEFORE SUNRISE IN THE VALE OF CHAMONIX

Hast thou a charm to stay the morning-star
In his steep course? So long he seems to pause
On thy bald awful head, O sovran Blanc!
The Arve and the Arveiron at thy base
Rave ceaselessly; but thou, most awful Form!
Risest from forth thy silent sea of pines,
How silently! Around thee and above
Deep in the air and dark, substantial, black,
An ebon mass: methinks thou piercest it,
As with a wedge! But when I look again,
It is thine own calm home, thy crystal shrine,
Thy habitation from eternity!
O dread and silent Mount! I gazed upon thee,
Till thou, still present to the bodily sense,

The Message

Didst vanish from my thought: entranced in prayer
I worshipped the Invisible alone.

Yet like some sweet beguiling melody,
So sweet, we know not we are listening to it,
Thou, the meanwhile, wast blending with my thought,
Yea, with my life and life's own secret joy:
Till the dilating Soul, enrapt, transfused,
Into the mighty vision passing – there
As in her natural form, swelled vast to Heaven!

Awake, my soul! not only passive praise
Thou owest! not alone these swelling tears,
Mute thanks and secret ecstasy! Awake,
Voice of sweet song! Awake, my Heart, awake!
Green vales and icy cliffs, all join my Hymn.

Thou first and chief, sole sovran of the Vale!
O struggling with the darkness all the night,
And visited all night by troops of stars,
Or when they climb the sky or when they sink:
Companion of the morning-star at dawn,
Thyself Earth's rosy star, and of the dawn
Co-herald: wake, O wake, and utter praise!
Who sank thy sunless pillars deep in Earth?
Who filled thy countenance with rosy light?
Who made thee parent of perpetual streams?

And you, ye five wild torrents fiercely glad!
Who called you forth from night and utter death,
From dark and icy caverns called you forth,
Down these precipitous, black, jagged rocks,
For ever shattered and the same for ever?
Who gave you your invulnerable life,
Your strength, your speed, your fury, and your joy,
Unceasing thunder and eternal foam?
And who commanded (and the silence came)
Here let the billows stiffen, and have rest?

Ye ice-falls! ye that from the mountain's brow
Adown enormous ravines slope amain –
Torrents, methinks, that heard a mighty voice,

And stopped at once amid their maddest plunge !
Motionless torrents ! silent cataracts !
Who made you glorious as the Gates of Heaven
Beneath the keen full moon? Who bade the sun
Clothe you with rainbows? Who, with living flowers
Of loveliest blue, spread garlands at your feet? –
God ! let the torrents, like a shout of nations,
Answer ! and let the ice-plains echo, God !
God ! sing ye meadows – streams with gladsome voice !
Ye pine-groves, with your soft and soul-like sounds !
And they too have a voice, yon piles of snow,
And in their perilous fall shall thunder, God !

Ye living flowers that skirt the eternal frost !
Ye wild goats sporting round the eagle's nest !
Ye eagles, play-mates of the mountain storm !
Ye lightnings, the dread arrows of the clouds !
Ye signs and wonders of the elements !
Utter forth God, and fill the hills with praise !

Thou too, hoar Mount ! with thy sky-pointing peaks,
Oft from whose feet the avalanche, unheard,
Shoots downward, glittering through the pure serene
Into the depth of clouds, that veil thy breast –
Thou too again, stupendous Mountain ! thou
That as I raise my head, while bowed low
In adoration, upward from thy base
Slow travelling with dim eyes suffused with tears,
Solemnly seemest, like a vapoury cloud,
To rise before me – Rise, O ever rise,
Rise like a cloud of incense, from the Earth !
Thou kingly Spirit throned among the hills,
Thou dread ambassador from Earth to Heaven,
Great Hierarch ! tell thou the silent sky,
And tell the stars, and tell yon rising sun,
Earth, with her thousand voices, praises God.

Poems

The Message

PERCY BYSSHE SHELLEY

MONT BLANC[1]

(Lines written in the vale of Chamouni)

The everlasting universe of things
Flows through the mind, and rolls its rapid waves,
Now dark – now glittering – now reflecting gloom –
Now lending splendour, where from secret springs
The source of human thought its tribute brings
Of waters, with a sound, but half its own,
Such as the feeble brook will oft assume
In the wild woods, among the mountains lone,
Where waterfalls around it leap for ever,
Where woods and winds contend, and a vast river
Over its rocks ceaselessly bursts and raves.

Thus thou, Ravine of Arve – dark, deep Ravine –
Thou many-coloured, many-voicèd vale,
Over whose pines, and crags, and caverns sail
Fast cloud-shadows and sunbeams: awful scene,
Where Power in likeness of the Arve comes down
From the ice-gulfs that gird his secret throne,
Bursting through these dark mountains like the flame
Of lightning through the tempest; – thou dost lie,
Thy giant brood of pines around thee clinging,
Children of elder time, in whose devotion
The chainless winds still come and ever came
To drink their odours, and their mighty swinging
To hear – an old and solemn harmony;
Thine earthly rainbows stretched across the sweep
Of the aethereal waterfall, whose veil
Robes some unsculptured image; the strange sleep
Which when the voices of the desert fail
Wraps all in its own deep eternity; –
Thy caverns echoing to the Arve's commotion,
A loud, lone sound no other sound can tame;
Thou art pervaded with that ceaseless motion
Thou art the path of that unresting sound –

[1] July 23, 1816.

207

Dizzy Ravine! and when I gaze on thee
I seem as in a trance sublime and strange
To muse on my own separate fantasy,
My own, my human mind, which passively
Now renders and receives fast influencings,
Holding an unremitting interchange
With the clear universe of things around;
One legion of wild thoughts, whose wandering wings
Now float above the darkness, and now rest
Where that or thou art no unbidden guest,
In the still cave of the witch Poesy,
Seeking among the shadows that pass by
Ghosts of all things that are, some shade of thee,
Some phantom, some faint image; till the breast
From which they fled recalls them, thou art there!

Some say that gleams of a remoter world
Visit the soul in sleep – that death is slumber
And that its shapes the busy thoughts outnumber
Of those who wake and live. – I look on high;
Has some unknown omnipotence unfurled
The veil of life and death? or do I lie
In dream, and does the mightier world of sleep
Spread far around and inaccessibly
Its circles? For the very spirit fails,
Driven like a homeless cloud from steep to steep
That vanishes among the viewless gales!
Far, far above, piercing the infinite sky,
Mont Blanc appears, – still, snowy and serene –
Its subject mountains their unearthly forms
Pile around it, ice and rock; broad vales between
Of frozen floods, unfathomable deeps,
Blue as the overhanging heaven, that spread
And wind among the accumulated steeps;
A desert peopled by the storms alone
Save when the eagle brings some hunter's bone,
And the wolf tracks her there – how hideously
Its shapes are heaped around! rude, bare, and high,
Ghastly, and scarred, and riven. – Is this the scene
Where the old Earthquake-daemon taught her young
Ruin? Were these their toys? or did a sea
Of fire envelop once this silent snow?

The Message

None can reply – all seems eternal now.
The wilderness has a mysterious tongue
Which teaches awful doubt, or faith so mild,
So solemn, so serene, that man may be,
But for such faith, with nature reconciled;
Thou hast a voice, great Mountain, to repeal
Large codes of fraud and woe; not understood
By all, but which the wise, and great, and good
Interpret, or make felt, or deeply feel.

The fields, the lakes, the forests, and the streams,
Ocean, and all the living things that dwell
Within the daedal earth; lightning, and rain,
Earthquake, and fiery flood, and hurricane,
The torpor of the year when feeble dreams
Visit the hidden buds, or dreamless sleep
Holds every future leaf and flower; – the bound
With which from that detested trance they leap;
The works and ways of man, their death and birth,
And that of him and all that his may be;
All things that move and breathe with toil and sound
Are born and die; revolve, subside, and swell.
Power dwells apart in its tranquility,
Remote, serene, and inaccessible:
And *this*, the naked countenance of earth,
On which I gaze, even these primaeval mountains
Teach the adverting mind. The glaciers creep
Like snakes that watch their prey, from their far fountains,
Slow rolling on; there, many a precipice,
Frost and the Sun in scorn of mortal power
Have piled: dome, pyramid, and pinnacle,
A city of death, distinct with many a tower
And wall impregnable of beaming ice.
Yet not a city, but a flood of ruin
Is there, that from the boundaries of the sky
Rolls its perpetual stream; vast pines are strewing
Its destined path, or in the mangled soil
Branchless and shattered stand; the rocks, drawn down
From yon remotest waste, have overthrown
The limits of the dead and living world,
Never to be reclaimed. The dwelling-place
Of insects, beasts, and birds, becomes its spoils;

O

Their food and their retreat for ever gone,
So much of life and joy is lost. The race
Of man flies far in dread; his work and dwelling
Vanish, like some smoke before the tempest's stream,
And their place is not known. Below, vast caves
Shine in the rushing torrents' restless gleam,
Which from those secret chasms in tumult welling
Meet in the vale, and one majestic River,
The breath and blood of distant lands, for ever
Rolls its loud waters to the ocean-waves,
Breathes its swift vapours to the circling air.

Mont Blanc yet gleams on high : – the power is there,
The still and solemn power of many sights,
And many sounds, and much of life and death.
In the calm darkness of the moonless nights
In the lone glare of day, the snows descend
Upon that Mountain; none beholds them there,
Nor when the flakes burn in the sinking sun,
Or the star-beams dart through them : – Winds contend
Silently there, and heap the snow with breath
Rapid and strong, but silently ! Its home
The voiceless lightning in these solitudes
Keeps innocently, and like vapour broods
Over the snow. The secret Strength of things
Which governs thought, and to the infinite dome
Of Heaven is as a law, inhabits thee !
And what were thou, and earth, and stars, and sea,
It to the human mind's imaginings
Silence and solitude were vacancy?

Poems

PIERRE DALLOZ

ZENITH

. . . Just as the sea gives us a vision of unlimited breadth, so do high mountains open up for us the unmeasured depths of the firmament. We love clouds for the way they move in fantasy across the sky, the way light plays among their ever-changing forms, but in the impression they produce on us there is no trace of giddiness; they float above us at heights unknown with no attachment to the ground beneath our feet. A tree, on the other hand, encloses a well-defined amount of space within its branches; a church spire brings to our knowledge a space that is far greater, and mountains are the greatest spires on earth. They stir the emotions by an excess of continuity to which our senses are not accustomed. By a transition so gradual that we are unconscious of it, our eyes are led from one point of interest to another, up to regions which still belong to earth but are no longer accessible, and wrap themselves in veils of air of deepening blue. Amazed by these heights conceived on a scale so different from his own diminutive dimensions, man fancies he can see in them the image of the infinite. Mountains are not the infinite, but they suggest it. They have been confused with altitude: as well confuse the soul with the faces that reveal it, or truth with the evidences of itself. . . .

When the blood throbs in our temples, and the ice-cold air dries up our throat and penetrates our whole being like a fluid, life-giving, infinitely precious;

When we no more feel hunger, but only thirst, when nothing exists for us but effort, thought and gesture;

When the cold freezes the ice-axe to our hand and the horizon is blurred by the tears with which it fills our eyes;

When the face the earth shows us is the face of a living thing, but the lined face of one who has suffered much;

When in a single picture are laid bare the old rents and wounds, the intricate joints and foldings that built up the mountain chains, the meetings and the partings of the waters;

When all life, animal and vegetable, is absorbed into the great crucible below;

When there comes up from the valleys to die at our feet the voice of geological ages, the groan of the earth in travail, made up of countless murmurs from below, the plaints of erosion, of water and the wind;

When we realize that this groaning, exhausted by its long ascent, can never break in upon the great silence that reigns above;

When that silence itself is so complete and so perfect that it pains our senses;

When we feel a tremor thrill through space itself;

When we see the stars shining in the light of day;

When the light shoots straight down to us out of unfathomable, dark, transparent depths, like a light that has lost its reflector;

When this light strikes directly on our eyes without hurting us, but is reflected from the newly fallen snow with blinding violence;

Then we know altitude again.

Haute Montagne

Mont Blanc

EDOUARD WYSS-DUNANT

THE LIBERATING EFFECT OF MOUNTAINS

The mountains are a world to the discovery of which man has devoted himself for two centuries, moved by what Irving has rightly called a large dose of curiosity, the love of adventure, and the passionate search for a revelation.

It was entirely the large dose of curiosity, the desire to see and to know, which actuated pioneers like de Saussure, Agassiz and Tyndall, and the explorers of mountain ranges then little known. Mountaineering for these pioneers was a means of geographical, geological, ethnological, phsyiological and botanical investigation; but in bringing these contributions to knowledge, they also opened up ways into little known mountain areas. With such men as Whymper, Mummery and Young, to name only the very great, exploration became identified with mountaineering. The Alps had been conquered and while exploration moved on to the Himalayas or the Polar regions, mountaineering became a sport. The perfection of climbing techniques and the knowledge of ice, snow and rock conditions, enabled climbers to reach the highest levels of performance.

The love of adventure was undeniably the second indispensable factor. Any ascent is an adventure, but to go in pursuit of danger, freely to accept the idea of expending one's energy to the extreme physical and moral limit, requires a strong love of risk, a paradoxical fact, opposed to the instinct of self-preservation, with all its fears and anxieties.

Is a man on a mountain the same creature as on the plain, or does his personality undergo such changes as will explain this contempt for the instinct of self-preservation, or for that law of the least expenditure of effort which drives him to invent machines to make life easier and lessen the calls upon his reserves of energy?

It seems that very special psychological elements intervene to break intellectual barriers, to defeat terror or nervousness, and to turn into bliss the hardships the body has to endure. More, the love of mountain risks may become a passion. That is why Julius Kugy wrote in *Alpine Pilgrimage*: 'For me, mountaineering is a thing of the heart.'

Yet, the cause of that love has not been explained. It remains a paradox: why run such deadly risks? Why this love of mountains?

Over and over, in mountain literature, the word *freedom* can be heard. 'Mountains make me free. . . . I take you along with me, you radiant summits.'[1]

'Happiness at last! Freedom from the usual slavery in equally usual prisons.'[2]

'A state of great spiritual freedom.'[3]

[1] G. Sonnier: *Où règne la lumière.*   [2] Betty Favre: *Les Alpes*, June 1959.
[3] Paul Guitton: *Le livre de la montagne.*

The Message

Come now! body and legs, get up! Bring back a happy soul to the prisons of the plain. That is more or less how the *leitmotif* may be summarized. In his Olympic serenity, Goethe expressed the same feelings: '*Auf allen Gipfeln ist Ruh!*' (On all peaks there is peace!) That feeling of freedom, or better, of being made free, is common to all mountaineers. . . .

As soon as he emerges from the forest, when the high pastures open to a distant vision of the coveted summit, out of the plainsman emerges this other self, which for a time will belong wholly to the mountain. This is not the place for him to look back on a former life: his look is forward towards the summit, observing the route and reckoning the obstacles to overcome. He feels a sort of physical well-being, and a moral euphonia: his mind, freed from the limitations of the plain, now soars. Eager curiosity drives him to study new routes or follow unbeaten tracks, a great hope fires him and his body, thanks to its training, enjoys all its elasticity.

Psychical and physical energies all have the same aim. He enjoys a single mind, in full accord with himself. It seems that part of his unconscious being, the most troublesome, has been shed, giving an impression of utter freedom. . . .

A sort of bond unites mountain lovers, springing from spontaneous ethics. There is direct contact and mutual aid where nature faces man with an imperative order: to be or not to be. Far from his social surrounding, and placed suddenly in the midst of a mineral world, the human spirit is caught by the mastery and coolness required by adventure. An instinctive defence reaction comes into play: vital functions are called to act, away from secondary reactions which find neither the place nor the opportunity to express themselves. Here everything is vast and there are no artificial boundaries: the spirit seizes its integration into the cosmos. This first liberation is the benefit everyone obtains, whatever his psychical structure. He who has felt it once will always try to recapture it by answering to what he terms the call of the heights. . . .

We live in a time when young people are filled with a desire to be freed from tradition, social servitude, and a past which has lost its attraction. They seek to be free, and to master a new world which they vaguely sense. . . . To those rebellious young people mountains can bring a progressive peace not only by allowing their aggressiveness to exhaust itself against an inert world, but by mastering this universe to attain an ethical fulfilment which removes from their innermost hearts that feeling of inferiority against which they are rebelling. With modern mountaineering technique, the younger generation have surpassed us: they can overcome obstacles which were thought beyond human capacity when we were young. . . . Yet the law which was the basis of our own mountaineering feats is their law too. . . .

213

There is a fundamental difference between clear-eyed young mountaineers who feel they can rely on themselves and the beatniks without an ideal in life. Some have found their true destiny there, although society had relegated them to a category of indeterminate beings, unable to orientate themselves, puzzled by inner contradictions from which they should have been liberated, so that they failed in choosing a profession. But the mountains, by deconditioning them, and by becoming their chosen milieu, have enabled them to achieve alpine careers of the first order. . . .

Les Alpes, 1960

GENERAL JACQUES FAURE

RECOLLECTIONS

The little train left Le Fayet, creeping up towards the valley. I was on my way to take up a new appointment. This was October 1932. General Dosse, the Military Governor of Lyons, commanding the Army Corps of the Alps, had decided to create a military mountain training school in Chamonix. It was commanded by an Alpine officer of high repute, Captain Pourchier; Lieutenant Villiers and I were instructors. Villiers came from the 7th Batallion of the Chasseurs Alpins, which was stationed throughout the Tarentaise with headquarters at the Redoute-Ruinée; as for myself, I came from the 13th Batallion at Maurienne.

The little train was plodding along, following the curves of the slope, leaving and returning to the bed of the Arve, pushing deeper into the mountain gorges. I was thinking of what was in store for me. I was remembering my brief sojourn in Chamonix in winter, long trips on ski, and the French ski competitions. Now the 'Valley' and the 'Range' belonged to us; it was a staggering thought.

I was resurrecting numberless memories. Images arose, without order, overlapping the years, built of all that from childhood on had been consciously or unconsciously overshadowed by the size and the majesty of the shapes we were to discover in a single vista after a last creaking of the train and a last jolt: Mont Blanc and the Aiguilles.

When we were children at our family home in the little village of Seyssinet, between Grenoble and St Nizier, at the foot of the Moucherotte and the Trois Pucelles, we used to be taken out on fine evenings to admire, far away at the back of the Gresivaudan gap, above rounded blue summits and framed between the fine precipices of the Dent de Crolle and the summits of Belledonne, and the Sept-Laux, something immaterial and dazzling high in the sky: Mont Blanc.

Sometimes the mountain stood there, like a last rosy flame, a great presence when all the neighbouring summits had already sunk into night. Alone in the sky, while the Gresivaudan gap grew darker and the hills on either side dissolved into a single mass of deeper and deeper blue, it seemed that the mountain remained alive just for us, to haunt our childish dreams.

It still dominated my dreams when we were older and mountains on our horizon gradually lost their mystery. We had conquered all their summits on long expeditions, already rich with the recollections suited to our years. Yet Mont Blanc stood there still, like a dream.

As the little train crept upwards, my thoughts still drifted back to the Haute Maurienne, to quiet hours when the night was falling over the Turra fortress, above Mont Cenis, whence we gazed down into the far Italian plains, or distantly descried the Dent Parrachée, the Vanoise, the long gap of the Arc leading towards the Albaron, the Levantinas and the Iseran. Those summits had all been land-marks in our lives as Ski Scouts. Now I was leaving them all and I felt as if it were something of a betrayal. The rough Maurienne, with her deep charm, the silent nights in our fortress, high up on the hills, our wonderful solitude, those mountains which belonged to us, the asperity and difficulty of which made us proud: a realm infinitely dear to us, filled with recollections of friendly faces, of a life spent among its villages, of the strength of our youthful years, when we trained to become officers and mountaineers. . . .

I was really feeling something akin to remorse, but I was never going to forget my Maurienne, even if I became enthusiastic about what was in store for me. Possibly, too, what was to become my new territory would lose its grandeur. Was not the mountain at its best when seen from the Grande Casse, the Pourri or elsewhere, in all its majesty?

As we reached the station of Les Houches, I remembered how we had skied down the Col de Voza a few years earlier. We did not give a very impressive show, overcome as we were by fatigue and lack of sleep. We had left Lanslebourg thirty hours earlier on a fine winter day, intent on getting to Chamonix in one stretch over the Col de l'Iseran, the Val d'Isère, the Chapieux, and the Col du Bon-homme. We had spent two nights on the way. The great lines of light and shadow endowed the mountains with most unexpected shapes which made us suddenly lose our balance, already precarious because of our heavy sacks. But all that was of little consequence now when weighed against the tremendous feeling of having conquered the 'valley' and Mont Blanc. For our little team, composed mostly of Maurienne people, it was our first meeting with the 'range' and we were overpowered by the extraordinary setting.

The train wound around the last curves. One more and the whole of that fantastic landscape would be in view, the wonder which strikes one dumb each time the valley reveals itself in all its splendour. It has been described so often that I can say nothing more; only silence and thoughtfulness seem equal to what we are allowed to admire and feel.

Within a second I forgot the slow musing in which I had been indulging. I was alert: instructor now at the Ecole de Haute-Montagne, very proud and also slightly disturbed. Everything was so big. To train men in such a setting, teach them their profession, turn them into officers or NCO's able to lead a party on difficult mountains, over routes of increasing difficulty, to fulfil the mission they have been given, enable them to realize their possibilities, to bring out the basic qualities which enable them to display their worth under tricky circumstances. . . . In such a setting were we strong enough to solve all the problems which faced us?

In Maurienne the setting seemed to fit the human scale. I knew all that could be made of it. In summer as well as in winter I knew what was possible on any route and what was not. It had been very easy to organize and time a training course there. But what about here? Everything looked gigantic, out of proportion, of overpowering beauty and difficulty, fit only for supermen. How would we tackle such a place?

The EHM settled down in the annexe of the Hotel Balmat. It was a very unassuming beginning, and we had to start from scratch. First of all, to get ourselves accepted in that mountain holy of holies, we had to listen to advice and information from experts: the guides. Then, little by little, we got ourselves integrated into the local life and became part of the valley people. Each day mutual trust and esteem increased and we were soon at home among friends.

In deciding to create the school, General Dosse effected quite a revolution. By deciding that this Alpine centre was made for young leaders and was meant as a real national school, he was breaking from the tradition that all military skiers were trained at Briançon.

The EHM was not to be another ski-ing school, but a genuine national military mountaineering school. Technique and teaching would be rationalized, equipment carefully studied, altered and improved, and rules would be evolved to regulate our work.

Dosse had selected Chamonix because of its many possibilities; also because any human task requires a setting, one which induces in a man the will to do his best.

Chamonix, at the foot of Mont Blanc and the Aiguilles, was just such a place. It was up to us to make the school live.

We were not restricted to mere technique. The school was to become the centre where young officers of the Alpine army were to get to know each other, to forge powerful ties of friendship, become integrated into an ensemble and get to know better the part they were to play. The mountain was to be no mere stadium for difficult performances, but a realm in which technique, physical effort, daring, self-control and poise could be blended in perfect balance in an atmosphere of mutual trust and truthfulness.

The EHM was to be imbued with all that typified the magnificent spirit of the Alpine army, its teaching and training, which turned our ski scouts into the world's best soldiers. Later, in 1940, their outstanding bravery along the frontier, when Italy entered the war, and their victory in Norway proved that General Dosse had been right when putting great hope in his Alpine army and the EHM.

Men of my generation are immensely in its debt, for it gave us two priceless things: pride in our calling, and joy in life, while doing our jobs properly. It enabled us to understand better what an extraordinary school for human training a mountain is.

The rhythm of the seasons, probations, training for competitions and, during empty periods, the study of our equipment or personal training, made months and years pass fairly quickly. The range was ours. Early anxieties had disappeared, and my youthful dreams had come true.

Instructors changed every other year. As I was commanding the National Military Ski Team, each winter brought me back to the valley. Mont Blanc kept all its mystery, but it was also a friend, the witness of so many hours filled with deep meaning and true happiness.

Years passed. The year 1940 and the consequences of defeat weighed upon the life of the whole nation. Two-thirds of France were occupied by the enemy; there was an unbelievable number of prisoners; all we had known, and which had upheld us, was destroyed and we had the painful feeling that we had been betrayed. It was impossible that the country we had known in victory was now prostrate, mutilated, cut to pieces and invaded. Then the first amazement gave way to secret anger. But we could not remain like that; we had to till the ground out of which everything would one day blossom again. Some of the members of the Expeditionary Forces to Norway made this real by staying in England; others thought that action, starting from within the country, would be more fruitful and effective.

Such was our state of mind when we arrived at Grenoble after a brief stay in Morocco, where we had thought we could remain.

In this huge confusion the destiny of the men of twenty was clearly tragic. Called up a few months earlier, their short time in the army had given them only a brief training and then defeat.

On August 1, 1940, Air-General d'Harcourt summoned me. He explained that the young men of the Air Force, massed round airfields without planes, without missions, in spite of all that had been done, were moral wrecks. 'You have got to give them back a feeling for life,' he told me, 'a taste for action, to place them in a climate which exalts them, and makes them proud of themselves, makes fighters of them. Mountains seem to be the best place for such a transformation.

Your mountaineering experience will enable you to do this job, so I ask you to come.' I accepted.

A fortnight later, everything had to be got ready to welcome them. *Jeunesse et Montagne* ('Youth and Mountain') was born. Organized along the lines of the Ski Scouts, the boys lived on the mountainsides in little groups. We had to begin in the Alps and later got to the Pyrenees.

The first thing was to get the help of the local specialists; without them, 'Youth and Mountain' would never become what I wanted – a tightly organized unit, with the mountains as a hard setting that would produce something real and strong. These young men needed first-rate teachers, born leaders of men, trained during their hard struggles against the mountains, humane and strong at the same time, and able, through their presence and talents, to make the young men love the life. It had to be an adventure, one that had been carefully conceived.

I began in Chamonix. The Compagnie des Guides, in which I had so many friends, welcomed me, and I have never forgotten the answer I received from one of them at the end of my talk: 'How many of us do you need?' It was the first trial, and the great alliance which was to be 'Youth and Mountain' was born. After that, I was sure it would come to life. I had found real friends, those who help in the hours of darkness. I was reaping the harvest of our communal living, of our simple, solid, mutual trust. It was the same in Oisans and in the Pyrenees.

The whole mountain region and its veterans were getting ready to welcome their new guests. The centres were organized and alive. The lads who had sprawled about, scowling and unkempt, were becoming sunburnt men, properly dressed, with open looks. The guides told me of their extreme goodwill and of the astonishing talent some of them possessed.

It is better not to speak of the daily problems: they cropped up constantly and we were constantly on the brink of tragedy. The Italo-German armistice committee looked askance at this proliferation of mountain posts, this renewal of activity along the frontier. I must confess they were not altogether mistaken. A few years later, the J. M. maquis fully justified their apprehension. Quite apart from the fact that we were able to hide numerous pilots who later joined us in North Africa, we got many members of J.M. across the Pyrenees.

One day, only a hair's breadth saved us from discovery. The head of the centre, a magnificent fighter pilot, who a few months later was shot down in an air fight, on the strength of our decisions concerning the future had made a list of all the men in the valley who could be called up, and what tasks they could be given in the branches to be organized subsequently, with the JM group as a centre. Incidentally, they had settled in the former quarters of the EHM, more or less as its successor. He kept the lists in his office, not thinking how very useful they might prove to some inquisitive person. They were found. There was much ado and the JM groups seemed doomed. But heaven protected us. Explanations concerning food requirements brought the whole thing back to normal. The centre headquarters were changed and taken to Le Tour. It was a gain in height. As for the lists, we used them later.

During those hard times, 'Jeunesse et Montagne' had been a connecting link, bridging a gap. All through the dark years the mountains played their part, bringing strength and hope where there had been none. Now the EHM could start again, supplied by many officers of the Alpine army, guides and teachers trained by J.M. It had fulfilled the mission that General d'Harcourt had given it.

It is hard to decide which is my dearest recollection. The long tramps when the approach to a mountain was marked by the babbling of a torrent and the fragrance of the low thick grass; or the moment when, gathering all my strength to reach a poise, the pitch was overcome; or when the summit was finally conquered? Or possibly the joy of the constant sense of discovery of a mountain in winter.

As with all great realms the air, the sea, the desert, those who have been modest long enough to realize that they can conquer may attempt to venture there.

However far technique may develop as a result of material progress, the mountains will stay as a magnificent place of trial, where every man must reveal his true face. The mountain may not be cheated, nor can one cheat on a mountain. Everything there is expressed in terms of balance: physical effort, technique, daring, moderation. Yet, above mountain beauty and the joy of success, the partnership and friendship developed there stand out. A stout thread spun over many days, made of full trust and self-expression, when each man emerges as he is, with all his possibilities, failings, renewals, where everything is true. Mountains are a great school.

I slowly turn the page so that none of my precious recollections may escape. Other generations of soldiers will know such joys and endeavours. At the foot of Mont Blanc, young men trained by the EHM will scatter their generosity and devotion along our high valleys. One day, they will look back to their past and from the depth of their souls express their deepest thanks.

(Hitherto unpublished)

12
BIOGRAPHICAL APPENDIX

ADAMS-REILLY (Anthony Miles), 1836-1885. Irish mountaineer, painter and cartographer.

ALDEBERT (Max). Contemporary writer, novelist, poet and mountaineer. He has written *Conquête de la Montagne* and, together with André Chamson, *Royaume des Hautes Terres*.

ALMER (Christian), 1826-1898. Born at Grindelwald. A first-rate guide, who liked mountains to the point of ascending the Wetterhorn with his wife to celebrate their silver wedding. He climbed with Sir Alfred Wills, A. W. Moore, Sir Leslie Stephen, Hardy, Horace Walker and his sister Lucy, W. A. B. Coolidge, Miss Brevoort, Whymper and others. He ascended the Mönch, the Eiger, the Viescherhorn, the Sesiajosh; traversed the Ecrins, the Col du la Pilatte, the Moming Pass, the Grandes Jorasses; made the first ascents of the Aiguille Verte, the Jungfrau on the Guggi side, the second ascent of the Meije, and the Jungfrau in winter.

ANDEREGG (Jakob), 1827-1878. Born at Zaun near Meiringen. Climbed with the Walkers, Stephen, Moore, Morsehead, Cordier, Maund and others. Made the first ascent of the Brenva face of Mont Blanc, of the Verte, the Courtes on the Argentière side, a new route on the Lyskamm, etc.

ANDEREGG (Melchior), 1828-1912. Jakob's brother. Born at Zaun. One of the best guides of his time. Climbed with most of the leading mountaineers, the Walkers, Stephen, Kennedy, Grove, Moore, Matthews, Walroth, Loppé, etc. He made the first ascent of the Brenva, of the Bosses ridge, of the Dent d'Hérens, the Disgrazia, the Mont Mallet, the Col des Hirondelles, etc.

ANGEVILLE (Comtesse Henriette d'), 1793-1871. Born at Hauteville (Ain), of an old and very noble family, to which belonged naval officers and Knights of Malta. She was a canoness. She fell in love with Mont Blanc and determined to ascend it, activated by romantic motives and also by the desire to be one of the 'lions' of her time. She was vaguely jealous of George Sand. She organized her expedition minutely and carried it through successfully in 1837. She wrote various accounts of it. I have selected here the least known of them, from a letter to Markham Sherwill.

ARENTHON D'ALEX (Mgr d'). Bishop of Geneva at the end of the seventeenth century. As all Bishops of Geneva since the Reformation, he lived in Annecy.

BALMAT (Auguste), 1808-1862. Chamonix guide and a very distant relative of Jacques Balmat. He was cultured and refined, a good guide and a pleasant companion. He climbed with Forbes (on the High Level Route), Tyndall, and Wills, who, when he retired took him as the keeper of his chalet above Sixt, the Eagle's Nest. He ascended Mont Blanc often, also the Wetterhorn, and traversed the Adler Pass.

BALMAT (Jacques), 1764-1832. Guide and crystal hunter, who accompanied Dr Paccard during the first ascent of Mont Blanc, and was one of de Saussure's guides during his own ascent and during his stay on the Col du Géant. He did many more ascents of Mont Blanc, went to Saas Fee and the Val Anzasca, and was killed when looking for gold ore above the Glacier des Fonds. Alexandre Dumas met him.

BARRY (Martin). Scottish doctor who ascended Mont Blanc in 1834 and published his account in 1838. He was a Quaker : hence some slightly surprising terms in the letter quoted.

BECKFORD (William), 1759-1844. One of the strangest characters of English Romanticism. He came several times to Switzerland and visited Chamonix while living there.

BLAIKIE (Thomas), 1750-1838. Scottish landscape gardener, who worked for several years at the French court. He was employed by the Comte d'Artois, the Duc d'Orléans, the Princess de Lamballe, Mme Vigée-Lebrun, etc. He worked on the gardens of Bagatelle. He went to Switzerland and Savoy in 1775 and happened to meet and climb with Dr Michel Gabriel Paccard. His *Diary* was published in 1931 by Francis Birrell.

BOELL (Jacques). Contemporary writer. Mountaineer and novelist. Author of *Oisans, Cimes d'Oisans, Le trésor de la Muzelle* and the one book about the part played by Alpine troops during the last war, *Eclaireurs-Skieurs au Combat.*

BONATI (Walter). Contemporary writer. One of the greatest mountaineers of the present day. He has climbed in the Himalayas and the Andes, to say nothing of the Alps. Author of *Le mie montagne.*

BOURRIT (Marc-Théodore), 1739-1819. Precentor in the Cathedral of Geneva, painter, engraver, traveller and writer. He was enthusiastic about Mont Blanc, made many expeditions to Chamonix and various Alpine valleys and was very soon convinced that Mont Blanc could be climbed. Accordingly, he tried to climb it and always failed. He discovered several little-known valleys, mainly in the Valais. He was a profuse writer and had a vile temper, which led to violent quarrels with many people. He was jealous, and, when abused, likely to become tearful. He wrote *Description des Glacières du Duchée de Savoie* (1773), *Description des aspects du Mont Blanc* (1776), *Description des Alpes Pénines et Rhétiennes* (1781), *Nouvelle description des Glacières de Savoie* (1785), *Itinéraire de Geneve, Lausanne et Chamonix* (1791),*Description des ols et Passages des Alpes* (1803), *Itinéraire de Genève des Glacières de Chamonix, du Valais et du Canton de Vaud* (1810).

BUHL (Herrmann), 1924-1955. Outstanding German climber who, after a number of first-rate ascents in the Alps, made the first ascent of Nanga Parbat, unaccompanied. He was killed two years later in the Karakoram. He wrote *Achttausender drüber und drunter.*

BURGENER (Alexander), 1846-1911. Born at Eisten. A very great guide, he was killed by an avalanche below the Bergli Hut. Climbed with Mummery, Dent, Donkin, Güssfelt, etc. First ascents of the Dru, the Teufelsgrat on the Täschhorn, the Mitteleggi ridge on the Eiger. He went to the Caucasus with Dent and Donkin.

BYRON (George Gordon, Lord), 1788-1824. He was in Switzerland between May and October 1816, where he met Shelley. He went to Chamonix in August with John Hobhouse. He did not like Chamonix and hardly refers to it in *Manfred*, though he mentioned the Alps in the third Canto of *Childe Harold.*

CHABOD (René). Contemporary writer. A lawyer, a senator of the Italian Republic, and one of the leaders of the drive for autonomy in the Val d'Aosta. With Guido Gervasutti he made the second ascent of the north face of the Jorasses. He has written a guide book to Mont Blanc.

CHARLET (Armand). Contemporary writer. One of the best Chamonix guides, a specialist of the Aiguille Verte and the Aiguilles du Diable. Author of *Ma vocation alpine.*

CHATEAUBRIAND (François-René de), 1768-1848. He hated mountains in a violent, clever, argumentative way, mostly because they had been praised by Jean-Jacques Rousseau. Yet his denunciation of Mont Blanc is quite striking, though written in bad faith. He also has outstanding pages on the St Gotthard in the *Mèmoires d'outre tombe.* He also has outstanding

CHENEDOLLE (Charles de), 1767-1833. A friend of Mme de Stael and her group; also of Chateaubriand. He lived in Switzerland during the Revolution and returned later. He wrote about mountains in his diary, and also in a terrible epic poem, *Le génie de l'homme*, and in a few odes, written after Byron's poems.

CHENIER (André), 1762-1794. In 1784, he came to Switzerland and Savoy with his friends, the two Trudaine brothers. From Geneva they went to Chamonix, ascended the Montenvers and left by way of the Tête Noire and the Col de la Forclaz. They spent about two months in Savoy and Switzerland (September and October). Chénier wrote about his journey in *Les Amitiés, aux frères de Trudaine*, and in the VIIe *Elégie*.

COLERIDGE (S. T.), 1772-1834. He never went to the Alps: *Chamonix by Sunrise* is a very clever imitation of *Chamonix bei Sonnenaufgang* by the Danish poetess Fredericke Brun.

COURTNAY (William). William Beckford's very dear friend.

COURTOIS DE BALLORE (Mgr de). Bishop of Nîmes at the time of the Revolution; he escaped to Savoy first and then by way of Chamonix, Vallorcine and Tête Noire to Valais.

DALLOZ (Pierre). Contemporary writer. Mountaineer, writer and architect. He has written *La Pointe Lagarde* and *Haute Montagne*.

DAUDET (Alphonse), 1840-1897. He went twice to Switzerland and Savoy, in 1882 and 1886, to gather documents for *Tartarin sur les Alpes*; his documents were perfectly accurate. The book came out at the end of 1885.

DELILLE (Abbe Jacques), 1738-1813. As a diplomatic secretary, he went to Malta and Greece with the Comte de Choiseul-Gouffier. He was a poet endowed with no genius but with boundless fertility. Part of the Third Canto of *L'Homme des Champs* is about Chamonix. His house near Paris now belongs to Jacques Boell.

DENT (Clinton Thomas), 1850-1912. Surgeon, mountaineer, traveller and one of the first specialist photographers. Among many outstanding first climbs, he made those of the Dru, the Bietschhorn and the Lenzspitze.

DESNOUS (Abbé). Dates unknown. A priest of the diocese of Orleans, he was exiled from France in 1792. He went first to Chambery and, when French troops entered Savoy, he got to Chamonix and then to the Valais. His booklet *Mon Emigration* is the delightful account of the discovery of mountains by a man who had never seen one before.

DEVONSHIRE (Georgina, Duchess of), 1757-1806. Member of the most fashionable London society and a writer, she was on the Continent in 1791-1793, and met Saussure and his wife in Geneva. The letter quoted here has been published by her biographer and descendant, Iris Leveson-Gower, in *The Face Without a Frown*.

DICKENS (Charles), 1812-1870. He knew the Alps and liked them. He crossed Switzerland in 1844-45, when coming back from Italy. In 1846 he spent several months in Lausanne and then went to Chamonix with his wife and son. On his return he wrote to Forster the letter quoted here. In 1858, with Wilkie Collins, he went back to Chamonix in winter and they both used their impressions in a rather dull tale, *No Thoroughfare*.

DISRAELI (Benjamin, Earl of Beaconsfield), 1804-1881. In 1826, when making the Grand Tour which was to take him through Europe, Palestine and Egypt, he traversed Switzerland, staying in Geneva some time. He used the impressions he gathered in *Contarini Fleming* (1832).

DOLOMIEU (Commander Déodat Tancrède de), 1750-1801. A knight of Malta and an outstanding naturalist. He was still very young when he was elected to the Academie des Sciences. Owing to his Malta career, he travelled extensively. During the Revolution, his friend, the Duc de la Rochefoucauld d'Enville, was murdered before him and he managed to save his wife and mother. After the Revolution, as an inspector of mines, he went all over the Alps and even thought of ascending Mont Blanc, but bad weather prevented him from doing so. He often mentions the Alps in his letters. He was Saussure's devoted friend.

DUMAS (Alexandre), 1803-1870. Went to Switzerland and Savoy in 1832; one of his first expeditions from Geneva was to Chamonix. He interviewed everybody – possibly adding a little of his own to the information they gave: Jacques Balmat, Marie Paradis, the first woman to ascend Mont Blanc, and Marie Couttet, survivor of the first Alpine accident in 1820. He knew how to make the most of a story. He published three volumes of *Impressions de Voyages* about that journey.

DZIEDUSZCKI (Comte Laurent-Martin), 1772-1836. A young Polish nobleman who came to Western Europe in 1786-88. He went to Switzerland, France and Italy, keeping a diary and writing to his brothers at home. He left his notes in Switzerland to a Mr Sylvestre, whose descendant by marriage, M. Roux-Devillas, lent them me. The bulk of his memoirs is unpublished. Dzieduszcki went back to Poland, was Kosciusko's a.d.c. in 1794 and married Countess Anastasia Mier.

FAURE (General Jacques). Contemporary writer. As a senior officer of the Chasseurs Alpins, he was one of the creators of the Ecole de Haute Montagne at Chamonix, of the *Jeunesse et Montagne* organization during the war, and an organizer of paratroops. An outstanding figure in the Alpine world.

FAY (Chevalier de), no dates. Dolomieu's friend; he also was a Knight of Malta.

FLORIAN (Chevalier de), 1755-1794. Voltaire's nephew. A very sentimental novelist and dramatist. In 1788, after a pilgrimage to Ferney, he went to Chamonix and gathered material for his Savoyard story, *Claudine*. In spite of the title, there is nothing Savoyard in it, except the introduction, which I quote.

FORBES (J. D.), 1809-1868. He taught at Edinburgh University, travelled extensively over the Alps and even went to Norway to ascertain his theories about glaciers. He wrote *Travels in the Alps of Savoy* (1843), *Norway and its Glaciers* (1853), *the Tour of Mont Blanc and Monte Rosa* (1855).

FRENDO (Edouard). Contemporary writer. He made the first French ascent of the north face of the Grandes Jorasses with Gaston Rebuffat (*La Face Nord des Grandes Jorasses*, 1946).

FRISON-ROCHE (Roger). Contemporary writer. Novelist, traveller, and guide. He has written several mountaineering novels, *Premier de cordée, La grande crevasse, Retour à la montagne*.

GAUTIER (Théophile), 1811-1872. Art critic, poet and novelist, one of the leaders of Romanticism in France. Gautier often went to Geneva where his mistress, Ernesta Grisi, lived. He saw Mont Blanc from Geneva and went to Chamonix and also to Zermatt in 1868. He was the first French writer to describe a mountaineering party returning from a big climb, but that was in Zermatt and not in Chamonix. He loved mountains and described them in *Tra los Montes, Voyage en Italie, Vacances du Lundi, España*.

GERVASUTTI (Guido), 1909-1946. Born in the Frioul. He was one of the first great specialists of the Dolomites and, after 1931, began tackling the most difficult routes in the Mont Blanc range. He was killed when trying a new route up Mont Blanc du Tacul. He wrote *Scalatte nelle Alpi*.

GLADSTONE (William Ewart), 1809-1898. It is most likely that his one connection with mountaineering was the answer to a request formulated by Queen Victoria, which is quoted here.

GOETHE (Johann-Wolfgang), 1749-1832. He went three times to Switzerland. In 1779-1780 he accompanied the Duke of Saxe-Weimar from Geneva to Chamonix and then to Martigny. He described his journey in *Reisen*.

GRINLING (Kenneth). Contemporary writer. A New Zealander, he was caught in France by the invasion of 1940. He remained hidden in Bourg d'Oisans and, when the whole of France was overrun by the Germans, he made his way towards Switzerland, finally crossing the Col du Chardonnet alone and at night. He was an excellent mountaineer, but even so it was an extremely daring feat of mountaineering.

HAMILTON (Douglas, 7th Duke of). He was very young when he made his Grand Tour, escorted by his physician, Dr John Moore, and the latter's son. The trio was painted in Rome by Gavin Hamilton.

HAMILTON (Sir William), 1738-1806. English Minister in Naples for many years. A friend of Saussure and Dolomieu. He was a talented amateur in many activities: music, geology, archaeology, numismatics.

HECKMAIR (Anderl). Contemporary writer. With Vörg, Harrer and Kasparek, he made the first ascent of the north face of the Eiger; later he went on with the north faces of the Matterhorn and the Grandes Jorasses. He published *Les derniers problèmes des Alpes*.

HOBHOUSE (John, Lord Broughton), 1786-1869. Byron's friend. They went together to Chamonix and Hobhouse published the story of the trip in his *Recollections of a Long Life*.

HUGO (Victor), 1802-1885. He went to Savoy in 1825. Later he travelled throughout Switzerland and described his trips in *Le Rhin* and *Alpes et Pyrénées*. He wrote a few poems about mountains, which are not among his best: *Désintéressement* and *Le régiment du Baron Madruce* in *La legende des siecles*, *Dicté en presence du Glacier du Rhone* (*Les feuilles d'automne*) and *Balma* (*Toute la lyre*).

IRVING (R. L. G.). Contemporary writer. Mountaineer and historian of the Alps, one of the early guideless climbers; he trained many outstanding mountaineers, George Mallory among them. (*The Romance of Mountaineering, The Alps, Ten Great Mountains, The Mountain Way*.

KUGY (Julius), 1858-1944. Born in Trieste; lawyer and mountaineer. The great specialist of the Julian Alps and of Monte Rosa. He also made very big ascents in the Mont Blanc range (*Aus dem Leben eines Bergsteiger, Anton Oitzinger, Fünfjahrhundertet Triglav, Im Göttlichen Lacheln des Monte Rosa*.

LABICHE (Eugène), 1815-1888. The great comic writer never set foot on the Montenvers: otherwise, he would have noticed that one did not drive there. His *Voyage de M. Perrichon* was acted in 1860, the year when Savoy was annexed to France. Probably, the play was already going through rehearsals when papers published the photos taken during the trip made by Napoleon III and the Empress in Savoy, and it was too late to alter the text — or he did not care.

LAGARDE (Jacques). Contemporary writer. One of the pioneers of guideless mountaineering in France in the twenties. With Henry de Ségogne as second man on the rope, he made — among other climbs — the first ascent of the Pointe Lagarde in the Aiguilles Rouges du Dolent.

LA ROCHEFOUCAULD d'ENVILLE (Alexandre, duc de), 1740-1792. Naturalist, traveller, and philanthropist. Friend of Saussure and Dolomieu. He was murdered in 1792 in Gisors. In 1760 he went to Chamonix at a time when it was still a feat to visit the valley, and he wrote an amusing account of the trip for his tutor. The ms was widely circulated: several copies of it are known to exist.

LE PAYS (René). No dates. Seventeenth century. Collector of taxes on salt in the Dauphiny. He went several times to the court of the Duchess of Savoy in Turin, and in 1669, while returning, made a detour to Chamonix. Many critics abused his letter, not being keen on the baroque style and not realizing the wit and gift for observation to be found there. It was published in 1671 in *Amitiés, amours et amourettes*.

LEPINEY (Tom de). Contemporary writer. A pioneer of guideless climbing in France in the twenties, together with his brother Jacques, who was killed in a mountaineering accident in Morocco. When the Pointe Lagarde was climbed for the first time, he was Pierre Dalloz's companion. He and his brother wrote *Sur les crêtes du Mont Blanc*.

MAGNONE (Guido). Contemporary writer. In spite of his Italian name, he is French. One of the leading guides today, the conqueror of the west face of the Dru and of many difficult summits in the Andes – Mount Fitzroy among them. Author of *La face ouest des Drus*.

MAILLIEUX (René). Contemporary writer. Vice-president of the Belgian Alpine Club. He often climbed with the late King Albert I, about whom he wrote *Le Roi Albert Alpiniste*. He ascended the north face of the Dru with Gaston Rebuffat.

MALCZESKI (Comte Antoine), 1795-1826. A Polish nobleman, and a poet, who served in Napoleon's army. He ascended Mont Blanc in 1818 and wrote a *Lettre au Professeu Pictet* to describe his expedition. The text quoted here is a long note he wrote for his poem *Maria* (1822), which is far less known than the letter. He led a very romantic life and died when 31.

MALLORY (George Leigh-), 1887-1924. He studied at Winchester and Cambridge and taught at Charterhouse. He had been trained as a mountaineer by R. L. G. Irving and G. W. Young. He did many first-class ascents in the Alps before the first World War and, as soon as the 1921 expedition to Mount Everest was organized he was invited to join it. He found the route up to the North Col in 1921, made several attempts in 1922 and, in 1924, together with Andrew Irvine, disappeared in an attempt to reach the summit. He published various articles in the *Alpine Journal*.

MASON (A. E. W.), 1865-1848. Mountaineer and novelist; member of the Alpine Club. There are several mountaineering episodes in his best novel, *Running Water*.

MATHEWS (G.), 1834-1905. An excellent mountaineer; President of the Alpine Club, 1878-1881. He was with Moore and the Walkers when they made the first ascent of the Brenva route. He wrote *The Annals of Mont Blanc*.

MICHELET (Jules), 1798-1874. One of his 'popular books', written in collaboration with his wife, is *La Montagne*. As often the case, the book is a mixture of very brilliant and very inaccurate pages; and those about Mont Blanc are not among the best.

MILLOT (Albert), 1835-1901. A French mountaineer, one of the founders of the French Alpine Club, and a member of the Alpine Club. Leslie Stephen's friend. His wife was also a mountaineer.

MONTGOLFIER (Elie-Ascension de), 1784-1864. The nephew of the two aeronauts; as he was born the year after their first balloon flight, he was given those two rather heavy Christian names. He came to Chamonix when 15, having run away from school. His long life was rather restless. His unpublished *Memoirs* belong to his descendants, who lent them to me.

MOORE (A. W.), 1841-1887. An excellent mountaineer who climbed with the Walkers, Whymper, Morsehead, etc. He went to the Caucasus with D. W. Freshfield. In 1865 his party made the first ascent of the Brenva route up Mont Blanc. He published *The Alps in 1864*. His very interesting diary is still unpublished.

MOORE (Dr John), 1729-1802. He accompanied the Duke of Hamilton on the Continent as his Doctor. His son became General Sir John Moore. He wrote *A View of Society and Manners in France, Switzerland, Germany and Italy*.

MUMMERY (A. F.), 1856-1895. He practically invented athletic mountaineering, either guided or guideless. The routes he opened on the Grépon, the Charmoz, the Réquin, the Verte, the Täschhorn were of unparalleled severity at the time. He climbed in the Caucasus and went to the

Himalayas, where he disappeared when attempting to climb Nanga Parbat. He wrote *My Climbs in the Alps and Caucasus.*

NODIER (Charles), 1780-1844. He went to Chamonix with Victor Hugo in 1825 and gave a hair-raising description of Hugo's harmless walk on the Mer de Glace; but he was really impressed by the landscape and put it into one of his short stories, *Les Aveugles de Chamonix.*

NOYCE (Wilfrid), 1920-1962. Besides his very fine climbs in the Alps and the Himalayas, Wilfrid Noyce was a scholar, a novelist and a poet. He was killed when climbing in the Pamirs. He wrote *Scholar Mountaineers, The Springs of Adventure, South Col, The Gods are Angry, Climbing the Fish Tail,* and books of verse.

PACCARD (François), 1734-1819. It seems that the guide described by Florian was this rather colourful person. When very young, he acted as guide to a well-known highwayman, Mandrin, after which he was exiled from Savoy. He was pardoned through the exertions of the Comte de Caylus and took to guiding less compromising people (William Coxe, Sophie von La Roche, Fredericke Brun), and made a few attempts to reach the summit of Mont Blanc. He was Dr Paccard's uncle or cousin, and sided with him against those who abused him, Bourrit and Balmat. Bourrit had him arrested and then pardoned.

PACCARD (Dr Michel-Gabriel), 1757-1827. He made the first ascent of Mont Blanc with J. Balmat on August 7, 1786, after various attempts, one of them with Thomas Blaikie when he was barely eighteen. It seems that, when on holiday in Chamonix, he acted as amateur guide to make a little money. He had studied in Turin and Paris.

PIERRE (Bernard). Contemporary writer. Stockbroker, mountaineer and explorer. He has made a number of very big Alpine climbs, mostly with Gaston Rebuffat, and has also climbed in the Hoggar, the Andes, the Himalayas, the Ruwenzori, etc. He has written *La conquête du Salcantay, Une montagne nommée Nun-Kun, Escalades au Hoggar, Les montagnes de la lune,* etc.

POCOCKE (Richard), 1704-1765. When he came to Geneva and agreed to accompany William Windham to Chamonix, he was returning from an extensive journey, later described in *Description of the East.* His only reference to his Savoy trip was a single sentence. He was a clergyman and became Bishop of Ossory.

RADCLIFFE (Mrs Anne), 1764-1833. She never went to Savoy and got her faint local colour from Saussure's books.

RAMBERT (Eugène), 1830-1886. He taught literature in Lausanne and Zurich. Disgusted by the very dull descriptions of the Alps which were far too frequent, he decided to write a book about mountains, to make people understand what they really were like: hence the four volumes of the *Alpes suisses,* which are full of very charming pages.

RAMBUTEAU (Comte Claude-Philibert de), 1781-1869. He was one of Napoleon's high officials, his chamberlain, then a prefect and finally a peer of France. Under Louis-Philippe he was made Prefect of the Seine. In 1813 he was prefect of the Simplon (Sion), and when the Austrians were progressing into Switzerland, he managed to get all the members of his staff back into France without loss or accident, though it meant crossing the Col de la Forclaz and Tête Noire in the dead of winter. He related this episode in his *Mémoires.*

REBUFFAT (Gaston). Contemporary writer. One of the best contemporary guides and climbers, and a leading Alpine writer. He was a member of the French team which conquered Annapurna, and among other ascents he lists the six main north faces of the Alps. He has written *L'Apprenti montagnard, Etoiles et tempêtes, Calanques, Neige et rocs, Entre terre et ciel, Mont Blanc, Jardin féérique,* etc.

REY (Guido), 1861-1935. A leading Italian mountaineer who found lyrical inspiration among mountains. He spent most of the last years of his life in his big chalet at the foot of the Matterhorn in Breuil. He wrote *Il Monte Cervino, Alpinismo Accrobatico, Famiglia Alpinistica*.

ROBERTS (Michael), 1902-1948. Professor, poet, literary critic and mountaineer. He often took his students climbing in the Dauphiny or Savoy. He has written many fine Alpine poems, one of the best being his *Elegy for fallen climbers*.

ROUSSEAU (Jean-Jacques), 1712-1778. In spite of a persistent legend, Rousseau did not like mountains and discovered nothing about them. He borrowed most of his ideas from Haller's poem, *Die Alpen*, re-telling them in his own beautiful style. High valleys did not interest him. When he was in Cluses, he did not push on to Sallanches, which is quite near, though he was a first-rate walker.

RUSKIN (John), 1819-1900. He loved mountains as a poet and an aesthete. He made numerous trips through Savoy, the Valais, the Bernese Oberland, the Mont Cenis, the Italian Alps, etc., and wrote about them in *Modern Painters, The Stones of Venice, Sesame and Lilies, Praeterita*, etc. But he never thought of doing any real mountaineering, which he did not understand and loathed from the bottom of his heart.

SALES (St Francois de), 1567-1622. When going over the Chablais, he pushed as far as Chamonix and mentioned the valley – but not Mont Blanc – in various letters. The letter in which he speaks of Mont Blanc by name is a forgery.

SAND (George), 1804-1876. She went to Chamonix in 1836 with her children and one of her lovers, Gustave de Gévaudan, to meet Marie d'Agoult, Liszt and Major Pictet. She was not interested in the landscape and spent her time playing practical jokes on everybody in the Hôtel de l'Union. She describes the trip in the *Lettres d'un voyageur*. One of her later novels, *Valvèdre*, has an Alpine setting which is meant to be Zermatt – where she never went.

SAUSSURE (Horace-Bénédict de), 1740-1799. Naturalist and traveller; a leading Alpine figure. He had a beautiful style and keen observation, together with a personality which impressed all those who met him. He crossed the Alps fourteen times, according to what he says in the preface of his big *Voyages dans les Alpes*, and not only ascended Mont Blanc, but camped for a fortnight on the Col du Géant, explored the Valley of Zermatt, crossed the Théodule and went over the Alps from the Oberland to the Tessin. He also went to England, Italy and Sicily. Some of his travel diaries are still unpublished.

SHELLEY (Percy Bysshe), 1792-1822. He was in Geneva from May to August 1816, and went for a few days to Chamonix, where he wrote *Mont Blanc*, after having related that trip to Peacock in a long letter.

SHELLEY (Mary), 1797-1851. She was in Chamonix with Shelley and she wrote about that trip first in *Frankenstein*, then in *The Last Man*.

SHERWILL (Captain Markham). No dates. He ascended Mont Blanc in 1825, after which he published *A Visit to the Summit of Mont Blanc*, and then in 1832 *A Brief Historical Sketch of the Priory of Chamonix*. He collected the accounts of former climbs, a number of autographs from their authors, a large quantity of prints, and had the whole bound under the following title: *Fourteen Narratives written by those travellers who have successfully attained the Summit of this mountain between the year 1786 and 1837, collected by Markham Sherwill, one of the intrepid adventurers*. In 1840 he presented it to the Bibliothèque Royale in Paris. It is now in the Prints department of the Bibliothèque Nationale.

SMYTHE (Frank), 1900-1949. His main achievements in the Alps were the opening of the two major new routes up the Brenva face, over the Sentinelle Rouge. He made many great ascents in the Himalayas, including Kamet. He published many mountaineering books, *Climbs and Ski*

Runs, *Kangchenjunga Adventure, Kamet Conquered, The Spirit of the Hills, The Valley of Flowers, Again Switzerland, An Alpine Journey, Over Tyrolese Hills, Edward Whymper, Camp VI, Secret Mission, Climbing in the Canadian Rockies*, etc.

STANLEY OF ALDERLEY (Lady). Maria Josepha Holroyd was the Earl of Sheffield's daughter. She wrote charming letters about her trip on the Continent at the beginning of the Revolution. They were published by J. H. Adeane.

STEPHEN (Sir Leslie). 1832-1904. A great scholar, he was also one of the great early mountaineers. His *The Playground of Europe* is one of the first Alpine classics. Chamonix was one of his favourite centres.

TERRAY (Lionel). Contemporary writer. A leading guide and explorer. He has been to the Himalayas, the Andes and Alaska and has also made most of the outstanding climbs in the Alps. He has written *Les conquérants de l'inutile*.

TALFOURD. Dickens' friend the author of *Recollections of a Visit among the Alps* (1841) and *Vacation Rambles* (1845); he tramped all over Switzerland and attempted Mont Blanc.

TOEPFFER (Rodolphe), 1799-1846. A Genevese novelist, humourist and schoolmaster. Each Summer he took a number of schoolboys to the Alps, trying to induce in them some feeling for nature and the mountains, and to prevent them from playing pranks. He loved mountains passionately, but tried to avoid sounding too lyrical and romantic. He edited the *Partie pittoresque des voyages de Saussure* and wrote *Les nouvelles Genevoises, Voyages en zig-zags* and *Nouveaux voyages en zig-zags*.

TWAIN (Mark), 1835-1910. Long before Daudet, he was acutely aware of all that was ludicrous in Alpine matters and devoted *A Tramp Abroad* to the subject. The page I have reproduced is, however, not in the least humorous.

TYNDALL (John), 1820-1893. Scholar and mountaineer. Though he pretended to see mountains from a wholly scientific viewpoint, he loved them passionately. He made several great first climbs, the finest being the Weisshorn, and he travelled extensively over the Alps. He wrote *Glaciers of the Alpes, Mountaineering in 1861* and *Hours of Exercise*.

VIGEE-LEBRUN. (Elisabeth), 1755-1842. A charming portrait painter and Marie-Antoinette's favourite. It seems that, according to her *Souvenirs*, she painted a view of Mont Blanc from the Bossons: but it has been lost. She was in Switzerland and Savoy in 1807 and 1808. She visited Mme de Staël at Coppet.

VIOLLET-LE-DUC (Eugène), 1814-1879. A leading but very questionable architect. He loved mountains, stayed often in Chamonix (where he built a big chalet at the top of the village) and, though he loathed mountaineers, made several trips around Mont Blanc and Monte Rosa. He had a rather stupid accident on the Schwartzberggletscher, going to Saas, and gave a hair-raising account of it. His *Mont Blanc* can still be read with interest.

WALKER (Frank), 1808-1872. When young, he undertook minor climbs, but became increasingly daring; he trained his son Horace and — what was quite extraordinary at that time — his daughter Lucy.

WALKER (Horace), 1838-1911. An outstanding mountaineer. He climbed with his sister Lucy, with A. W. Moore, the Pilkingtons and Whymper, all over Valais, the Dauphiny, Savoy, Italy and even the Caucasus. It is great pity the Walkers never wrote about their climbs.

WHYMPER (Edward), 1840-1911. During five years, from 1860 to 1865, he went all over the Alps, collecting the most magnificent summits. He was soon attracted by the Matterhorn and concentrated on its conquest. After the accident which marred its first ascent, Whymper did not quite abandon climbing, but made no more first ascents. He ascended Mont Blanc several times. He published *Scrambles amongst the Alps* and *Travels amongst the Great Andes of the Equator*, and guide-books to Zermatt and Chamonix.

WILLS (Sir Alfred), 1828-1913. A judge and a mountaineer. With his guide, Auguste Balmat, he explored all the secondary valleys near Chamonix and bought a chalet above Sixt, the 'Eagle's Nest'. He ascended Mont Blanc several times. He published *Wanderings among the High Alps* and *The Eagle's Nest*.

WINDHAM (William), 1717-1761. While studying in Geneva, he indulged in amateur theatricals (*Macbeth*) and visited the 'Glacières'. He then went to Hungary to fight in the army and, returning to England, entered Parliament. He was keenly interested in military matters. His account of his journey to Chamonix is one of the earliest reliable descriptions of the valley.

WORDSWORTH (William), 1770-1850. He went to Chamonix in 1792, and described the valley, first in *Descriptive Sketches*, and then in the *Prelude* (Book VI). He went back in 1822, and mentioned the valley again in some of the sonnets of the *Tour on the Continent*.

WYSS-DUNANT (Dr Edouard). Contemporary writer. A doctor, an explorer and a mountaineer. He has climbed throughout the world and he was the leader of the Swiss Expedition to Everest. He has published *L'Appel des sommets*, *Au dela des cimes*, *Cimes et forêts himalayennes*, *Mes ascensions en Afrique*, etc.

YOUNG (Geoffrey Winthrop), 1876-1958. The main part of his Alpine career was before the 1914 War. With Franz Lochmatter or Joseph Knubel, he ascended some of the most difficult summits and ridges of the Alps, giving his name to several of them. He lost a leg on the Italian front during the first World War, yet managed to climb still for several years, in spite of the difficulty of dragging an artificial leg uphill. He published *On High Hills*, *Mountain Craft*, *Climbing with a Difference* and a book of *Collected Poems*.